R

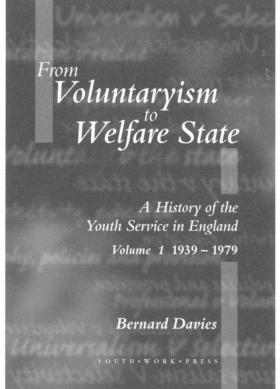

From
Voluntaryism
to
Welfare State

A History of the
Youth Service in England

Volume 1 1939 – 1979

Bernard Davies

YOUTH · WORK · PRESS

One
Week
Loan

One Week Loan

A History of the Youth Service in England comprises two volumes:

Volume 1: 1939 – 1979
From Voluntaryism to Welfare State
ISBN 0 86155 207 5   £14.99

Volume 2: 1979 – 1999
From Thatcherism to New Labour
ISBN 0 86155 208 3   £14.99

Published by

17–23 Albion Street, Leicester LE1 6GD.
Tel: 0116.285.3700. Fax: 0116.285.3777.
E-Mail: nya@nya.org.uk
Internet: http://www.nya.org.uk

© September 1999

Editor: Denise Duncan
Cover design: Sanjay Kukadia

Y O U T H • W O R K • P R E S S
is a publishing imprint of the National Youth Agency

Contents

Glossary of Acronyms

AJY	Association for Jewish Youth
BYC	British Youth Council
BYCWA	Black Youth and Community Workers Association
CBI	Confederation of British Industry
CDF	Community Development Foundation
CHE	Campaign for Homosexual Equality
CETYCW	Council for Education and Training in Youth and Community Work
CHAR	Campaign for the Homeless and Rootless
CYSA	Community and Youth Service Association
CYWU	Community and Youth Workers' Union
CRC	Community Relations Council
CRY	Campaign for Rural Youth
CSV	Community Service Volunteers
DES	Department of Education and Science
DfE	Department for Education
DfEE	Department for Education and Employment
EPA	Educational Priority Area
ESG	Educational Support Grants Scheme
GEST	Grants for Education Support and Training
GLC	Greater London Council
HMI	Her Majesty's Inspectorate
ILEA	Inner London Education Authority
INTEP	Initial Training and Education Panel
INSTEP	In-Service Training and Education Panel
IPPR	Institute for Public Policy Research
IT	Intermediate Treatment
JNC	Joint Negotiating Committee
JOC	Juvenile Organisation Committee
LEA	Local Education Authority
LEATGS	Local Education Authority Training Grants Scheme
LUYC	London Union of Youth Clubs
MAYC	Methodist Association of Youth Clubs
MSC	Manpower Services Commission
NACYS	National Advisory Council for the Youth Service
NABC	National Association of Boys' Clubs

NAGC	National Association of Girls' Clubs
NAYCEO	National Association of Youth and Community Education Officers
NALGO	National Association of Local Government Officers
NAYPCAS	National Association of Young People's Counselling and Advisory Services
NAYSO	National Association of Youth Service Officers
NAYC	National Association of Youth Clubs
NAYLO	National Association of Youth Leaders and Organisers
NCTYL	National College for the Training of Youth Leaders
NCVYS	National Council for Voluntary Youth Services
NCSS	National Council for Social Service
NOW	National Organisation for Work with Girls and Young Women
NUT	National Union of Teachers
NYA	National Youth Agency
NYB	National Youth Bureau
OFSTED	Office for Standards in Education
OPCS	Office of Populations Censuses and Surveys
SCPYCO	Standing Conference of Principal Youth and Community Officers
SCNVYO	Standing Conference of National Voluntary Youth Organisations
SRB	Single Regeneration Budget
TAG	Training Agencies Group
TEC	Training and Enterprise Council
TUC	Trades Union Congress
YCWTA	Youth and Community Work Training Association
YMCA	Young Men's Christian Association
YODU	Youth Opportunities Development Unit
YOP	Youth Opportunities Programme
YSA	Youth Service Association
YSDC	Youth Service Development Council
YSIC	Youth Service Information Centre
YSWU	Youth Social Work Unit
YTS	Youth Training Scheme
YVFF	Young Volunteer Force Foundation
YVRU	Young Volunteer Resources Unit
YWCA	Young Women's Christian Association
YWU	Youth Work Unit

About the Author

Bernard Davies first got involved in youth work in 1948 aged 13, as a member of a youth club and a Jewish Lads' Brigade unit. He went on to professional training via senior member and part-time leader and, after graduating with a history degree, took the one-year course for 'youth leaders and organisers' at University College Swansea during the year of Albemarle, 1958–59.

During the early 1960s he was a tutor at the National College for the Training of Youth Leaders and, after 18 months in the USA, for seven years ran a teacher-youth worker course at a mature student teacher training college in Lancashire. He served on advisory and review groups for NYB and CETYCW during the 1970s and 1980s and also served on a local authority education subcommittee and on local youth service review panels. His extensive experience of the voluntary sector includes chairing and being a member of local management committees and involvement as a local community activist. In 1983–84 he was president of the Community and Youth Workers' Union.

Throughout his career Bernard Davies has written extensively on youth work, the youth service and youth affairs. He contributed regularly to *New Society* in the 1960s and 1970s, co-authored *The Social Education of the Adolescent* with Alan Gibson, published in 1967, and has written pamphlets and a book, *Threatening Youth* (1986), on youth policies. Since taking early retirement as youth officer (training) from Sheffield Youth Service in 1992 he has acted as consultant for a number of voluntary organisations and local authorities including, with Mary Marken, carrying out a review of Sunderland Council's youth services.

About the Publisher

The National Youth Agency aims to advance youth work to promote young people's personal and social development, and their voice, influence and place in society. It works to: improve and extend youth services and youth work; enhance and demonstrate youth participation in society; and to promote effective youth policy and provision.

The NYA provides resources to improve work with young people and its management; creates and demonstrates innovation in service and methods; supports the leadership of organisations to deliver 'best value' and manage change; influences public perception and policy, and secures standards of education and training for youth work.

Acknowledgments

Though I of course take full responsibility for what follows, I want to record my thanks to the many people who, often in passing and perhaps even without realising it, have contributed information and above all ideas to the writing of this history. They include all those who took part in the Durham History of Youth and Community Work conference in November 1998 but in particular Colin Heslop, Doug Nicholls, Sangeeta Soni and Jean Spence. I am grateful, too, to Lady Albemarle and Sandra Leventon for some specific information and responses and to the students on the Durham Youth and Community Work course who allowed me to try out some early ideas on key 'threads' emerging from the youth service's history.

Over nearly three years, the staff of the National Youth Agency's library and information centre have been infinitely patient with my cries for help, particularly Judy Perrett and Carolyn Oldfield. Mary Durkin, then at the NYA, provided early inspiration. Mary Marken's reactions to drafts have invariably gone straight to the weak points in my arguments, been incisive but constructive and so have added greatly to the analysis. Sally Davies has also flogged her way through long drafts, in the process contributing valuable comment on the content and language as well as identifying errors which have saved me from much later embarrassment.

Above all, however, I want to put on record my thanks to Tom Wylie and Denise Duncan. Through their consistent support, encouragement – and critiques! – I have come to understand and appreciate just how crucial editors are for writing for publication.

Bernard Davies
September 1999

Dedication

This book is dedicated to **Stanley Rowe** (1924–92) – youth worker, youth work trainer, trade unionist and youth service policy-maker – who had a permanent influence on my own work and thinking and whose contribution to the youth service over five decades helped to ensure its survival and development.

Preface

Bernard Davies has written the definitive history of England's youth service during the last 60 years of the 20th century. It highlights the contributions and achievements made by diverse individuals and organisations to the development of a distinctive form of practice – youth work – and of a distinctive, if nebulous, pattern of social education provision for young people – the youth service.

There are many ways of presenting history: as a nostalgic reverie of better times; as a set of accidents or contingencies with unintended consequences; as an elemental struggle by heroes and heroines. Bernard Davies's book transcends all of these. It is a tale of continuities, of enduring – and sometimes resolved – struggles towards a better life for our young people, more often by those who worked directly with them than by those who made national policy about them. It is the text for generations of youth workers, and also a spur to greater effort based on a deeper understanding of our roots.

Tom Wylie
Chief Executive
National Youth Agency

Foreword

Beyond objectivity

In setting out to write the history of England's youth service, pure objectivity has for me never been a realistic option. This admission is not meant to suggest that I have allowed free rein to my personal prejudices and biases. It is merely to own up to the subjectivity which is part of the analysis of any human enterprise as this is filtered through the values, feelings and preconceptions of the analyst.

This, however, is a history which has stood even less chance than usual of being neutral and stand-offish. For most of the period it describes, I have had some sort of personal involvement in youth work. In the late1940s, just after my 13th birthday, I joined a (voluntary) youth club and boys' brigade unit. From the mid-1950s my awareness of the wider organisational context of these personal experiences was being sharpened by my deepening contact with Stanley Rowe, a full-time leader who had been actively and influentially involved on the national youth service stage for at least 10 years. After studying history at university – a not insignificant influence in itself on what follows – I found myself doing full-time training for youth work during 'the year of Albemarle' (1958–59).

Though for long periods straying into the worlds of both teaching and social work, I have never since got youth work or the youth service out of my system. For good or ill, therefore, I have a considerable personal investment in the history which I here try to record and interpret – hardly an ideal platform for objective appraisal or distanced judgment.

My objectivity has been further restricted by my unashamed intention to write a history which addresses institutional and professional concerns which have stayed *current* through most of the youth service's development. Precisely because so much of my own personal and career development over the past 40 years has been intertwined with that of the service, I have become highly sensitive to (even impatient with) how easily even its immediate past slips away, unnoticed and undervalued. This is a service, I am tempted to conclude, without a history – and therefore, if it is not very careful, without an identity.

Losses like these have real everyday consequences. For one thing, they have prevented (and still prevent) those who come later from 'standing on the shoulders of those who went before' – an essential (and humbling) viewpoint for anyone caught up in the daily pressures and aggravations of today's struggles. This deprivation of insights into why things are as they are, these gaps in historical awareness, also cut off practitioners and policy-makers from crucial analytical tools for current planning and action. In offering a historical framework, however partial (in both senses of the word), I hope therefore to give some distant support to these ongoing activities and engagements and maybe even to contribute a little to them.

Limitations

On the assumption that another history of the youth service in England may not be written for some time, I have tried to make this one as authoritative as possible – that is, to put together a comprehensive and accurate document of record. Even so, some crucial limitations are built into what follows.

- In striving to give due weight and space to the range of cultural experiences and traditions which have gone to create the youth service in England, my class origins and my experiences as a Jew have hopefully added something relevant to my interpretations. Nonetheless, I have remained conscious throughout that this is history written by a white able-bodied heterosexual man.
- This is a history of the *youth service* and not of youth work. Moreover, it starts from the assumption that, far from being amenable to some non-controversial definition, this will always involve a degree of

arbitrariness. What follows sets this definition quite narrowly. It, for example, assumes that the service was created as an institution when the state achieved a recognisable and substantial presence in the sponsorship of youth work – and it dates this from November 1939 when the Ministry of Education published Circular 1486, *The Service of Youth*. It also assumes that, by definition, it constitutes a complex set of relationships and negotiations between the state and voluntary organisations – though conceptions of the latter, their boundaries and their much-hyped 'partnership' with the state are also treated as problematic and in crucial respects unresolved.

- This is quite explicitly a history of the youth service in *England*. It does make passing references to Scotland, the north of Ireland and particularly Wales, most often where significant overlaps into English events and learning occur. However – above all because the youth services in these other parts of the United Kingdom have developed in such often radically different ways – it makes no claims at all to writing their histories.
- This also is very largely a history *from above* – about national policies and policy makers, statutory and volun-tary, and how these have interacted with and helped to shape local developments. Though some use is made of local experience to illustrate and illuminate these top-down influences, no claim is made to in any way trace how local and national policies have worked their way out as provision and practice on the ground.

Sources

Though this account of the growth of the youth service in England is based on considerable 'research', only a small proportion of this has been archival in the sense that it has used original documents or records. Key published papers – government, voluntary sector and independent reports, policy statements and discussion papers, departmental circulars, HMI reports once they became public documents – have clearly been important sources. So, too have some 'semi-published' papers such as presidential addresses to union AGMs, other conference papers and reports, press releases and a range of similarly transient materials going back to the 1940s.

Most of the detailed 'evidence', however, has been drawn from the (often high-quality) journalism of what can at best be described the service's 'popular' press and periodicals. I have thus relied heavily on the monthly and quarterly publications of the Ministry and later Department of Education, the Youth Service Information Centre, the National Youth Bureau and the National Youth Agency. Most important here have been:

- The YSIC *Digest* of the late 1960s and early 1970s;
- *Youth Service* in its various forms;
- *Youth in Society*;
- *Youth Scene* and *Scene*;
- *Young People Now*;
- (*Youth*) *Policy Update*; and
- The *Newsletter* of the Council for Education and Training in Youth and Community Work.

I have also made use of NAYC/Youth Club UK's *Youth Clubs* and of cuttings from *Education*, the *Times Educational Supplement*, the *Times Higher Educational Supplement*, *The Guardian* and *The Observer*.

Other key sources have been trade union journals. Particularly important here have been *The Youth Leader*, the National Association of Youth Leaders and Organisers' quarterly published during the 1940s and 1950s; *Youth Review*, the National Union of Teachers' periodical published monthly in association with the National Association of Youth Service Officers and the Youth Service Association through most of the 1960s; and since the early 1970s the Community and Youth Service Association/Community and Youth Workers' Union journal and then newspaper *Rapport*.

Throughout, I have striven to remain critical of these sources – and indeed self-critical where I have drawn on my own previous writing and publicly expressed views. Though most would hardly be classified as respectable academic sources, they have nonetheless proved a mine of information on what happened, when, and with and through whom. They have also conveyed a strong sense of what was important to the service at different times and so have caught something of the mood, even the passion, driving events.

Where I have ridden on the back of others' original research and findings, references are listed at the end of each chapter. However, in order to avoid over-burdening further two already lengthy volumes, most of the detailed sources have not been listed. They are for the most part recorded and can be made available to anyone interested – either from me through the National Youth Agency or via the NYA website http://www.nya.org.uk

Hopefully, too, such exchanges will help to achieve one of the main objectives of writing this history in the first place: to set in motion further debates on issues and concerns which have deep roots in the service's past and which continue to engage and preoccupy it at yet another critical moment in its development.

Bernard Davies
September 1999

Introduction

Chronology – with attitude

The overall framework of this history depends on that rather simplistic trick of dividing the past into significant periods and key events. By coincidence – and it surely *was* coincidence – influential reports on the youth service have been published at or very near the turn of each of the four decades which provide this book's main focus: Albemarle in 1960, Milson-Fairbairn in 1969, Thompson in 1982 and Coopers and Lybrand in 1991. In shaping the overall plan, each of these is used as a major signpost and transition point.

Other critical transition events and developments will also be dated and placed as accurately and as objectively as possible. These include state papers such as the 1967 Hunt Report *Immigrants and the Youth Service* and government discussion papers and circulars; the periodic attempts to get 'youth bills' through parliament; and the ministerial conferences of the late 1980s and early 1990s. What follows therefore is in many respects a very conventional chronological exposition intended to tell 'the story' as logically as possible.

The reason for wanting to fulfil this basic task, however, is not just to satisfy those who see history as 'getting the facts straight'. In this account, these have the more important purpose of providing a skeleton on which to flesh out more analytical themes. Far from being conceived and constructed as a description of who did what when, this book seeks as far as is possible to understand some of the 'whys' of those 'facts'. Above all, it attempts to locate them in the (changing) ideas and social, economic and political conditions of their time and in their broader educational and social policy contexts. Youth work, youth organisations and the youth service itself are thus treated, not as special or exceptional but, first and foremost, as examples of the way educational and welfare activity has been organised *and institutionalised* in our society.

One of the ways this book seeks to do this is to filter the past through present preoccupations in order to construct a *contemporary* history. Such filtering is to some extent an inevitable part of the subjectivity of historical description and analysis. What follows therefore, far from trying to deny or mask this effect, seeks deliberately to embrace it in order to try and produce a usable set of insights and comments on our own times. Date-stamping is thus interwoven with engagement in debates on key policy issues which have swirled around the service across the decades and continued to do so even as this book was being written.

Though overlapping, inherently ill-defined and far from exhaustive, these – in simple terms deliberately intended to convey something of their inherent and unresolvable tensions – include the following:

- **Universalism vs selectivity** – that is: How far should the youth service be an open-door provision, working with those young people who choose to participate. Or – especially assuming limited resources – should it concentrate its efforts on identified sections of the youth population specifically targeted because they are in special need; or because they are discriminated against and oppressed?

- **Education vs rescue** – that is: How far should the youth service's 'mission' be concerned with young people's self-realisation and personal (and indeed collective) development; or with their rescue from personal, family and/or societal risks and difficulties?

- **Professional vs volunteer** – that is: How far should the youth service move from a reliance on lay volunteers (that is, with limited training and specialist qualifications) to employing paid, trained and 'qualified' staff?

- **Voluntary vs the state** – that is: How far should the youth service move from sponsorship and control by 'independent' charitable bodies or self-help groups to state sponsorship and control underpinned by legislation, shaped by government policies and priorities and funded out of local and national taxation?

In negotiating these debates, other key elements of the service's philosophy, policies and provision are also passed through an analytical mesh. These include:

- **The changing perceptions of the youth service's clientele** including how, and how far, these have taken account of the ways in which young people differ because of their identity and self-identity – for example, as Black, female, disabled, gay, lesbian or bisexual, living in rural areas.

- **Changes in how the work has actually been delivered** – that is, in the methods and approaches adopted and the facilities provided; and in how these have been seen, described and justified by policy-makers and practitioners.

- **The service's changing structures and administrative arrangements**, including, for example, in some periods, the distinctive role and contribution of HMI; whether and how ministers have been provided with advice through national committees and councils; and the provision of 'intelligence' on what is going on (particularly information and research).

- **The changing nature and conditions of the workforce (paid and unpaid, full- and part-time).**

- **The evolution of training and qualifications for those workers.**

- **The rise and fall – and ultimately fall – of funding and other resources.**

In search of a critical history

Underlying this approach to historical writing, however, are some deeper assumptions – about the nature of society and the questions which need to be asked about its past development. These, too, need to be made explicit.

Inevitability

In reassessing any historical event, especially one which retrospectively is judged to have been significant, the wisdom of hindsight has huge power. Often its leads to the implicit (even unconscious) assumption that:

- the event was of course bound to happen; and
- it was bound to happen when it did.

A much more penetrating and textured history, however, demands a constant search for naivety. This helps to encourage a focus on what at the time individuals and groups thought and why they did what they did. Historical changes are then less likely to be treated as the result of some mysterious (and mystifying) process of inevitability than of human agency – of the conscious choices which people in the past have made. Though influenced by the dominant values and ideas of their time and constraints imposed by political or economic realities, events are then seen to unfold because women and men acted – and took responsibility for their actions.

Most often and influentially, these 'actors' have come from – or are seen to have come from – the more privileged sections of society. However, from the 19th century onwards, others who were less privileged and had had a less 'natural' grasp on power also gained some leverage on decision-making processes. This happened particularly as, 'from below', groups

organised themselves, acted collectively and thereby much more consistently wrote themselves into history.

Absences

However, at (sometimes crucial) moments women and men also failed to act – perhaps because they did not think to do so, or because certain actions were considered and rejected or because others, individually and collectively, prevented them from acting. Absences then acquire great potential significance – sometimes as telling as 'presences' – and so need if possible to be spotted, analysed and their significance judged.

Contradiction

In the context of education and welfare, denying that events occur inevitably also opens up the question: is everything that happens really for the best – simply part of that great march of human progress driven by altruistic aspirations and rational decision-making? This book does not operate on this premise. Rather it assumes that what eventually emerges as social policy is almost always the result of contradictory, even contested, motives, many of which may have more to do with self-interest on the part of those promoting the policies than with an unsullied desire 'to do good'.

Conflicting interests

Such a perspective points to another, of equal influence: that underlying such motives are processes of policy-making which are often (some would say always) rooted in some fundamental conflicts of interests between competing groups within the society. These social divisions are often most starkly outcrops of the divergent experiences which citizens have particularly because of their class, their gender, their race, their sexual orientation and/or because they are disabled. On occasion, these differences can run so deep that they challenge the very concept of society when this simply takes for granted (and so helps to reinforce) commonsense notions of a largely unblemished consensual culture and social structure.

Negotiation

Because of these inherent societal differences and even conflicts, the social policies which do eventually get agreed and implemented are thus seen as the product of a complex if at times barely discernible 'negotiation'. This in effect occurs among a society's varied interest groups, and especially among those within it with usable degrees of power. Necessarily therefore such political processes embody and produce significant practice and even principled compromises for those involved in the negotiation.

The state

In carrying through this negotiation – especially during the period in which the youth service has been constructed and developed – the state has played an increasingly influential part, often taking on direct responsibility for designing and implementing social, including youth, policies. Notionally 'neutral' in these

negotiations, in practice it usually reflects and indeed replicates prevailing balances of power among the competing interests while acting as the vehicle for operationalising the political, economic and/or social priorities which these have produced at any particular time.

Thus, though often implicit and (again) contradictory, throughout the youth service's 60-year history the state's 'mission' has to varying degrees endorsed some important and influential aspirations for individuals and their personal development. However, particularly because the focus is youth, the state has paid very special attention to nurturing a section of the population openly defined as society's 'seed corn' – or its emergent 'human capital'. Induction into those values, beliefs and practices particularly endorsed by dominant interests in the society and seen as essential to a stable social order have thus also been given considerable emphasis.

Though a highly complex concept, the state's key ways of expressing itself have for the purposes of this book been greatly simplified. In effect it is thus conceived as those organisations, institutions, services and facilities:
- which have been created or sometimes backed up by legislation;
- which are at least in part paid for out of public taxes;
- which operate under the auspices of central and/or local government or (sometimes) other 'statutory' bodies; and
- which are administered by elected and employed public officials.

Youth service as social policy

Implicit in all the above is the assumption, too, that within this society the youth service does *not* stand alone as a free-floating provision for a specified section of the population. Rather it has to be understood as one, albeit somewhat peculiar, outcome among many of the broader social policy negotiations in which the state has this century played an increasingly influential role.

In the past much historical writing has treated the service and the most influential voluntary organisations within it as entirely novel inventions for dispensing education and welfare to young people. The youth service may indeed have, and may have had, a range of unique and positive features and an important internal rationale. On their own, however, these cannot explain why it was conceived of in the first place, by the particular people who did the conceiving, at the particular moment in time that they did this; or why its development took the particular twists and turns it did. Such events and explanations need continually to be located in the wider shifts of thought, belief and action of the periods during which it has existed.

In these ways and for these reasons, material towards the history of England's youth service does not – indeed, cannot – simply 'speak for itself'. What this version of that history attempts to offer, therefore, is a critical pathway through some contradictory and 'unfinished' negotiations. The origins of these can certainly be traced back at least to the mid and late 19th century. However, in this interpretation the proper substantive starting point is taken to be much later – the moment Britain went to war in 1939.

1   Before Albemarle

Origins: Pioneering the voluntary youth organisations

In September 1939, Britain declared war on Germany. Within a year, its state machinery had mobilised over two million men and women and had organised two waves of evacuation. One of these, carried out even before the war started, moved nearly one-and-a-half million people from the cities to the countryside. After months of phoney war had persuaded most of these to return home, the exercise was repeated a year later, this time for one-and-a-quarter million people. As a measure of the priority attached to catering for the youth of the nation, within that same 12-month period the state also made two of its most decisive moves into what we now know as youth work. Through the Board of Education it issued two circulars which, for the first time, brought a 'service of youth' into existence.

The officials who drafted the first of these, *Circular 1486*, made it very clear that they had no wish to start this service from scratch: indeed, implicitly at least they conceded that they could not have done this even if they had wanted to. Their initiative was ground-breaking though. It gave 14 voluntary youth organisations the

right to nominate representatives to new local youth committees empowered to oversee the development of youth provision in their areas. These organisations were:

  Boys' Brigade
  Boy Scouts Association
  Church Lads' Brigade
  Girl Guides Association
  Girls' Friendly Society
  Girls' Guildry
  National Association of Boys' Clubs
  (seen also as including the Association
  for Jewish Youth)
  Girls' Life Brigade
  National Association of Girls' Clubs
  Welsh League of Youth
  Young Men's Christian Association
  Young Women's Christian Association
  National Federation of Young Farmers'
  Clubs

In this way, *Circular 1486* bestowed on these organisations an official status. It also implicitly endorsed an assumption which, then and since, has been largely taken for granted: that these 'independent' charitable bodies invented this distinctive if variable way of working informally with young people in their non-work time.

Such an account almost certainly over-simplifies history. During these decades, other ways of making such provision had been tentatively attempted or envisaged, often based on principles, not of patronage, but of mutuality and self-help within and between working class and other groups. These often continued to operate and in fact in the last third of the 20th century gained some public recognition as an 'independent' voluntary sector determined, particularly within Black and Asian communities, to keep the secular (and racist) state at arm's length.

For their part, with their high sensitivity to actual or potential threats of radicalism and socialism, key power-holders within the burgeoning state in effect treated such endeavours as 'non-organisations'. They therefore refused to support them financially or in other ways – offers which even if they had been made would probably have been rejected anyway. They subtly and sometimes not-so-subtly subverted such activity to the point where it was excluded from 'given' definitions of youth work and all but written out of its history.

The publicly mapped field of youth work was therefore in effect confined to the organisations to which *Circular 1486* finally gave its formal recognition and endorsement. Some of their founders – often charismatic, not to say idiosyncratic, individuals – were far from uncritical of a society shaped by such self-interest. Many were openly appalled at how young people were being treated by its usually ruthless economic system. As upper and middle-class philanthropists, they sought to offer some at least ameliorating experiences and opportunities. They thus added their zeal and their compassion to a broader 'child saving' movement which was by then campaigning, organising and

vigorously intervening on behalf of poor and exploited children who were the fall-out of Britain's exploding industrial society.

Thus in the early 1900s those involved in Salford Lads' Club made clear that one of their concerns was 'to brighten young lives'. And the founders of Ardwick Lads' Club in Manchester declared that:

> It is incumbent on us, fortunately placed as we are, to do something to help those who have to spend their lives in the mean and sordid districts and slums of our city.

Nor did these early youth work 'pioneers' always see the world in exactly the same way. Many concentrated on responding to young people's personal and developmental needs by, in their leisure time, offering 'whatever is most lacking in their everyday life, filling up gaps, broadening their lives, making them more complete women'. Others – for example, women like Lily Montagu – gave specific attention to the damaging consequences for young women of 'the monotony of the workshop life'. She like others, sometimes in the face of fierce male hostility, particularly concentrated contemporary minds on the extra economic and social disadvantages experienced by girls and young women.

Notwithstanding these oppositional stances, in crucial respects these first sponsors of youth work were products of their time. As most of their successors have continued to do, they claimed that their facilities were 'open' to all. Yet, as within most such commitments, their motives were at the very least mixed. Deeply interwoven with their compassion, for example, were anxieties about, in their terms, the social and moral unreliability of 'youth': that is, specifically, about young men's law-breaking and the failure of young women to live up to the feminine ideal then current. Unashamedly and unquestioningly, therefore, they targeted their efforts on 'the working-class boy' and 'the factory girl', expressing themselves with a directness and a certainty which the intervening hundred years have overlaid with liberal mystification and qualification.

Out of these anxieties emerged a number of positive and equally unambiguous objectives. For many, and perhaps the underpinning one, was a determination to win and hold these young people to a religious faith, usually though not always Christian, which was key to their own driving force. Thus, also in the early years of the 20th century, those running St Christopher Working Boys' Club in West London were clear that:

> Our aim is to teach them religion, and to help them learn that the service of God is the highest service ...

For the boys this meant, in the words of William Smith, founder of the Boys' Brigade, ensuring that they grew into a 'true Christian manliness' of, what is more, a particularly masculine kind:

> By associating Christianity with all that was most noble and manly in a boy's sight, we would be going a long way to disabuse his mind of the idea that there is anything effeminate or weak about Christianity.

The equivalent of this in work with girls and young women was also strongly and

openly articulated. In 1890, Maud Stanley made clear that clubs for the working girl were important because they could 'make her conscious of her own responsibilities both towards God and man' and in doing so 'give her an influence over her sweetheart, her husband and her sons'.

As these quotations also show, contained within such religious proselytising was a determination to 'moralise' young people – to instil in them some 'bedrock' social attitudes and habits. This view was again articulated by those running the St Christopher Working Boys' Club:

> It is our aim to ourselves mix with them freely, and give them, as far as in us lies, the advantage of better education and tone that a happier fortune has bestowed upon us from our circumstances ... The lads can appreciate and will learn for themselves that subtle something which is called "good form", which is such an important factor among the higher classes.

For the Boys' Brigade this required that its officers:

> ... promote cleanliness, discipline and obedience, and ... encourage physical, mental and moral culture ...

– an aspiration which was seen as particularly important because of the dangerous attractions of the music hall and other commercial leisure facilities. Though young men were certainly regarded as at risk here, so too were young women, not least because of the 'repressive' nature of the factory work in which so many of them were involved. As one writer noted in 1918:

> Much of the immorality of which the factory girl is accused may be put down to

sheer reaction. She is drugged with the monotony and long hours of physical labour, and feels the need for a strong and sharp stimulus.

As a result, it was felt, perhaps as a balance to Christian manliness, that young women should be encouraged to develop 'capacities of womanly helpfulness'.

Nor were such preoccupations confined only to those operating out of a Christian commitment. They were shared, for example, by the long-established, often aristocratic, Jews who at the turn of the century found themselves faced with mass peasant and working-class immigration from eastern Europe. For them the task was to Anglicise the newcomers – to convert 'the narrow chested, round-shouldered, slouching son of the Ghetto' into 'an erect and self-respecting man, a living negation of the physical stigma which has long disfigured our race'.

These religious and moral aims were closely integrated with some barely concealed political agendas. Around the turn of the century these focused increasingly on thwarting the class conflicts which were re-emerging both within and outside parliament and the threat these posed to what was still largely seen as a given social order. One deeply committed 19th century philanthropist, Lord Shaftesbury, had recognised very early that:

The middle classes know that the safety of their lives and property depends on having around them a peaceful, happy and moral population.

This was a view echoed some years later by the Archbishop of York who in 1878, just at the time that many youth organisations were emerging, warned:

If we in the Church of England do not deal with the masses, the masses will deal with us ...

– to which one of his contemporaries added:

The Church of England must either come into contact with the working classes of the country, or else her national position will suffer and her leading position be ultimately lost.

The early youth organisations often openly expressed these political concerns. In the late 1900s the founder of the Boy Scouts, Lord Baden-Powell, was urging that 'we must be careful that we do not let our differences of opinion on politics or other questions grow so strong as to divide us'.

For many of the youth work pioneers, as for others of their generation and class, the need to remoralise 'the lower orders' – especially at a time when imperialist passions were running high – arose, too, from fears for Britain's economic and military dominance in the face of new international competitors. It was seen as essential that young people grew up patriotic, fit enough physically to defend their country and committed to fulfilling its 'white man's burden' – that is, transmitting its self-evidently superior values to the heathen and uncivilised peoples of the world. Unquestioningly therefore, in Baden Powell's words, 'a scout is loyal and a scout obeys' – and:

Through esprit de corps, patriotism will grow; true patriotism will lead to a just

*appreciation of the duties of citizenship,
and the part which the Anglo-Saxon race is
called upon to play in the cause of progress.*

By the time the first world war had to be
fought these motives had transposed
themselves into an undisguised, if not
altogether uncontroversial, jingoism
which, for example, in the first eight
months of the war led to 169 out of the 217
members of the Hugh Oldham Lads' Club
in Manchester joining up:

> *We felt that, if properly handled and
> without delay ... a great opportunity had
> arisen to test the value of the Lads' Club
> Movement ... It was clearly our duty to
> place the general call before the lads ...*

The 'gift' of charity

These youth work motives and aims did
not emerge out of a social and ideological
vacuum, as if the early youth workers
thought them up from scratch for themselves. Underpinning them was a conception of charity as the proper and indeed
only framework for responding in a very
'targeted' way to those who were regarded
as in need – and as deserving help.

Moreover, within such a notion of
charitable activity financial donations
were in themselves never regarded as
sufficient. To be both morally justified and
effective, it required that the giver 'mix
freely' with the recipient in order also to
contribute to the encounter something of
their 'esprit de corps' – that is, their
values, beliefs and lifestyle. Through this

process the donors must also gain by
fulfilling their obligation (usually to God)
to maintain their personal commitment to
those less fortunate than themselves.

By the later decades of the 19th century, in
some charitable fields these standards of
'noblesse oblige' were already crumbling.
Much that was being done in the name of
charity was being severely criticised as
demoralising to the poor because its alms-
giving had become arms-length and indis-
criminate. Though caused in part by the
increasing individualisation and so
disorganisation of charitable activity, also
underlying this 'deformation of the gift' was
a growing geographical gulf between the
classes, especially in London and the other
large cities. As a result, defining features of
the charitable enterprise – the personal
relationship between giver and receiver; the
mutual obligations on them to be parties to
an exchange – got lost or were overlaid.

Together with the settlement movement to
which they were sometimes closely linked,
the emergent voluntary youth organisations could thus be seen as pioneering an
important new expression of the true
philanthropic spirit. By self-consciously
requiring their 'workers' to engage directly
and personally with young people, they set
out to bind giver and receiver very closely
together. Indeed these highly personalised
interactions were clearly seen as perhaps
the carriers of the moral education to be
achieved through youth work. From the
very start therefore, and on the grounds
that this was how its charitable mission
was best conducted, 'youth leadership'
placed 'relationships' at the very heart of
its practice and provision.

Should the state take a hand?

By the middle of the 20th century, the organising and philosophical under-pinnings of this practice and provision had shifted, in some respects very radically. The state, local and central, was assuming for itself considerable rights and responsi-bilities, albeit in partnership with the grandees of the voluntary youth organisa-tions. The result, as one influential report put it in 1948, was that 'something of the suggestion of charity from which youth units formerly suffered' had been softened.

The conversion to state sponsorship did not occur overnight, nor did it follow an unbroken straight line of development. Making its first moves in 1918, the state took at least 20 years to gain anything like a secure foothold in policy-making and provision and another 20 to establish a central role within these. This slow pace resulted partly from the resistance to state intrusion by the voluntary organisations themselves which, like all such long-established institutions, were prone to territorial defensiveness. Underlying such self-interest, however, were deeper ideological reservations, rooted in the organisations' charitable origins.

Indeed, well into the early 20th century – and despite its control normally by powerful and often highly privileged groups – the voluntary youth sector continued to define itself as the inde-pendent expression of democratic activity and community involvement. By touching such sensitive chords in public and especially political consciousness, youth work's 'traditional' voluntary organisa-tions were able to label the state as a potential threat to individual and family responsibility and to community self-help.

This critique of state intervention was articulated particularly strongly during the 1930s. By then 'the state' was liable to be regarded as synonymous with the 'totalitarianism' of the fascist and communist governments in Europe which were banning existing voluntary youth organisations and creating youth move-ments of their own. However, from its origins, suspicions of state intervention had been deeply embedded in the youth work of Britain and never ceased to have an impact. Indeed, in almost their original form, they gained a new currency within social policy thinking generally in the 1980s and into the 1990s. This came with the emergence of new right Conservatism under Margaret Thatcher and her successors and their renewed and explicit commitment to 'Victorian values'. They continued to have an unmistakable resonance, too, in New Labour thinking even after 1997.

In addition, influential state functionaries had a number of reservations of their own about whether they should be intervening – and how they should be doing this if they had. Many – probably most – central state policy-makers shared the same class origins and many of the attitudes and concerns of the men and women running and working in the voluntary organisations. (Indeed one of the most influential of the earliest boys' club pioneers, Charles Russell, was a senior civil servant during the 1914-18 war, with responsibility for implementing proposals which prefigured the creation of a service of youth in the 1940s.)

The role of the local state in the youth service's development – that is, usually, of the local education authority – would seem to have been more complex. The councillors and local government officials who became involved brought more varied and even contradictory values and interests to their task than their central government counterparts, especially in the areas where the Labour Party became dominant. As a result, they were certainly liable to be less respectful of the whole notion of 'voluntaryism', certainly as it had been handed down from the 19th century.

However, the mandarins at the centre largely started from the assumption that the voluntary principle was fundamental to youth work's policy-making and practice and that, if the state had to get involved, it must as a minimum operate in 'partnership' with philanthropic bodies. More pragmatically, too, they saw the voluntary sector as capable of providing a relevant, flexible and cost-effective service for a demanding and changing clientele. Notwithstanding the fact that most of these organisations came increasingly to cater mainly for children, for the first half of the 20th century this commitment to voluntaryism stopped the central state seeking full-blown sponsorship of, or taking a major financial stake in, youth work facilities. Even after that, its approach remained ambivalent at best, helping to generate a repeating hesitation over strengthening the youth service's legislative base.

For many state policy-makers (local as well as central), what went on in the name of youth leadership was anyway an essentially recreational provision, concerned mainly with providing 'fun' for young people, albeit in uplifting and healthy ways. The incentive, indeed drive, for the state to get directly involved was therefore much weaker than when the nation's workforce had to be educated (or trained) in vital vocational skills and attitudes; or when neglected, abused or abandoned children had to be rescued and cared for; or when teenagers who were robbing, assaulting or even killing other citizens, had to be controlled and punished. As youth work thus seemed to require a noticeably less directive and mandatory legislative base than for other key areas of youth policy, if state intervention was seen to be needed at all, it could remain cautious and strictly limited.

Above all, however, unlike schooling, childcare or juvenile justice, youth leadership continued to allow young people to choose to attend. The return on the state's investment (of credibility as well as actual money) was therefore uncertain and (even when it was measurable) often seemed marginal to the state's dominant concerns about youth. As a result, its intrusions were less direct and less assertive.

However, through the 20th century, state policy-makers found themselves contending with an increasingly complex industrialised and urbanised society operating in a very (sometimes militarily) competitive world. The unprecedented social upheavals brought about by two world wars added hugely to the pace and the destructiveness of these developments. Much more coherent and well resourced responses were called for to emerging social and educational as well as economic needs. This seemed especially necessary when dealing with that societal 'litmus test', the younger generation – and, what is more, when trying to reach and influence them in that 'discretionary' and largely unregulated time, their leisure.

The youth work being carried out by the voluntary youth organisations was clearly seen, at least potentially, as a powerful instrument for achieving such a goal. However, at best its reach remained limited and its impact uncertain, especially on those whom it usually picked out as its target population: that urban underclass of young men and young women who were least interested in 'improving' recreational programmes. What is more, because youth work remained firmly committed to young people's voluntary attendance, users' resistance to what was on offer could be highly effective.

From youth work's earliest days, therefore, 'take-up' was low as a proportion of the total youth – or even target – population. Some young people, it seems, actively and even on occasions violently opposed the intrusion of youth work into their neighbourhoods and culture – 'hooligans', for example, could make life very uncomfortable for those attending the early Scout and Boys' Brigade sessions held in working class areas. Despite this, between the wars the membership of these organisations grew impressively – the Scouts from 152,000 in 1913 to 438,000 in 1938; the Boys' Brigade from 65,000 to

161,000. The Girl Guides, too, expanded from its initial 8,000 members in 1910 to become the most popular girls' youth organisation in the country by the Second World War.

Other organisations such as the Church Lads' Brigade and the Army Cadet Force lost members in this period. At various times, too, the providers – for example, key figures in the boys' club movement – acknowledged that 'every year large numbers fall away', especially apparently when faced with 'a standard of discipline'. That is, 'a leakage' took place whereby 'a fair percentage of boys leave the club before reaching the age of 13'. Estimates of attachment to the voluntary youth organisations from the later 1930s onwards ranged from 15 to at best 30 per cent of the potential clientele. By the 1940s and 1950s providers were openly defining 'the unattached' as 'a challenge' and were developing experimental and detached work projects well before the *Albemarle Report* gave them its seal of approval. Meanwhile, many of those who did join up used the facilities in very instrumental ways, taking as their starting point: 'What can I get out of this on my terms?'

However, particularly at moments of national crisis, it became increasingly difficult for the state to ignore the threats to social stability apparently posed by young people. These drew them more directly into – even forced them to become responsible for – educational and welfare provision and especially for achieving a greater and more reliable impact on youth. To these pressures were added those of the organised labour movement which, for example, pressed throughout much of the 1930s for secondary education for all.

In due course these spreading state tentacles embraced youth work, too. Initially the focus was on strengthening and extending its existing structures and facilities so that its reach and impact could be increased and made more effective. However, as happened in other spheres of charitable endeavour, in its efforts to get such practice to address some key state-defined priorities in sharper and harder ways, in due course the state also found itself trying to mould the voluntary organisations' philosophy, values and priorities.

From charity to a 'service of youth'

It was the impact of the First World War, especially on the home front, which gave this process its first significant push. The war itself had some very obvious effects on how youth work was explained and justified within some youth organisations: as we have seen, recruiting young men into the armed services was the 'natural' thing to do. In addition, wartime conditions at home generated their own tensions and problems, not least as a result a serious juvenile crime wave. A Home Office committee chaired by Charles Russell recommended that 'somewhat nebulously defined' juvenile organisation committees should be set up locally to coordinate and stimulate youth provision. Until his death in 1917 Russell himself chaired a national Juvenile Organisation

Committee which for the first time drew the voluntary youth organisations into a policy-making relationship with the state.

After the war these powers were formalised by the 1918 and 1921 Education Acts. Where voluntary organisations had failed to do so previously, local authorities were empowered to set up their own committees. Though usually still operating largely through voluntary bodies, these were permitted to spend public money on youth facilities. In 1932 Gordon Ette, a teacher who was later to become one of the first local education authority youth officers and an influential youth service commentator, set about establishing such a committee in Cheltenham. Another key figure in the boys' club movement, Sir Basil Henriques, was, as late as 1934, urging leaders to go to their local Juvenile Organisation Committee to get cheap railway fares for boys travelling to camp.

However, 'though a few authorities … provided generously and pursued a vigorous policy of development', the practical long-term effects of these initiatives were limited. The key factor here, as so often in the history of youth work right up to the present day, was economic: when the financial going got tough, state support for it was treated as wholly dispensable. By 1936 only 36 local authorities had kept their committees going. Only six had full-time paid secretaries, so that 'in many of these areas its chief function seemed to be the holding of an annual sports day and/or organising a football, netball or swimming league'. They had also largely been divorced from the educational machinery.

theless, for state policy-makers a psychological and practical threshold had been crossed. What is more, during the 1930s, with many of them convinced that a new war was unavoidable, concerns were increasingly being expressed about the physical health of the nation and especially about whether young men were fit enough to fight for their country. Indeed, this preoccupation with 'national efficiency' – with improving the health of the (male) nation – seemed at the time to override, not just financial constraints, but even the social and moral imperatives which had traditionally driven youth work's development. The result was a further tentative step towards state sponsored provision. The 1937 Physical Training and Recreation Act empowered local authorities to pay for facilities designed to raise the level of national fitness. Some, interpreting this power very broadly, for the first time went beyond merely supporting the programmes and provision of existing voluntary organisations by opening up and operating their own youth centres.

Though in retrospect it may seem that such developments were inevitable, that was not necessarily how they were seen at the time. In fact their pros and cons were sharply debated. One highly influential report on the needs of young school-leavers, commissioned by the King George's Jubilee Trust and published just before the war started in 1939, struggled hard to make the case for a stronger state presence which did not undermine the voluntary sector. Its starting point was a restatement of that mixture of motives which had driven youth work from its beginnings:

> If this country is to continue as the heart of

> a great empire it cannot afford to allow its resources to run to waste. Apart from the suffering which appeals to the humanit-arian sense, we are compelled on purely economic grounds to act, and act swiftly …

By focusing on those young people who were leaving school at the earliest opportunity, the report again, albeit implicitly, defined youth work's target clientele as those who were less able and less privileged. It took it as given that what they required were forms of education. However, it went one step further:

> This does not imply that the great amount of invaluable work done by the voluntary bodies should be taken over by public authorities today, or tomorrow. This is not our British way … while the voluntary system should be strengthened to carry on its already valuable work, the problem can be solved satisfactorily only by largely increasing the supply of public funds and services. If we are wise, we shall not abolish or strangle the voluntary system, but as in the past, public authorities will utilise and aid what exists and supplement it with their own services.

It concluded that:

> There is very high value in the effort inherent in the voluntary system, but it can and has become a burden too great to be borne if efficiency is to be attained or maintained.

And in doing this, the Trust's report at least implicitly reflected the steady attrition of management committee time and leisure available for philanthropic activity. Perhaps for the first time but certainly not for the last, it juxtaposed this modified defence of the voluntary principle with a call for a professional service, predicting that 'the number of paid leaders ... is bound to increase'. By 1938, so significant had they become that a group of women workers and organisers had come together to form the first youth workers' trade union.

This intrusion of the state into youth work seems to have contributed to another significant long-term development: the coalescence of otherwise fiercely independent local voluntary 'units'. National networks and umbrella bodies of course already existed. Indeed movements such as the Boy Scouts, the Girl Guides and the various Boys' and Girls' Brigades had begun as national (even international) organisations. With the death of so many potential male leaders during the First World War and the increased openings for women's paid employment, local voluntary effort and even the regional cooperation needed anyway to be supplemented by increasingly formalised national networks. Hence, for example, the emergence in the 1920s of such bodies as the National Association of Boys' Clubs (NABC) and the National Federation of Young Farmers' Clubs (NFYFC). Where these did not actually lay down policy and programme, they at least provided support and a variety of resources for their constituent and often isolated groups.

By the late 1930s, however, some 'political' rather than purely organisational or curriculum considerations were encouraging these bodies into an at least loose alliance. The central state's growing interest in their territory was clearly one of the 'push' factors. But so too was the

history of their unhappy relations with the local juvenile organisation committees. As one commentator who was a participant in these events recalled over a decade later:

The hope that local authorities and voluntary bodies might unite in an independent and powerful new organism (the local JOCs) was defeated by the obstinate desire of both sides to cling to their own independence, their powers and their right of access to central authority and its largesse.

The result in 1936 was a Standing Conference of National Voluntary Youth Organisations (SCNVYO). This gave 11 organisations – all with 19th century or early 20th century origins – a more collective voice for speaking to government, local as well as central: indeed, its very first move was to release an agreed statement to ministers.

However, the new body's terms of reference were not just shaped by such immediate concerns. It very clearly embodied some of voluntaryism's historic sensitivities and constraints. It, for example, reasserted the view that 'any element of compulsion must imperil the essential quality of their work'. And, again reflecting a rejection of the monolithic, state-sponsored work with young people then emerging elsewhere in Europe, the member organisations collectively went on to assert that:

The value of variety and competition in maintaining a high quality of work with young people has been fundamentally proved. The whole service of youth would suffer if this fundamental principle were ignored for the sake of administrative convenience and simplicity.

Notwithstanding this somewhat defensive stance, the almost throw-away use of the term 'service of youth' suggests that by 1936 at least one fundamental change had already taken place: even the voluntary organisations were having to accept that the state had a role to play in providing youth work facilities. Quite explicitly, in fact, they were acknowledging that, provided their essential freedom was respected, 'the full potential of work with boys and girls could only be realised if such work were aided by public funding'.

Through the filter of history, such a concession can seem both minor and inevitable. In the context of the time, however, it was neither. It represented an acceptance by what in due course came to be identified as 'the voluntary sector' that the state – 'the statutory sector' – had a right itself to provide youth work facilities. This represented a historic shift which, once formalised by the Board of Education circulars, in effect brought into existence that ill-defined and poorly delineated but nonetheless distinctive state institution, 'the youth service'.

From a 'service of youth' to 'the youth service': The effects of total war

When war did come, concerns about 'the condition of youth' again escalated. Once more the adolescent young were seen to be particularly at risk because, in addition to the huge number of men (many of them

fathers) who were called up, many women – including mothers – were working long hours in the factories. The air-raids on the large cities, the evacuation of children away from families and home areas and the consequent disruption of schooling were all recognised as likely to bring major disturbance into young people's lives.

Fears that all this would lead to more juvenile crime again dominated much public and political thinking. The number of under 17-year-olds in England and Wales found guilty by the courts rose by over a third between 1939 and 1941. Rather than abolishing corporal punishment as the government had intended, the total of under 16-year-old boys punished in this way rose from 65 in 1938 to 531 in 1941.

Circular 1486

In responding to these pressures, state policy-makers drew quite explicitly on some of the precedents from the First World War period – for example, to justify proposals contained in two key government circulars. The first of these, *The Service of Youth* (1486), was issued in November 1939. Like the Jubilee Trust's report of the same year, it just assumed that youth organisations were an educational resource and that therefore it was necessary to 'give the service of youth an equal status with the other educational services conducted by the local authority'.

However, the circular openly acknowledged that, in spite of all the efforts made in the previous 20 years, 'in some parts of the country clubs and other facilities are almost non-existent'. To remedy this it concluded that 'coordination is not enough: a new initiative is needed'. It made the Board of Education (the predecessor to today's Department for Education and Employment) directly responsible for youth welfare and proposed that a special branch of the Board be established to administer grants for maintaining and developing facilities. It also suggested that a National Youth Committee should advise the minister. With over five thousand copies of the circular distributed, the then Archbishop of Canterbury talked of the events as 'the beginning of an epoch'.

Developments at the centre were quickly mirrored locally with the establishment of youth committees designed 'to strengthen the hands of local authorities and voluntary organisations' – though 'not … directly to conduct youth activities'. (By August 1940, 129 LEAs had submitted schemes with nine others under consideration: only eight LEAs were deferring decisions.) Money was to be made available – again through the voluntary organisations – to help clubs hire premises, buy equipment and provide 'competent leaders' with the result that by September 1940 some 1,700 new units or clubs had been started. The Central Council of Recreative Physical Training was also given grant aid to ensure that these leaders were trained – something which was further encouraged by the Carnegie Trust's decision in the following year to make bursaries available to full-time youth leaders undertaking training.

Circular 1486 did stress that 'the association of voluntary effort with the public system is typical of the history of the growth of the education services in this country'. And Kenneth Lindsay, the Parliamentary Secretary to the Board of Education who drafted this and the later circular, made it clear that there was to be no 'imitating the totalitarian states': it was after all against just such regimes that Britain was 'fighting for its life'.

Nonetheless, these developments added to the voluntary organisations' pre-war anxieties over creeping state control. Ten years later, for example, a King George Jubilee Trust report talked of:

> *The traditionalists of youth work, being also stout champions of the voluntary principle … (feeling) themselves moved by a certain claustrophobia. The war-time partnership between private and public enterprise in youth welfare looked like losing its balance. The field the voluntary bodies had made their own over more than half a century was, it seemed, being recklessly overrun by official provision and statutory requirements.*

Speaking in 1951, Jack Longland, the Director of Education for Derbyshire, also recalled how alarmed the voluntary sector had been 'at the company they were expected to keep':

> *Local authorities belonged traditionally to the servants' hall, their unsympathetic bureaucrats were the last people to be trusted with so delicate and esoteric a mystery as youth leadership.*

Though, according to Longland, the 'ill-assorted members' of the new youth committees did in due course find that they 'really rather liked each other', their arrival clearly generated confusions and doubts within the statutory sector too:

> Some Directors of Education – old style – and perhaps a civil servant here or there, were shocked at being told to initiate a service so imprecise, without compulsory sanctions or troops of school attendance officers, with no proper buildings or salary scales or qualifications for staff, and they were terrified (justifiably) lest these strange voluntary members of youth committees might prove to be that dreadful thing, enthusiasts.

Circular 1516

Circular 1516, issued in June 1940 with the title The Challenge of Youth, was concerned less with overall organisation and administration than its predecessor. It focused rather on philosophy and purpose and on forms of delivery on the ground. It, for example, identified a 'general aim ... which links all youth organisations to one another and to the schools'. This it summarised as 'social and physical training' whose 'overriding purpose' it defined as:

> The building of character: this implies developing the whole personality of the individual boys and girls to enable them to take their place as full members of a free community.

For delivering this training it saw three elements as necessary: social facilities, physical recreation and 'continued education'. And it emphasised that 'leadership is essential and (that) much of this must spring from the corporate life of youth itself'.

After briefly summarising the history of state intervention in youth work, the circular also reiterated that 'any attempt at a state-controlled uniformity or regimentation would be both stupid and perilous'. On the premise that 'there need be no clash between statutory and voluntary effort', it went on to define the function of the state as:

> to focus and lead the efforts of all engaged in youth welfare; to supplement the resources of existing national organisations without impairing their independence; and to ensure through cooperation that the ground is covered in a way never so far attained.

The following year (1940), the president of the Board of Education made the limits of such a state role quite explicit:

> The last thing I want to see ... in a movement of this kind is the rigid uniformity, the regimentation, and the standardised practice which inevitably results from placing such a movement under the sole control of central Government, or the supervision of some super-functionary.

Moreover, as the role of the local state was still being defined as to 'fill in the gaps not covered by these (voluntary) organisations', at that stage the approach to the state's sponsorship of youth work endorsed by the two circulars broke little new ideological ground. Rather, it reached back to well before the Education Act even of 1918, to that of 1870. The (substantial) extension then of state control over schooling was justified by the education minister of the day on the grounds that it would 'complete the present voluntary system … (and) fill up gaps, sparing the public money where it can be done'. In taking their first substantial steps into youth work territory, ministers clearly felt they must adopt an equally self-denying formula.

Given these starting assumptions, it is perhaps not surprising that, even after the war, the service's 'very name (was) still unknown to many people'. Nonetheless, though not too much should probably be read into small differences of language and presentation, one significant change had occurred: the 'service of youth' to which *Circular 1486* referred had, by the end of *Circular 1516*, quite definitely become a 'Service of Youth' and even, within the body of the text, a 'youth service'.

From Board of Education circulars to Act of Parliament

In fact, even while service of youth policy-makers were struggling to achieve an acceptable balance between voluntary and statutory, the massive mobilisation of human and material resources required by total war was accustoming the British people to unprecedented degrees of state intervention into their lives. These experiences particularly prepared the ground for the Beveridge report on social security. Not only did this – that rare phenomenon, a government bestseller – escalate expectations that post-war Britain could and would finally slay 'the five giants' of want, sickness, squalor, idleness (that is, unemployment) and ignorance. It

also made respectable, even self-evident, the belief that this could only be achieved by extending or creating a wide range of public services. What Beveridge in fact advocated, almost in spite of his own liberal instincts, was the construction of a welfare state.

Though still often only after sustained labour movement pressure, generous and imaginative responses to young people, especially through extended schooling and further education, were placed at the heart of these aspirations. Youth work got caught up, almost as a matter of course it seems, in this thinking. A Board of Education White Paper, *Educational Reconstruction*, published in 1943 (and significantly also a bestseller) devoted a separate sub-section (four paragraphs) to the youth service – perhaps the first time this had happened. It made clear that:

> With the extended period of full-time education and the introduction of compulsory part-time education, it may be anticipated that the interest of young people in worthwhile pursuits will be further stimulated, and that there will be an increased demand for the facilities offered by clubs, youth centres and the national associations of the various voluntary bodies, which the youth service is designed to expand.

Symbolically as well as in very practical terms, the youth service was being actively considered as integral to the state's efforts to deliver on its populist educational promises.

Indeed, in May 1940, just before *Circular 1516* appeared, Kenneth Lindsay had made just this commitment on behalf of the government when he spoke at a large public meeting in Central Hall, Westminster – 'the culmination of similar regional meetings ... all over the country'. In his address he talked of the youth service as 'a fourth province' of the education service which was being added to those of primary, secondary and adult. Similar aspirations were reflected in the brief given to the Youth Advisory Council which replaced the National Youth Committee in 1942. This was asked to ensure that the service was not just a 'wartime expedient' and to consider how it could be integrated into the radically reformed post-war educational system which was by then being vigorously debated.

The two reports produced by the new council, in 1943 and 1945, helped to keep state policy-makers focused on the service at a crucial moment in the development of British social (and especially educational) policy. So too did a 1943 Board of Education circular on *Training and Service for Girls of 14-16* which acknowledged that girls' opportunities 'for training and service ... may appear to be less adequate than those open to boys'. The Youth Advisory Council's first report, *The Youth Service After the War*, reflected critically on the conditions affecting young people's lives and on the (strongly Christian) philosophy which it believed should inform youth work. It also spelt out how it saw the voluntary-statutory partnership developing, endorsing a central role for the voluntary organisations but concluding that the public funding they were by then receiving 'should be accompanied

by some measure of public control over their activities', including some 'scrutiny and inspection' of their work.

The 1943 report did acknowledge that such inspections needed to be carried out by 'people with special knowledge and understanding of the informal type of youth work which is done in voluntary organisations'. Nonetheless, this almost throw-away proposal was to have profound long-term consequences. Most obviously, it laid the foundation for the increasingly active role played subsequently within the youth service by the education system's own inspectorate (originally HMI, now OFSTED, the Office for Standards in Education). As happened to voluntary church schooling in the late 19th century, however, the introduction of an inspection system in its own right also underpinned a significant extension of state leverage over how youth work provision was made and what it did.

Such reports were certainly significant in moving forward thinking and action, with the second Advisory Council report published in 1945, *The Purpose and Content of the Youth Service*, taking a more 'theoretical and speculative' approach and opening up questions of purpose and philosophy. However, it was the 1944 Education Act which produced the most coherent move to establish the state's role within youth work.

Specifically, its Sections 41 and 53 are usually seen as having substantially strengthened local and central state responsibility for and control over youth work policy, financing and provision – and as having done so in a new and radical way. Section 41, for example, stated that:

> ... *it shall be the duty of every local education authority to secure the provision ... of adequate facilities for further education, that is to say ... leisure-time occupation, in such organised cultural training and recreative activities as are suited to their requirements, for persons over compulsory school age ...*

Section 53 reinforced these expectations by making it:

> *the duty of every local education authority to secure facilities for ... further education ... including adequate facilities for recreation and social and physical training ... (They) shall have regard to the expediency of cooperating with any (appropriate) voluntary societies or bodies.*

In crucial ways the Act represented considerable continuity with the recent past, especially in the way the state strove to maintain the delicate balance in its relations with the voluntary sector. It, for example, still required LEAs to 'have regard to the expediency of cooperating with any voluntary societies or bodies'. Their responsibility as laid down by the Act was not actually to provide the facilities – only to 'secure' them (that is, to ensure they existed).

Moreover, in setting out its own role, it remained extremely coy. It required a backbench amendment to the Bill to persuade the government that Section 53 should place a duty on LEAs rather than simply giving them the power to act if they so chose. Nowhere in the Act or in any subsequent guidance was clarification offered on what the Government had in mind when it talked of 'adequate' facilities being provided. Finally, given subsequent local interpretations of the relevant clauses, the legislation contained one highly significant gap: nowhere did it actually name the youth service (or even a service of youth).

Fifteen years later, the Albemarle Committee, appointed to review – and revive – a by then rapidly declining service, did acknowledge that this omission was 'strange'. However, it convinced itself that the resultant powers were 'so wide as to justify almost any reasonable provision for any group of the population' – that is, that they allowed local authorities to be generous and imaginative. In a period of assumed affluence, such optimism may have been justified. When times turned hard, however, another interpretation of the Act's vagueness of terminology came to seem more convincing: it justified the state's continuing reluctance to take on major and direct responsibility for providing youth work facilities.

At most, in fact, the 1944 Act, together with subsequent Ministry of Education circulars such as the one in 1947 which required LEAs to produce development plans for their youth services, was designed to strengthen the role of the local state in making such provision. It was at pains, however, to leave this as broadly discretionary as possible. Many years later Jack Longland, the Director of Education for Derbyshire, was able to point out 'how faithfully this new principle of non-interference has been observed by the Ministry' – that is by the central state.

Nonetheless the 1944 Act did extend what the law had previously permitted and required of local and central government in the field of youth work. Together Clauses 41 and 53 placed a duty on every local authority to ensure that their area had adequate facilities for further education which were to include 'leisure time occupation … for any person over compulsory school age', including 'play centres and other places' and which could be used 'for recreation and social and physical training'. In referring specifically to Clause 53, the junior minister who helped pilot the Act through the Commons insisted that 'the Government desire to see this clause fully implemented by local authorities'.

Surviving the peace: Can a youth service take root?

Within months of the passing of the 1944 Act, these ambivalent attitudes and stumbling approaches to central state involvement in this area of educational activity were again demonstrated. Following the publication of the Youth Advisory Council's second (1945) report, in a move which was repeated on at least three subsequent occasions over the next four decades, the Government disbanded the Council. In part its work was taken over by the Central Advisory Council on Education in England which was set up by the 1944 Education Act and which in 1947 in its report *School and Life* did give some attention to youth work. However, the loss of a central advisory body with a specific youth service brief proved to be the first

step in a steady withdrawal of the newly-established Ministry of Education's commitment to the service.

Some LEAs did enthusiastically accept the opportunities provided by the 1944 Act. By 1948 one survey was reporting that the new system had, for the voluntary organisations, 'considerably eased their financial and other difficulties' and that they had 'not suffered the standardisation and even suppression which some had feared in 1939'. This, however, was far from the whole story. Some – again not for the last time – were seriously at odds with their local statutory 'partners' who were operating in highly territorial ways to the point on occasions of openly empire-building:

> The county or county borough is apt to regard the area associations (of the voluntary organisations) … as superfluous in view of the help which any properly constituted local unit can obtain from the LEA's own organisers and advisers, and the authority may withhold grant-aid from the area associations.

Others apparently were showing 'abysmal ignorance of the work and intentions of voluntary agencies' which may help to explain some of the LEAs' failures to communicate adequately with them:

> In some places, particularly industrial towns … LEAs have managed the service of youth with the minimum of consultation with the voluntary bodies, and efficiency has been secured at the expense of humanity.

In view of these difficulties, it was therefore perhaps only to be expected that there would be anxieties that:

> LEAs may come to evaluate clubs simply in terms of the amount of instruction they purvey and, in allocating money and other assistance, may tend to underestimate the value of more informal activities.

Or as Jack Longland was later to put it, 'it brought the fear that the clumsy-footed State, in its quest for numbers, would sacrifice the quality, and traditions and standards which (the voluntary organisations) had laboriously built up'.

Despite these ambivalences, 'the Second World War proved to be a turning point. The concept of youth work as one kind of informal education crystalised and was generally accepted'. A youth service had emerged, with significantly increased recognition and a clearer identity. Though far from an unqualified success, the requirement in 1942 that all 16 to 18-year-olds register with their LEA to receive 'advice and encouragement' on the constructive use of their leisure had helped to raise its profile. According to the 1943 White Paper *Educational Reconstruction*, the service had shown 'remarkable expansion'. And a 'broadsheet' on the service published in 1948 by Political and Economic Planning (PEP), an independent research organisation, concluded that the appearance and growth of the service had 'greatly increased the interest which the general public takes in youth work'.

Indeed, a basic infrastructure of policies, resources and facilities emerged from the war period into the late 1940s and early 1950s within which, even as early as 1940, 'the old distinction between official and voluntary agencies (was) breaking down'.

- A variety of forms of grant aid from central government was available to key national bodies to support administration and training programmes.
- HMI were involved in assessing youth work provision and activity.
- Four one-year full-time university courses for youth leaders – at Bristol, Durham, Swansea and Nottingham – were operating, with additional shorter non-university courses being run at various times by the YWCA, the YMCA and the National Association of Boys' Clubs.
- A local government committee structure had been established with a specific youth service remit. In some places this included youth parliaments or youth councils acting 'as a medium through which the young worker's point of view can be expressed and passed up to the authorities'. (By 1949 some 240 of these had been created throughout the UK, though – adult-inspired as most of them were – few survived for very long.)
- Usually through the activities of these youth committees, local education authorities were providing voluntary organisations with more than grants. They were also offering staff and secretarial services, help with premises and their maintenance (including making school buildings and playing fields more easily available), equipment and help in finding leaders.
- By 1948 an estimated 1,800 full-time youth leaders were in post – with the McNair report *Teachers and Youth Leaders* recommending in 1944 that,

post-war, a total of between 5,000 and 6,000 would be needed, all to be trained on specialist courses. According to one estimate, in 1949 113 of these full-timers (in addition to 843 part-time leaders) were employed by the 113 local authorities surveyed and the concept of 'professional' youth work was being used in quite taken for granted ways.

- Indeed, the professional association for full-time leaders formed in 1938 had a membership of 255 by the 1940s.
- By 1946 nearly 250 full or part-time local authority youth organisers had been appointed, with other local authority staff also having some responsibility for supporting youth work activities. (Their first national conference held in 1942 was attended by over 70 people representing 70 LEAs – 'the maximum permitted by the accommodation available'.)
- LEA-run youth centres, often in school buildings, had seen 'prolific new growth', with one enquiry published in 1949 estimating that 70 of 113 local authorities contacted had between them opened some such 900 centres. A 14-day residential course arranged by the Board of Education in Birmingham in August 1940 attracted over a hundred leaders – and turned away several hundred more.
- Some local authorities – including, for example, Essex, Derbyshire, Staffordshire, the West Riding of Yorkshire and Glamorgan – though adopting a variety of patterns of provision, were very proactively developing distinctive, often predominantly statutory, youth services.

These were gains on the ground whose impact was not to be underestimated. Nonetheless – and notwithstanding the 1943 White Paper's assertion that the service was not to be a temporary expedient – the future need for it was still not entirely taken for granted. According to the PEP report, 'organised provision for the leisure of young people, whatever form it may take, raises some fundamental questions', for example:

> First, does it tend to disrupt family life? Secondly, does it isolate youth, so that youngsters do not grow easily and naturally into membership of the adult community? Thirdly, does it lead to an undesirable separation of boys and girls at a crucial stage in their emotional lives?

On the premise that county colleges and compulsory part-time further education would shortly be established, it also openly debated whether the service could remain as important as it had by then become.

Clearly, the fact that such questions were being raised suggests that the continuing support even of those who were sympathetic to the idea of a youth service could not be taken for granted. Nonetheless, on balance – even if, it would seem, only on balance – the PEP pamphlet was ultimately optimistic about the service's survival. No less significant, in its discussion of structures, its main doubts did not focus on whether the state had a part to play in providing youth work-type programmes. Rather, its concern was which state institutions could and should take on this role.

Post-war ups – and downs

Even so, subsequent events were to show that the continuing active backing of the state for such provision was by no means guaranteed. The concessions which to that point had been made to a state presence, still more to a central state role, had been partial and often grudging. State resources had been made available mainly as a result of wartime pressures or the threat of war, which had again converted the historic fear of 'youth' into a moral panic. Basic ideological and political objections to state involvement may have weakened, but they had certainly not disappeared altogether. Once economic conditions began to return to what passed for normal – that is, once serious financial constraints on state spending had to be re-imposed – the fragility of this state presence was again exposed.

This did not happen instantly or straight-forwardly: indeed during the late 1940s some of the youth service's wartime momentum seems to have been main-tained. Between 1945 and 1949, for example, four Ministry of Education pamphlets 'took it (the service) seriously into account'. According to Sir John Maud, Permanent Secretary at the Ministry in 1951, the amount provided centrally in direct aid to the service had risen over the previous five years to £300,000. Most of this went to voluntary organisations though some was also committed to local capital expenditure and a small proportion to training. In addition local authorities were spending some £1.8 million directly on the service.

This, however, was the good news. The bad news for the youth service was that wider government policies were deliberately designed to reduce the support it was getting. Thus, in order to prioritise schools, all building for youth welfare was stopped and grants to national voluntary organisations reduced by 10 per cent – a cut which was not to be restored until 1959. As a Ministry of Education circular in October 1948 noted:

> Expenditure under Section 53 of the 1944 Education Act during the current year is estimated to amount to £4.5 million. This is a higher figure than can be justified in present conditions for these purposes, valuable though they are. Authorities are therefore asked to reduce their expenditure under this head by curtailing or cutting out the less essential or more costly facilities.

At its annual meeting in the previous year, the National Association of Youth Leaders and Organisers (NAYLO) debated a number of resolutions deploring the decline of the youth service. One of these asserted that:

> … local education authorities have made drastic cuts in youth service estimates to such an extent that the maintenance of essential facilities has been impaired.

Sir John Maud's positive spin on these policies and their effects was given to a highly prestigious Ashridge College conference sponsored by the King George's Jubilee Trust and held in April 1951. Attended, it seems, by anyone who was anyone in the youth service, this was called to mark 10 years of voluntary-statutory partnership and to take stock of

27

the relationship as it had developed to that point.

The mood at the conference was, on some issues, quite positive. The value of local youth committees was recognised. A broad if slightly guarded consensus also existed that 'the partnership between statutory authorities and the voluntary organisations is, on the whole, developing satisfactorily'. A questionnaire circulated before the conference revealed that 130 local authorities (out of 136) were still supporting voluntary organisations both financially and in kind (though at what levels was not made clear), 115 were making grants towards capital costs and 134 towards building maintenance.

Not surprisingly, however, discussions at the conference were run through with financial anxiety and even foreboding – and with good reason. The conclusion of the Conference's second keynote speaker, the Director of Education for Derbyshire Jack Longland, was that the youth service was operating with 'not enough money, not enough buildings, and too few real people as leaders (and with) fewer organisations and fewer organisers and administrators'. Indeed, conference delegates, clearly accepting the inevitability of further cuts, were already looking for ways to tack to the new cold financial winds. One recommendation to the Jubilee Trust's Research Committee – which was speedily referred back to Sir John Maud and the local authorities! – was that it consider 'what economies could be made in order to allow for expansion and the introduction of new activities'.

It took little time for the fears of the conference delegates to be translated into an even grimmer reality. Within months another Ministry of Education circular was stating that:

> The Minister is satisfied that substantial economies can and should be made in work covered by Section 53 of the (1944 Education) Act.

The Ministry of Education Report for 1952 summed up the consequences:

> The further restrictions on financial expenditure and so on building work virtually called a halt to all new developments in the youth service. There was evidence too that local education authorities' expenditure on the youth service was reduced during the year.

The King George's Jubilee Trust's next intervention into youth service policy-making coincided with even further deterioration. *Citizens of Tomorrow*, its 'study of the influences affecting the upbringing of young people' published in 1955, pointed out for example that:

> The continuing pressures of economy both in capital investment and current expenditure on education has borne with special severity on a service in which urgency is less obvious.

As this last quotation clearly shows – and despite the existence of the 1944 Education Act – the service was in effect already being treated as discretionary. Indeed, many at the time felt that 'cuts in education should have been confined to the frills, of which the youth service was the most extravagant and bedraggled'. Moreover, as throughout the youth service's history, these cuts started from a very low base. In 1955, for example, 'the expenditure of the Ministry of Education and the local education authorities for the youth service is but a small fraction of the Further Education figure'. As we shall see later in this chapter, during the 1950s, when all public services were being held back by building restrictions and by competition for qualified staff as well as by wider economic imperatives, state policy-makers seemed willing, perhaps were even intending, to allow the youth service to wither away.

The best that could be said about some of these policies was that they were stop-go: in the mid-1950s, for example, some increased capital investment was again allowed and grants to support premises were revived. However, the very lurches in financial support and policy commitment contributed to the service's confusions and insecurities. By the mid-1950s contemporaries were clear about their long-term effects. There had been no circular since 1948 devoted solely to the youth service or to clarifying its direction and role. Those which had made mention of it had usually done so to limit or remove the resources coming from central and/or local government.

Local authorities were thus being reduced once again to gap-filling or at best, in their own provision, to emphasising the instructional side of the work. Josephine Macalister Brew, one of the few national figures who promoted the service positively and optimistically through some of its most depressed times, noted the consequences of such policies for the voluntary sector:

> Many local authorities made drastic cuts in their own youth service so that ... there was less money available for voluntary bodies to carry out their established programme. Since the war the voluntary organisations have found it increasingly difficult to raise funds ...

Citizens of Tomorrow also highlighted money as the youth service's 'cardinal lack' and went on to reach a very gloomy conclusion:

> Local authorities and the general public have lost the sense of urgency which informed Circular 1416 ... the youth service is at the parting of the ways. The nation must decide ... whether it wishes the youth service, and all it stands for, to survive and prosper, or whether it is prepared to see it ... shrivel away and perish.

The same deep pessimism about the service's future was reflected in the title chosen by Lord Aberdare for his address to the NABC annual conference in 1956: *The Youth Service in Grave Danger*. This prompted conference delegates to pass on his message to both Houses of Parliament.

In a situation in which anxieties about the younger generation were again building, Parliament did begin to react. Most notable was a highly critical Commons Select Committee on Estimates report, released in 1957, which doubted:

> ... that the Ministry of Education is properly exercising its responsibility for the money voted. The impression gained from the enquiry is that the Ministry is little interested in the present state of the service and apathetic about its future.

Though rejecting the criticisms made of his Ministry, the minister eventually acknowledged that financial restrictions meant he 'could not at present spend more money on the youth service'. Soon after it emerged that this was only part of the truth and that the minister and his officials were playing a rather more actively collusive role in the deterioration of the service. At the very time that he was making what the Select Committee called a 'tepid' response to its report, one of his senior civil servants was admitting that 'the youth service is one (service) which it has been definite policy not to advance'. A few months later the minister himself confirmed to the House of Commons that, 'the Ministry ... has felt that it ought not to encourage (the service) too much'.

Unfinished business at a time of change

Though two years later the Albemarle Committee believed that 'the line (had) at least been held', substantial evidence existed of real decline in the range and extent of state resources for youth work during the 1950s.
- On the ground, in Albemarle's own words, there was little willingness 'to break new ground' – 'to try new things, to adapt tried methods of work to the changing needs of young people, and to seek out new groups in need of help'.
- The youth service had no national group to advise ministers.
- As we have seen, central government grant aid to national voluntary

organisations was reduced while, according to Albemarle, the machinery for allocating it remained undeveloped.
- Youth service building had been severely curtailed and often stopped completely, with the result that youth work was often being carried out 'in dingy drab premises' and with 'a lack of equipment to do the job (and) insufficient provision for outdoor recreation'.
- The contribution of the local education authorities was 'somewhat haphazard', in part reflecting 'the apathy of some authorities or their loss of confidence in the service'. Indeed some of the more important LEAs had neither a youth committee nor a youth officer, so that by 1959 'very few (LEAs were) show(ing) evidence of possessing a coherent policy applied consistently over a period of years'.
- This latter assessment was made by one of the few academics of the period actively committed to the service – T.G. Jeffreys Jones who, against huge odds, had kept alive the one-year full-time course for youth workers at University College, Swansea. Indeed, of the four full-time university courses which had emerged from the war period, this was the only one to survive into the late 1950s. Two non-university courses, one at Westhill College in Birmingham and one run by the National Association of Boys' Clubs at the Liverpool University Settlement, were also operating. Between 1946–47 and 1952–53 the number of students undertaking training had fallen from 79 to 65 – and by 1954–55 to 54. Indeed, despite a series of major reports – McNair in 1944, Jackson in 1949, Fletcher in 1951 – youth

workers still did not have a nationally recognised structure for training and qualifications.

- The number of full-time leaders actually in post – estimated in 1948 at 1,800 – had fallen to 825 by 1953–54 and to about 700 by the end of the decade.
- Despite frequent calls for the situation to be rectified – for example, by Sir John Maud at the Ashridge Conference and in *Citizens of Tomorrow* – and despite a sustained campaign throughout the 1950s by NAYLO, those who remained were still not employed on a nationally recognised salary scale or conditions of service.

Indeed, the state of full-time youth leadership was a focus of repeated concern throughout this period. As early as 1948 the PEP report commented on the lack of comparability between youth leaders' salaries and those of teachers; their 'greatly curtailed social life'; their professional isolation; the inadequate support they received from management committees; and how overburdened they were. Understandably, as the professional body most directly involved, NAYLO was strongly echoing these concerns. In the year the PEP report appeared its journal noted that:

> Many leaders find it impossible to live on the salaries they receive. They have to act as caretakers, stokers and handymen. Some clubs spend more on the wages of the cleaners than on the salary of the leader.

No doubt reflecting what was happening nationally, membership of the Association fell to 94 in November 1950 and to 45 six years later.

Should the youth service survive?

By the mid-1950s what NAYLO was calling the youth service's 'precarious state' even led to some ruminations on the adequacy of its statutory base – though never, it has to be said, with much conviction about what could or should be done.

At the Ashridge Conference Jack Longland had reflected on the variations of support for the service across the country and wondered whether 'the local education authority which does not help voluntary youth organisations within its area … is disobeying the instructions of the Education Act'. In his view 'the vagueness of Section 53 is an entirely proper vagueness' because decisions on what to provide needed be exercised locally. Nonetheless, he acknowledged that where local authority variations were occurring 'because of politics, or because of an unjustified belief in their own self-sufficiency, or because of laziness, or because of meanness and desire to save ratepayers' money at all costs', then it was:

> … at least technically possible, if persuasion will not suffice, for the minister to insist that this defaulting authority should obey the law …

Very quickly, however, he added that 'in practice it is not quite as easy as that'!.

Four years later the King George's Jubilee Trust again pointed out, in its report *Citizens of Tomorrow*, that:

> The 1944 Education Act puts responsibility for the youth service as firmly on the

local education authorities as the obligations to provide more orthodox and traditional 'education'.

Even a Ministry spokesperson acknowledged in 1957:

> *It has not been the policy to expand this service to any definite standard. One must have a standard to which one is working of fairly general application before one can apply anything in the way of a fairly vigorous prod to a local authority ... there is no national standard in this matter.*

Even though the Albemarle Report regarded the service's statutory powers as provided by the 1944 Education Act as 'ample', it recognised the huge variations in local authority provision and pointed to 'there (being) no accepted minimum of services which voluntary bodies of standing can expect from every authority as a matter of course'. This perturbed others more than it did the Albemarle Committee. In 1961 the Conservative Party's progressive wing, the Bow Group, used Albemarle's own figures to highlight the 'wide variety of methods and different standards in financing' employed by local authorities and labelled this the service's 'confusion of organisation'. Concern was clearly lurking over the strength of the service's legislative mandate and so about the 'adequacy' of the provision being made to fulfil this.

However, times were changing – and in some respects radically. One crucial difference was that by the late 1950s, largely uncontroversially and at a rapid rate, the modern welfare state had been substantially constructed. It was during this period, for example, that a deliberate break was made with the tradition of charitable provision of hospital care; that the Poor Law had finally been laid to rest; that voluntary (church) schooling was finally integrated into the public education system; that state functionaries had been drafted in numbers to supplement and even override the work voluntary organisations had done for decades with orphaned, neglected or abused children. In such conditions, principled objections to a burgeoning state presence in providing for young people's informal education in their leisure time were bound to be greatly weakened.

In addition to the ideological and political defence of voluntaryism, however, what in the past had also blocked a full-hearted state engagement with youth work had been a reluctance or inability – or both – to invest public money in it, even on a very modest scale. Indeed, it could be argued, at a time when the hold of the voluntary tradition was repeatedly being breached by the state, it was lack of money which best explains why state provision did not advance much further and much faster in the years after 1945. Once these financial constraints reduced or were at least seen to reduce, this major obstacle to a more expansive state role in the provision of youth work was removed.

One final factor helped to tip this balance. The ideological, political and economic shifts within social policy-making, including within youth policy, were taking place just as major changes were occurring in the extent and nature of young people's leisure. For policy-makers and indeed the public at large, these were experienced as worrying trends which – peacetime though it might be – seemed to call for vigorous and well-targeted action. In such a climate it was hardly surprising, not just that a House of Commons Select Committee should decide to focus for the first time on the youth service, but that its report should touch a raw political nerve. Nor that, when NAYLO lobbied the two major parties on the report, it should get a 'very sympathetic hearing'.

In broad historical terms this turned out to be but a brief moment in the development of youth work policies. Nonetheless it produced an unusual combination of possibilities: dominant ideological assumptions and political ideas favouring state intervention, albeit to certain limited ends; a somewhat more favourable economic climate; and changing social conditions which were apparently radically altering young people's behaviour and their leverage on opinion formers and power-holders. The outcome of this moment was the Albemarle Report.

Main references

Ashridge Conference Report, *Youth Service Tomorrow*, King George Jubilee Trust, 1951

L. J. Barnes, *The Outlook for Youth Work*, King George Jubilee Trust, 1948

J. Macalister Brew, *In the Service of Youth*, Faber and Faber, 1943

J. Macalister Brew, *Youth and Youth Groups*, Faber and Faber, 1957

Michael Blanch, 'Imperialism, nationalism and organised youth', in John Clarke et al, *Working Class Culture*, Hutchinson, 1979

Sidney Bunt, *Jewish Youth Work in Britain*, Bedford Square Press, 1975

Bernard Davies and Alan Gibson, *The Social Education of the Adolescent*, University of London Press, 1967 (Chapter 2)

H. C. Dent, *The Education Act of 1944*, University of London Press, 1947

Carol Dyhouse, *Girls Growing up in Late Victorian and Edwardian England*, Routledge and Kegan Paul, 1981 (Chapter 3)

Gordon Ette, *For Youth Only*, Faber and Faber, 1949

W. M. Evans, *Young People in Society*, Basil Blackwell, 1965

Catherine Green, *In the Service of Youth: A History of the National Council of Voluntary Youth Services 1936–1986*, NCVYS, 1986

Basil Henriques, *Club Leadership*, Oxford University Press, 1934

Richard Hoggart, *The Uses of Literacy*, Chatto and Windus, 1957

Anthony Jeffs, *Young People and the Youth Service*, Routledge and Kegan Paul, 1979

Peter Keunstler, *Youth Work in England*, University of London Press, 1954

King George Jubilee Trust, *Citizens of Tomorrow*, 1955 (Part IV)

Kenneth Lindsay, 'What went wrong with the Youth Service?', *Youth in Society*, Sept/Oct 1975

Matthews et al, 'Local Places and Political Engagement: youth councils as participatory structures', *Youth and*

Policy, Winter 1998–99

A. E. Morgan, *The Needs of Youth*, Oxford University Press, 1939

Alicia Percival, *Youth Will Be Led*, Collins, 1951

Political and Economic Planning (PEP), *The Service of Youth Today*, PEP, 1948

Don Potts, 'Some notes on the history of the National Association of Youth Leaders and Organisers', NAYLO, 1961

Charles Russell and Lilian Rigby, *Working Lads' Clubs*, MacMillan and Co, 1908

John Springhall, *Youth, Empire and Society*, Croom Helm, 1977

Pauline Wharton, 'An Examination of the Conceptual Foundations of the Youth Service in England', unpublished Masters thesis, Department of Social Administration, University of Birmingham, 1979

2 The Albemarle Report: A New Beginning?

Was Albemarle inevitable?

With the wisdom of hindsight, Albemarle and all that flowed from it can seem inevitable: the establishment of the Committee, its actual proposals, their instant acceptance by the government of the day, the expansion that followed. Given the state of the youth service by 1958, to say nothing of what was happening to young people, how could such a review not have been agreed? Once in place, how could the Committee not have recommended in the relatively generous and even visionary ways it did? Once it had made the case, how could the government of the day not implement its proposals?

Yet, favourable though the moment was – and notwithstanding the deferential way in which this 40-year-old historical document is now often treated – such outcomes cannot just be seen as obvious and natural. *Citizens of Tomorrow* did recognise that the youth service's approach was distinctive when compared with some other actual or potential providers of informal adolescent education:

> There is a fundamental difference in spirit
> and attitude between attending an evening
> institute class … and being a responsible
> and contributory member of a girls' club …
> The underlying principle of the (proposed

> county college) is not, as it is in the youth
> service, voluntary choice by the young
> themselves; and that fact in itself is enough
> to make a clear and abiding difference
> between anything the county colleges can
> do and what the youth service does.

However, even these arguments now read as rather defensive. Indeed, throughout the 1950s, doubts were being expressed about whether the service could – even whether it should – survive. Even *Citizens of Tomorrow* – sympathetic though it was to the youth service – acknowledged that:

> There are serious doubts abroad as to the
> purpose of the youth service in these days
> of full employment and the claims it can
> make on the already over-pressed resources
> of the state and local authorities … There is
> widespread (though seldom articulated)
> doubt whether in fact the youth service has
> a part to play in the life of young people …
> The reasons for a youth service, whether
> they date from the 19th century or from the
> stresses of war, have gone; what need is
> there, then, to perpetuate arrangements for
> situations which have vanished, we hope
> for good?

Nor did Albemarle's terms of reference dispel these uncertainties. True, these did charge the Committee to think positively by considering how the service could help young people 'play their part in the life of the community, in the light of changing social and industrial conditions'. It was also asked, however, to take into account 'current trends in other branches of the education service' which, decoded, could just mean: 'Now that the schools and further education are diversifying their roles and approaches, is a youth service still needed?' According to some of the sceptics at the time, the request to the Committee 'to advise according to what priorities best value can be obtained for the money spent' could have been reinterpreted as: 'Suggest the least painful and least contentious ways of diverting youth service funding to more deserving sectors of the education service.' Some years later one Committee member, Denis Howell, who was by then 'minister for youth' in the Labour government, admitted that the Committee had started with 'very fundamental questions as to whether we want a youth service at all'.

Even after the Committee had started its work, scepticism, sometimes it seemed bordering on cynicism, remained. In his presidential address to NAYLO's annual conference in May 1959 – that is, six months into the Committee deliberations – Fred Bush spoke on behalf of 'those … who have been plugging away for years trying to get the government to act'. From his perspective the decision to initiate the review was the product of 'something brewing up at the top'. It was linked too, he assumed, to the Ministry's wish to prevent discussion on the 1957 Select Committee report which had so savaged its performance over the previous decade – an avoidance tactic to which later governments turned when their guardianship of the service attracted

criticism. Bush in fact went on to wonder: 'Why all the hurry?' And, not altogether convincingly, he concluded 'we can only wait and hope that the outcome of all this effort will mean a new life for the youth service'.

Some six months after the report had appeared, his successor, Charles Smales, strongly echoed his doubts:

> Last year … a small ray of light was trying to break through … the Albemarle Committee had commenced its delibera-tions … Even the most pessimistic thought some good might come out of it, although they also reminded us of the fate of the McNair, Jackson and Fletcher reports.

Both Fred Bush and Charles Smales ultimately gave optimism a chance. Nonetheless, with powerful forces, from the responsible minister downwards, having actively colluded in the service's run-down for most of the 1950s, 'the field', though still hoping for the best, could be forgiven for fearing the worst. And for some the worst included a government plot to rid itself of the service altogether – and to use the Albemarle Committee as a front for doing this.

In fact, according to research done much later by David Smith, official motives were rather more complex. Civil servants' impatience with the service, though real, stemmed less from a repudiation of a youth service as such than from what they saw as an outdated ethos and style, especially of the voluntary organisations. Far from ruling out a review of its work, Lord Hailsham, the government spokesperson in a 1958 Lords debate, looked to the Albemarle Committee to carry out a full scale enquiry. What is more he wanted this to 'raise questions about the type, pattern, scope, extent and standard of the service'. Hailsham also quoted a *Times Educational Supplement* comment that 'many organisations regarded as youth service organisations are no such thing, they are children's organisations'.

In Smith's view, the government was thus wanting the Albemarle Committee to provide innovative proposals which would allow it to justify reversing past policies of neglect. Even so, though the Committee ducked the tricky question of whether the service's legislative base was strong enough, the Ministry of Education probably ended up with more than it bargained for. The main recommendations constitute an impressive – and for the 1990s inconceivable – list of proposals for new initiatives and improvements including:

- a 10-year development programme;
- a Youth Service Development Council of not more than 12 people to advise the Minister;
- LEA education subcommittees ('not subcommittees of subcommittees') to oversee local youth services;
- young people as partners in the service;
- a youth service building programme;
- an emergency training college to be established within 18 months of the report being published to increase the number of full-time leaders from 700 to 1,300 by 1966;
- longer-term training programmes for full-timers which would allow easy

transfer to teaching and social work;
- a committee to negotiate salaries and conditions of service for full-time workers in both the statutory and voluntary sectors;
- more paid part-time workers;
- more cooperation between LEAs and the voluntary organisations to organise part-timers' training;
- Ministry of Education grants to national voluntary organisations both for headquarters costs and for 'experimental and pioneering work';
- capital grants by LEAs to local voluntary bodies and increased and more consistent LEA revenue support to the voluntary sector;
- matching central government grants to LEAs to ensure they increased their expenditure on the youth service; and
- via the new Development Council, the collection and collation of information and research on 'young people who find it difficult to come to terms with society'.

The who of Albemarle ...

Albemarle thus faced the (Conservative) government of the day, not with a winding up notice for the youth service, but with a blueprint for an ambitious expansion programme. One reason for this was that, whether knowingly or naively, it appointed to the Committee a number of people who, shrewdly and sympathetically, were capable of riding a wave of changing popular attitudes, not least among young people. Some of these

Committee members also had the skill and the contacts to make their proposals politically acceptable.

Not surprisingly, the key figure here was Lady Albemarle herself who, behind her aristocratic title, operated as an experienced committee professional. By the time she took over the youth service review, she had for 10 years chaired what became the Rural Development Commission. Originally appointed by Sir Stafford Cripps, then Chancellor of the Exchequer, she had stirred the Commission out of its moribund state, revitalising its membership and refocusing its work on industrial and social development. In addition, she was vice-chair of the British Council, a life trustee of the Carnegie Trust (which, as we have seen, had for long been committed to supporting youth work developments) and a member of the University Grants Committee. She had also sat on the Royal Commission on the civil service and was chair of the National Federation of Women's Institutes.

An *Observer* profile at the time insisted emphatically that she was not a crusading amateur like Elizabeth Fry or Florence Nightingale. Her energy had for long been devoted 'to working the machinery by which public services of all kinds are performed', using as one of her main 'professional tools … her personal friendship with strategically placed people in authority (particularly in the civil service)'. Through this, she had learnt 'precisely how much her contacts will swallow and at what point they will choke'. Indeed, her approach was 'to negotiate unofficially each committee

suggestion with the authorities, tempering it to what they will inevitably reject'. According to an HMI of the period, that meant in this case that 'while the Committee was still sitting, interim arrangements had been made (within the Ministry) to deal with an expanded service and a high ranking official with assistants had been put in charge of the administrative work'.

As apparently Lady Albemarle herself was the first to admit, such an approach to policy-making did not make her a great reformer. Indeed, because compromise was at the heart of her style, the price of her achievement often involved 'the watering down of any really radical suggestion'. As a result, 'the Albemarle Report was in a sense accepted before the report itself had been written'. Though for some critics, the *Observer* concluded, this meant that it ended up being 'too mild and unadventurous', it made history by being endorsed in its entirety by the Ministry within hours of its publication.

Other members of the Committee, however, though hardly wild radicals, were determined to respond to some rapid and fundamental changes which they saw taking place within society generally and especially among young people. One whose national and international reputation was to grow hugely in the intervening years was Richard Hoggart. His *Uses of Literacy*, subtitled *Aspects of working-class life, with special references to publications and entertainments*, had appeared in 1957. In it, the picture he painted of young people, albeit in very broad brush strokes, was not especially sympathetic. He, for example, talked of 'juke-box boys … who spend their evening listening in harshly-lighted milk bars to the "nickelodeons"'. Though, he acknowledged, a few girls were in evidence, he saw most of them as 'boys aged between 15 and 20, with drape suits, picture ties and an American slouch'. They were being offered an 'almost entirely unvaried diet of sensation without commitment', resulting in 'a peculiarly thin and pallid form of dissipation'. They were also contributing to what he saw as an 'unbending of the springs of action' which had sustained working-class communities for generations.

Policy-makers had for years denounced popular, especially commercialised, entertainments and facilities as seriously damaging to the development of the younger generation. In 1929, for example, Lord Baden Powell, the founder of the Scouts, had apparently seen a sinister connection between 'cinema stars, Test matches, cup finals and murders', all of which he judged to be encouraging 'interest in false values'.

However, the analysis of contemporary cultural change being offered by Hoggart – at the time a lecturer at Leicester University who saw serving on the Albemarle Committee as 'fulfilling a sense of duty' – was sharply drawn, vividly expressed and rooted in a deep personal as well as academic appreciation of the past. The contrasts he highlighted between the inherent strengths of traditional working-class culture and the superficiality and transience of the newly emergent mass media reverberated

strongly with the chattering classes of the day. They were also apparently seen by policy-makers as having special relevance to their growing 'youth problem'. As one of the two committee members charged with drafting the report, Hoggart's influence on the sections dealing with the changing social scene and the world of young people is unmistakable.

His co-writer in the drafting process was Leslie Paul, whom Hoggart himself later described as 'part of the cultural history of Britain over the past 40 years'. Paul, founder of the socialist youth movement the Woodcraft Folk in 1925, published an autobiography in 1951. Its title, *Angry Young Man*, became something of a media catchphrase, not least because it caught a changing popular mood about youth. It also reflected the critical edge to his own views and his openness to what an unconventional, even iconoclastic, younger generation could contribute to their society.

Other Committee members, though from different starting points, also brought to bear critical understandings of young people. Pearl Jephcott had been active in the National Association of Mixed Clubs and Girls' Clubs and its predecessor organisations for at least two decades. She had also researched and written extensively on young people and particularly on girls and girls' clubs. Denis Howell had been active in the voluntary youth sector in Birmingham for many years and was later to become Labour's minister for youth. The Committee's secretary Ted Sidebottom was a very experienced HMI who, as the founding principal of the Albemarle-inspired National College for the Training of Youth Leaders, exerted a significant if often indirect influence on the service's post-Albemarle development.

... and the why

The experience and ideas brought to the Albemarle Committee by the individuals who served on it did much to shape its analysis and proposals. However, like their pioneering predecessors, they too were, to a significant degree, products of their time. To explain why the Committee was so determined to revive a faltering and unfashionable service requires some examination of those wider social, economic and cultural shifts about which Richard Hoggart and others were already so exercised. As one contemporary commentator put it, for 'stimulating interest in youth service ... conditions are now arising when the pressure of events will probably do more than any committee'.

Not that Albemarle was the first to recognise the significance of these conditions or the way they were reformulating 'the youth question'. A changing societal context for the youth service had been trailed at the very start of the decade, at the Ashridge Conference. Jack Longland, for example, in his keynote address, had been clear even then that 'the youth service must ... operate against the background of, and indeed as part of the apparatus of, the welfare state'. Its creation meant that 'many of the major reforms for which the early pioneers of youth work had fought and prayed ... have in fact been achieved'. Already, he concluded, the result was 'the better-paid, better-fed, better-clothed, more comfort-loving and gadget using youth of today' – a 'rapid revolution in the conditions of life' which, he believed, had not yet been sufficiently taken into account. Four years later *Citizens of Tomorrow* was even blunter: 'the under-privileged ... no longer exist'.

The House of Lords' debate in February 1959 in which Lord Hailsham spelt out his hopes for the Albemarle Committee was dominated by voices which, in expressing similar concerns, exposed many of the motives driving the review. One of the less damning and more sympathetic contributions repeated some of Longland's phrases word for word:

> ... *certainly, taking the young of the nation as a whole, (they are) better fed, better clothed and better educated than any of their predecessors. But it seems to me ... that they are less deferential to their parents; they are quicker to expect the rewards of maturity; they expect more of life ... The vast majority who leave school at the age of 15 ... are surely more neglected in relation to their moral needs than any other section of our community today.*

Cumulatively, contributors to the Lords debate drew up a disturbing list of examples of how youth was (once again) going to the dogs: 'many of the old taboos in the relations between the sexes have vanished'; young people were indulging in 'a high rate of anti-social behaviour'; 'many adolescents ... (had) not found very satisfactory outlets for the money and leisure they have' and so were becoming the target of 'bidders in the commercial world'; parents were 'prepared to surrender their responsibilities for oversight' and thereby were leaving the young 'unguided by traditional values'.

Fears about what all this might do to a society which prided itself on its stability and coherence were never far from the surface. In 1961, for example, RAB Butler, Home Secretary and chairman of the Conservative Party, contributed to a collection of 'Oxford lectures', *Accent on Youth*, published by the Conservative Political Centre. His warning was to 'not only our own Party, but also the nation':

> *The prosperity which has brought us our power may rob us of our meaning and purpose, either by selfishness or else by forgetfulness of the real standards by which a nation is measured as great … We must inculcate into the "new rich" the old virtues of thrift and economy. We must widen the circle of those who use their leisure not for the pursuit of mindless and mechanical pleasures but for the development of discriminating tastes.*

For Butler this particularly meant persuading the younger generation 'in this age of flux, that the immemorial traditions, sanctions and responsibilities of English (sic) society still hold good'.

Though much of this – especially in the late 1990s – reads like the conventional tale of adult woe about society and its youth, some harder social and political realities were intruding. The post-war baby boom meant that by the early 1960s the number of 14 to 20-year-olds would

increase by some 800,000 (or nearly a fifth). What is more, this was going to occur at the very moment that National Service was to end, depriving up to 170,000 young men a year of what was widely regarded as the very best training in discipline.

What, however, made all this especially threatening was the nation's perceived moral deterioration. The most powerful carrier of this message over the decade were the statistics on rising levels of crime among young people – for example, the increases (highlighted by Albemarle) in the rates of convictions among 17 to 20-year-olds for drink offences, violence, sexual offences and disorderly conduct. As David Smith pointed out, for reasons of inter-departmental rivalry the Ministry of Education was not anxious to use the fears produced by these and similar figures to justify a review of the youth service since crime was a Home Office responsibility. As Lord Hailsham argued in the Lords:

> *I do not by any means say that … if we could put forward a better service for youth there might, as a by-product of the service, be less juvenile crime … The youth service is not, and does not like to be thought just a more attractive alternative to Borstal.*

In any case, the precise meaning of such 'evidence' was as always far from straightforward. It could, for example, have been a result of changing police priorities and practices or even of how the figures themselves were collected and analysed.

For public, politicians and other policy-makers, however, the statistics stood as proof positive of the existence of an increasingly anti-social and less law-abiding younger generation – a conclusion which dramatic high-profile events seemed constantly to confirm. In 1952 the trial of two teenagers, Derek Bentley and Christopher Craig, for killing a policeman, generated a hysterical media reaction which even corrupted the Chief Justice who presided over the case. Equally panicky media campaigns developed over other assumed examples of teenage dangerousness: the spread of flick knives; 'rock and roll' riots, especially in cinemas showing Bill Haley's film *Rock Around the Clock* when it was first released in Britain in 1956; the 1958 race riots in Nottingham and particularly Notting Hill in West London in which Teddy Boys were later shown to have played a significant part. The result was a growing panic that youth was getting increasingly out of control.

Bill Haley's impact was significant for other reasons, too: in so far as any single event or set of events can do this, it marked the moment when a distinctive and assertive youth culture was born in Britain. In an article in *Twentieth Century* in February 1958, Colin McInnes cautioned his readers (some of whom would certainly have included members of the Albemarle Committee which was by then three months into its work) that the pop songs about which he was writing did not mean 'crooners'. It was not just, he pointed out, that the word was 20 years out of date. It was much more that it 'at once betrays the cultivated person who's never listened to pop'.

In the late 1950s and through most of the 1960s, the class and generational differences thus exposed were more and more sharply delineated as – usually in the teeth of their elders' derision and hostility – young people instantly embraced Presley, the *Beatles*, the *Rolling Stones* and their many (even if not always as talented) successors. It was not just the music of the new youth culture, however, which was seen as generationally divisive. With (some) extra money in their pockets, young people were making public presentations of themselves which adults found more and more discomforting. What some sections of teenage population wore, how they did their hair or applied their make-up, how they danced, where they shopped and what they bought, the things they did in their leisure time, the drugs (in addition to alcohol and nicotine) which even then they preferred – all these came to act as undeniable markers of a whole generation's break with their parents and their parents' past. As if the core statements about liberation apparently embedded in these activities were not explicit enough, they were repeatedly driven home by a new relaxation and openness in young people's sexual relationships as (in common with their elders) they made increasing use of more reliable and accessible forms of contraception.

In all this, radio and the new medium of television played a crucial part. They did not just disseminate the new teenage messages to the point where more and more young people were able to own them for themselves. Through 'illegal' commercial stations like Radio Caroline and Radio London (to say nothing of Radio Luxembourg) and through television programmes like *Six-Five Special, Ready, Steady, Go, Juke Box Jury* and in due course *Top of the Pops*, a powerful extra ingredient was added to this apparently rebellious and certainly non-deferential teenage dynamic. In the process the whole generation was widely assumed to be caught up in it until, according to one influential journalist at the time, youth had become 'the last foreign country'. 'You need to learn a language', he proclaimed, 'to spend an evening in their territory'.

With people like Hoggart, Paul and Jephcott as their antennae, the Albemarle Committee was quick to pick up on these novel generational signals as well as on the public and political concerns, both objective and alarmist, which they were producing. The improved opportunities and protections provided by education, housing, social security and the National Health Service were identified as crucial context for youth service development. So too were the ending of National Service, 'the bulge' in the birth-rate and the 'changing pattern of women's lives' as they married earlier, spent less time child rearing and joined the labour market in increasing numbers. The report also expressed what turned out to be exaggerated concerns about a juvenile crime wave.

Above all, however, the Committee was struck by the new spending power of the young. As well as drawing on official statistics, it was given a preview of what at the time were treated as sensational new findings on teenage consumer spending. Produced by Mark Abrams, research director of Britain's largest

advertising agency, the London Press Exchange, these contained clear echoes of Hoggart's critique of modern youth and were seen by the Committee as a whole as having major implications for its work:

> … much of the spending is clearly – and naturally – on goods designed to impress other teenagers (e.g. dressing up) or on gregarious pursuits (e.g. coffee bar snacks). This is spending which is, to an unusually high degree, charged with high emotional content – it helps to provide an identity or to give status or to assist in the sense of belonging to a group of contemporaries.

One of the most striking features of this and other passages was the report's use of the term 'teenager' – still new enough in 1959 to be rather faddish. (Colin McInnes's novel *Absolute Beginners*, which is often credited with having invented the whole teenage phenomenon, had been out only a few months when the report appeared). From this taken-for-granted starting point, the Committee went on to paint a picture of young people '*of* a new world of adolescents' (emphasis in the original). This, it made clear, was defining itself, not just at a time when 'old habits, old customs, old sanctions and responsibilities will be called into question and new relationships demanded' – but as a direct response to these very changes.

In particular, the report suggested, young people were being faced with the 'contrast between what their parents tell them – if indeed they speak of the subject – are the foundations of a worthwhile personal life and the assumptions made on many a hoarding or at many a work-bench'. Faced with the 'persuasive voices' of the commercial providers:

> Why should they (young people) listen ...
> to the more sober and often drab voices –
> urging restraint, caution, discipline and (to
> them) similarly "old fashioned" attitudes –
> voices from that very world which has
> seemed, in its formal classifications, not
> greatly to care for them?

This analysis led the Committee to endorse the increasingly popular certainty that a generation gap was opening up between parents and young people whose starkest and most material expression was an unprecedentedly independent youth culture. Indeed, this was seen as replacing traditional social divisions:

> The parents now see these children as the
> teenagers of the early "sixties", well-fed,
> healthy, maturing early, well-clothed and
> prosperous. These young people have
> tastes, in dress, in amusements and in
> many other things, widely different from
> and more costly than any their parents
> were able to entertain ... A particularly
> strong imaginative effort is needed by
> anyone over 35 – by middle-class parents
> as much as working-class parents – to
> understand the true quality of the lives of
> this generation which is itself so often
> "classless" in appearance and in some of its
> habits.

Even before the 1960s were out, evidence was emerging that these apparently unbridgeable gaps between young and old were much narrower than was popularly assumed, and might even be real. This new research revealed wide agreement between the generations on the importance of marriage and the family, on which political party to support, on the need to send 'coloured' immigrants home and to restore the death penalty. For one contemporary commentator, the problem was far less their rebelliousness than 'repression of the young, their premature moulding according to adult models, their redirection into restricted channels'.

At times the Albemarle Committee came close to conceding some of these points – as when it acknowledged that the classlessness of the new youth culture existed in appearance only and only 'in some of its habits' and that it had 'found no body of evidence sufficient to suggest that teenagers as a whole have rejected family life'. It also brought a sharp focus onto the insecurity and even confusion of the young in a world of nuclear weapons and in a 'society which disagrees about or is unsure about its meaning and purpose'.

Nonetheless, for the purposes of most of what came later in its report, the Committee was convinced that young people's material expectations were rising rapidly and their values diverging radically from those of older and socially superior generations. The basic premise of its policy proposals therefore was that the youth service's target group was affluent, iconoclastic and, culturally, highly distinctive. With Hoggart's somewhat jaundiced eye probably providing the most powerful lens for viewing this bravish new teenage world, the overall conviction which drove the Committee was unambiguous: unless the youth service was re-quipped to penetrate the mysteries of a novel youth culture, its prospects were dim.

Beyond the language of the school speech day

To achieve this penetration the Committee made proposals aimed at forcing the youth service to develop a contemporary, youth-friendly approach. In the course of doing this, though apparently not always intending it or completely succeeding, it came as close to expounding an unselective ('universalist') set of aspirations for the youth service as have ever been proposed.

It was not of course unaware of the contradictions and dilemmas embedded in such aspirations. It defined youth work as 'a tense day-to-day walking on a razor edge between sympathy and surrender'. In a phrase which seemed to have come straight from Hoggart's pen, it explicitly distanced itself from 'an abdicating assimilation to the adolescent's view of the world'. It also denied that it saw the youth service's task as 'to remove tensions so as to reach towards some hypothetical condition of "adjustment" to individual and social life'.

At the same time it was determined that the service should free itself of its drab and ramshackle image and achieve a greatly extended and more heterogeneous take-up. It was particularly critical of its past reluctance to break new ground with the result that 'the type of boy or girl aimed at tends to be the same'. In its concern that the service should win many more 'unattached' young people, it identified variety and flexibility as two key guiding principles.

In advocating such targeting, Albemarle envisaged that it would help to broaden the youth service's reach and certainly not limit or narrow down entry to it to certain categories of youth. Its rhetorical starting point was that the service was and should remain open to all as of choice: it took it as given, for example, that those voluntary youth organisations which attracted a mainly middle-class clientele should stay firmly within its orbit. Yet, beneath this broad aspiration, the historic limit to such a universalist vision persisted, at least implicitly. The service's primary mission was, still, to reach and influence working-class young people, particularly those who were disadvantaged and so potentially or actually disruptive – which meant those who felt alienated from its own 'traditional' approaches and philosophies. The Committee's completely taken-for-granted assumption that university students would look elsewhere for their social education gave away this bottom line as clearly as any of its more explicit ruminations.

One of the ways in which the Committee sought to encourage an increased take-up was by seeking to reinvigorate the service's core values and purposes. Though it claimed that it had no wish or intention to challenge these fundamentally, its temerity in attempting even to re-interpret them was bound to raise the suspicions, if not the hackles, of some of the service's most powerful vested interests. Particularly influential and vocal here were those who continued to assume, not only that youth leaders needed to have a religious and indeed a specifically Christian commitment, but that, even in

45

'open' youth work settings, they must strive to win young people to this. For many of the individuals and organisations concerned, the (secular) state's intrusion into youth work provision over the previous two decades had given extra urgency to defending and indeed reasserting these traditional positions.

In 1950, for example, *Eighty Thousand Adolescents*, a substantial and influential report on young people in Birmingham published by one of the leading commercial publishers of the day, stated as an apparently self-evident truth that:

> *The ideal of a free democratic society ... which fully recognises the worth of the individual derives <u>alone</u> from Christian faith. It has grown out of faith in the Christian God, and will only be sustained as it continues to be derived from the same source.* (Emphasis added.)

The report concluded that all the other youth service aims it was advocating – experience of democratic living, discovering significance in daily work, the enrichment of home life, training for citizenship – 'can only be truly realised by those who can live in a truly Christian spirit'.

The following year a consensus around the same value base emerged from the Ashridge Conference. Though some 20 per cent of the 150-plus people present could be said to come from the statutory sector – and notwithstanding the fact that the Association for Jewish Youth had two representatives at the conference – one of the clearest points of agreement at the meeting was that:

> *All youth work should be based on the principle that the national wellbeing requires that there should be preserved or born a genuinely Christian civilisation in which belief in God sets the tone for society.*

As late as the mid-1950s, similar sentiments continued to be expressed by influential policy-making groups. Though *Citizens of Tomorrow* did not advocate for 'any specific religious affirmation' for youth leaders, it did at least consider – even if in the end declaring itself not competent to decide – whether its position assumed that Christian doctrine should be taught within youth work. It too concluded that 'work with young people must be founded on the Christian ethic and the recognition of Christian standards of thought and behaviour'.

At the Ashridge Conference, Sir John Maud sounded what was for a senior civil servant a strikingly blunt note of warning that this ground might be about to shift:

> *... do not let us, particularly those of us who happen to be Christians, allow any definition of the youth service which has a smell of the closed shop about it.*

However, despite an obvious and repeated nervousness ('we earnestly hope not to be misunderstood'), it was left to the Albemarle Committee to transform such personal doubts into something approaching a statement of public policy. It gave itself a mandate for doing this by paying a strong tribute to the 'strong ethical feelings (which) moved the pioneering voluntary organisations', stating baldly that it was 'obviously ...

deeply sympathetic' to the aim of many of them (including many which were non-denominational) of 'communicating Christian values'.

Moreover, it at no point acknowledged that the ethical dilemmas by then facing the service might perhaps reflect a plurality of often conflicting values within the wider society; and that this plurality might actually include rejection of organised religion or Christian belief. And it certainly failed to recognise that Britain was rapidly becoming not just multi-racial and multi-cultural, but also multi-religious. Instead, as an extension of its preoccupation with the generation gap, it explained the moral and ethical dilemmas it was describing as simply 'a failure of communication' – as the inability of youth service sponsors to 'connect with the realities of life as most young people see them; they do not seem to speak "to their condition"'.

This in itself was of course challenging for its day – indeed something of an analytical breakthrough in constructing youth policy. For a highly influential state policy paper, the report's gloss on this was also highly sensitive. It began by asserting, for example, that:

> ... for the youth service as a whole ... (its) way of embodying aims is mistaken. For many young people today the discussion of "spiritual values" or "Christian values" chiefly arouses suspicion.

It then raised the stakes further by demystifying some of the service's other 'magical' invocations of worthiness:

> We have been struck by the great number of occasions, in the evidence presented to us, on which words such as the following have been used <u>as though they were a commonly accepted and valid currency</u> (emphasis in the original): "service", "dedication", "leadership", "character building" ... (These words) recall the hierarchies, the less interesting moments of school speech-days and other occasions of moral exhortation ... (Young people's) failure to attend youth clubs may be less often a sign of apathy than of the failure of their seniors properly to adjust their forms of language.

Again the Committee excused itself for possible misunderstandings of its intentions. Again, too, it sought to secure its rear – or was it perhaps to preserve a basic consensus amongst its members? – by declaring that it wished 'in no way to challenge the concepts behind these words' and by defining its critique of the philo-sophical status quo as one simply of language and communication. Nonetheless, in what the report itself described as the increasingly 'open and demotic' climate of the times, such a critique was perceived by many youth service traditionalists as containing something much more substantive – and perhaps even subversive. By daring even to ask questions about some of the service's most revered beliefs and concepts, the Committee challenged those who, out of both religious conviction and class patronage, had previously assumed the right to act as the repositories of all youth work's moral wisdom.

Notwithstanding such reactions, by conducting its discussion of values as if the problem facing the youth service was merely out-of-date terminology and defective communication, the Committee portrayed considerable philosophical and ideological caution, if not conservatism. And yet, for practice and provision during the 1960s and into the 1970s, the report did have some more radical consequences – most of them almost certainly unintended. Over time its ruminations on values and purposes helped a range of more critical and even political perspectives to take root and even gain some legitimacy within the youth service.

One area where in due course this occurred – clearly unintentionally – was in the work done with girls and young women. Though the report's sub-section on *Preparation for marriage and home-making* was directed at boys as well as girls, elsewhere it revealed some very conventional views on the potential and roles of young women. (It, for example, took it as self-evident that it was a girl's 'job' to acquire 'technical competence … as home-maker'.)

Over time, however, its endorsement of a wider range of values and aims encouraged some feminist youth workers to see the youth service as a potentially valuable site for their more political as well as social educational practice. This did not occur in time to prevent the rapid swing during the 1960s to mixed provision which, as we shall see in the next chapter, made young women less and less visible and more and more marginal within youth service policy-making and planning. By the 1970s, however, as the wider feminist movement in Britain revived, the youth service's relative openness and flexibility offered women some opportunities – albeit usually in the face of considerable male resistance – to reclaim some lost ground by initiating a feminist practice with a contemporary relevance.

Nor was feminism the only such 'subversive' perspective eventually to penetrate youth work through the philosophical niches inadvertently opened up by Albemarle. The Committee was appointed only three months after the Nottingham and Notting Hill 'race riots' which, it was claimed at the time, so shocked the nation that judges were impelled to impose exemplary sentences on some of the (white) perpetrators. Yet the report itself made only one reference to these 'racial outbursts' and only then in the context of a discussion on housing. This response also seemed to betray the Committee's bewilderment, not to say hurt, at what had happened. How, they wondered out loud, could such violent antagonisms occur 'when young people of all races and nationalities … share common interests such as jazz and football and even a common culture'?

This focus on culture as the defining characteristic of such relationships came increasingly to dominate almost all social policy analyses of 'immigrants' and 'immigrant communities' in Britain at the time. It assumed that race relations were shaped by, and could most effectively be influenced through, the personal and inter-personal interfaces of family, peer group, neighbourhood, religion and recreational activity. According to Albemarle, for example, a sense of insecurity could sometimes develop within the established community as 'new and strange faces appear on the doorsteps and congregate in the streets' – a view which seemed to suggest that, by daring to be new and strange, it was the newcomers who were creating inter-racial tensions. In common with most of their contemporaries, therefore, the Committee concluded – again in a throw-away phrase – that the solution was 'the integration of these (immigrant) families', presumably into 'the British way of life'.

In so far as such integration assumed a one-way accommodation by the newcomers to an unchanged British society, it was not a solution which was to recommend itself to the Black and Asian youth workers. However, by in due course occupying the philosophical as well as the institutional territory opened up by Albemarle, they were able to inject some more explicitly 'Black liberationist' perspectives into youth service discourses. When complemented by racism awareness and then later anti-racist approaches to their work with white young people, these sought to locate responsibility for much of the Black and Asian young people's 'disadvantage': within the (white) 'host community'. The result was to convert Albemarle's nervous questioning of youth work's language and concepts into a substantive and often quite fundamental critique of its ideology – and its practice.

By the 1970s, as other oppressed groups – for example, the disabled and gays and lesbians – also asserted themselves and their interests, some youth workers and indeed some young people were also able to some extent to exploit the pluralist space which Albemarle had bequeathed to the youth service.

England – and Wales?

The Albemarle Committee's terms of reference were very clear: it was to review the contribution of the youth service in England *and Wales*. And in token ways it fulfilled this remit, primarily through a 4-page chapter on *The Position in Wales*. This acknowledged 'the existence of two languages (which) necessitates a different approach to the problems of youth and at the same time multiplies them'. It identified, too, 'the challenge (to the Welsh) to preserve their heritage against the threats to which it is exposed from modern means of mass communication'. In a specifically youth service context it also recognised that, as no Ministry grants were paid directly to national voluntary organisations in Wales, these depended on whether and how the parent bodies reallocated them.

In the end, however, though generally concerned about the levels and reliability of central government support to the voluntary sector in Wales, the Committee chose to regard this rather colonial process for deploying resources as simply 'a domestic matter' which did not justify any specific recommendation. Overall in fact it seemed as anxious to emphasise the similarities between the two countries as to draw attention to special Welsh character-istics and needs. It started from the proposition that 'the general features of the youth service in Wales resemble those of England' and asserted that, in spite of 'living side by side with one of the most culturally powerful nations in the world', the Welsh had (somehow) 'contrived to preserve their identity'.

As this latter statement makes clear, for the Welsh as for Black and Asian ethnic minorities, culture was taken as *the* determinant of social problems and policy responses, with economic and political factors apparently playing little, if any, part. It was therefore hardly surprising that, even though the Committee recognised 'the force of national sentiment' within Wales, it did not see a separate Youth Service Development Council for Wales as either 'necessary or desirable'. Indeed, not one of its 44 recommendations related specifically to the chapter on Wales nor directly addressed the circumstances of the youth service in Wales *per se*. Here too such changes had to await the later emergence of pressure from those most affected – that is, in this case, for the resurgence of more organised expressions of Welsh national feeling.

The Albemarle Report as social policy

As we have seen, some youth service interests were deeply suspicious of the Albemarle Report's call for changes in the language used to express youth work's purpose – particularly, it seemed, those running single-sex and uniformed organisations and organisations with a strong Christian orientation. They interpreted this as barely disguised advocacy of the permissive ideas which, by the 1960s, were endangering many of the service's and indeed society's bedrock values. The politics of the youth service

were to provide ample evidence on why the Committee felt the need to tread carefully in presenting some parts of its analysis and making some of its recommendations.

Other critics of the report had more pragmatic criticisms. There was, for example, the (apocryphal?) story circulating in the months immediately after its publication which had one LEA chair dismissing the document with: 'We're not paying for *fun!*' In contrast, there were those who asked why the Committee had not been more ambitious in its demands for resources. And then there was 21-year-old Ray Gosling, general secretary of 'the first "self-programming" youth club set up in the backwash of the Albemarle Report'. With the support of 'trendy' aristocrat Lord Stonham, he complained in his widely publicised Fabian pamphlet *Lady Albemarle's Boys* that the report had done nothing to shift real power towards young people. Moreover here he was not just thinking of the youth service as a service but even more importantly of what still needed to be done within the structures of individual clubs.

Yet, despite ruffling feathers of such very disparate hue, in the broad sweep of its thinking the report was very much a document of its time – part of a strengthening progressive consensus on why, how and by whom education and welfare should be provided. This particularly supported Albemarle's contention that, in both its ideology and its forms of delivery, youth work must become less autocratic, more individualistically focused and more professional (which also implied more secular). In this climate, the Committee's very openness to new concepts and revised forms of language, far from damaging its wider political credibility, fitted neatly into some of the period's most fashionable social policy assumptions.

These started from one 'fact' which, as we have seen, underpinned so much of the Albemarle Committee's own work: that, in the words of the prime minister of the day, Harold MacMillan, Britain had 'never had it so good'. A minority might continue to resist this newly affluent and consensual society and its blandishments. They were certainly likely to include some young people – especially those who broke the law – as well as the 'permissive' parents who so worried their lordships during their debate on the youth service. However, the problem which came to seem for many increasingly serious was, as RAB Butler put it, that 'people are divided not so much between "haves" and "have-nots" but between "haves" and "have-mores"'.

Moreover, with (it was argued) poverty thus all but eradicated, so too, it was widely agreed in policy-making circles, were most of the basic (particularly class) conflicts which had divided British society for centuries. Another of the slogans of the time, 'we are all middle-class now', confirmed that the cultural and value consensus which had been the cement of British society for centuries was now broader and firmer than ever.

It was not until the second half of the decade that this cosy social and economic mapping of Britain was challenged in any fundamental way. By then small and unfashionable groups of academic researchers, rights advisers and professional 'helpers' (including some youth workers) were rediscovering poverty, identifying casualties of the welfare state and recognising that some substantial sections of the youth population were decidedly 'non-swinging'. As well as posing new questions in its own right, this evidence also suggested that supposedly neutral terms like 'deprivation' and 'under-privilege' might after all be little more than class differences by another name.

Nonetheless, implicitly and sometimes explicitly, policy-makers continued to deny that any of this pointed to intrinsic fault lines within British society. Instead they insisted that all that remained were some residual social problems, little local difficulties and blemishes, mere technical blips and imbalances in what was otherwise an essentially effective and benign society. Unpacked, such explanations assumed that most if not all of society's outstanding deviancies could be traced back to small numbers of 'pathological' individuals and families and their defective personal characteristics and ways of socialising their children. In time, their rehabilitation would be achieved through the interventions of the newly emergent breed of trained and skilled human relations experts.

In 1956 Anthony Crosland, who was to become Secretary of State for Education during the 1960s, gave a remarkably clear account of these assumptions in his book *The Future of Socialism*. There was, he pointed out, a need for:

> ... *aid (which) will often take the form, not of cash payments, nor even of material provision in kind, but of individual therapy, casework and preventive treatment and for "the advice, not of economists, but of psychiatrists, sociologists and social psychologists".*

This, he also asserted, would lead to an increasing emphasis on 'the Family Planning Association, childcare committees, home visitors, almoners and mental health workers'.

The profession which perhaps had its thinking and practice most directly shaped by these ideas was social work. Increasingly employed by the state through childcare, mental health and welfare and probation departments, its practitioners, managers and trainers were often quite unambiguous about their responsibility to (re)-socialise 'inadequate' individuals and 'failed' and 'problem' families. For one contemporary commentator, their preoccupation with these kinds of 'diagnoses' of client situations and with the forms of treatment flowing from them pushed social workers increasingly into coercive forms of social policing which were concerned more with control than with care.

Education had its parallel – and for a time also extremely fashionable – theories. The unelaborated vocabulary of working-class children which got particular attention was interpreted (over-simplistically according to their originators) as indicating a need for compensatory education programmes. More positively, educational policy-makers and

practitioners justified the move to comprehensive secondary schooling in the late 1960s in part on the grounds that it would ease entry into the new opportunity society for many more able and deserving individuals.

In their underlying assumptions, the recommendations of the Albemarle Committee fitted well into this strengthening social policy ideology. Nods were given to some of the structural roots of society's problems and tensions. The youth service, it was agreed, 'cannot be expected to deal with the causes of delinquency' while theories which associated law-breaking with 'disturbed social conditions' and with poverty were also acknowledged. However, not only did the report rely on a notion of 'personal disturbance' to help explain the period's 'new climate of crime and delinquency'. More generally, the wider economic and social conditions shaping young people's lives – the 'hampering' effects of poor housing, the damage done to 'the young and immature' by educational and vocational selection, the 'impersonality' of life at work – were treated, not as key constraining factors on their use of leisure and their longer-term development, but in effect as interesting background.

The Albemarle Report thus envisaged few structural limitations on what the young could do, aspire to, even think – or on the goals it was setting the youth service. The corollary of this, however, was that, albeit sometimes naively, it adopted a generally very positive view of young people and of youth work's 'mission'. Though specifically highlighting the service's 'social and pastoral' functions, it never apparently even considered whether it should be located outside the structures of education, either locally or centrally. It was explicit in its view that the service 'is not … a means of keeping (young people) "off the streets" or "out of trouble"'. Instead it repeatedly emphasised both the young's potential and the pressing need for youth work to release this. It thus strongly reasserted the service's educational role and in particular, albeit in almost throw-away references, its responsibility for offering 'social education'.

In doing this it went on to argue at some length that, to deliver such an education, the youth service's activity programmes must provide three key kinds of experience: 'association' (which could be 'immensely educational, according to the imagination of the leadership'); 'training' (which, 'flexibly planned … can both connect relevantly with the experience of the students and be tough and demanding'); and 'challenge'. It also highlighted young people's role as 'the fourth partner' in actually running the service and gave participation and specifically self-programming a special prominence.

From such recommendations flowed the report's encouragement of a much wider and more disciplined use of small group methods. In addition to urging youth workers to provide individual 'counsel' to young people, it wanted them to make skilful use of the range of social situations which they so enjoyed in their leisure anyway. Despite its sceptical view of the youth service's usually taken-for-granted commitment to 'training young people in citizenship', it also emphasised its duty to provide 'new freedoms for the next generation to come to maturity, and so to social responsibility in their own way'.

Yet, for all its stress on group work, on social interaction and on the need for young people 'to make a significant contribution to society', the Albemarle prescription had little to say on the possible shared outcomes of its proposed programmes. The potential of group experience for motivating and preparing like-minded people to work together for collective outcomes which might, even marginally challenge the status quo was neither acknowledged nor, it would seem, even considered. Social contact and interaction was valued as a vehicle for encouraging a person-centred practice – as merely a means by which individual growth, self-expression and self-realisation could be achieved.

For the Committee in fact the youth service's main rationale was that it would 'help many more individuals to find their own way better, personally and socially'. It thus strongly reflected the basically individualistic perspectives on human motivation and need then current among social policy makers. In the process it endorsed an essentially 'up-by-your-bootstraps' philosophy of personal development and advancement which was at the heart of 'the meritocratic society' – a notion which was specifically identified, named and popularly internalised at the very moment that the Albemarle Report was being written.

Such individualised values and aspirations were of course far from novel to Albemarle's conception of youth work. They were deeply embedded not just in its own 19th century origins but also in what had been proposed and supported by the state since it first got directly involved. As we have seen, both *Circular 1516* and the 1943 White Paper *Educational Reconstruction*, in emphasising the need to provide what they called 'social and physical training', endorsed a focus on individual boys and girls as the route to their taking up responsible community roles. The 1943 report of the Youth Advisory Council, for example, used very 1990s language when it talked of each young person needing to see that 'the fullest life, both for himself (sic) and his community demands that he should recognise duties and responsibility as well as enjoy rights and benefits'.

The Advisory Council's second report published two years later reiterated these themes as did the widely quoted definition of youth service purpose which Sir John Maud presented to the Ashridge Conference in 1951:

> To offer individual young people ....
> opportunities ... to discover and develop
> their personal resources of body, mind and
> spirit and thus better equip themselves to
> live the life of mature, creative and
> responsible members of a free society.

Finally, only three years before the Albemarle Committee was appointed, *Citizens of Tomorrow* was emphasising that a youth service existed to provide:

> Opportunities for young people to live and
> move in the fields of desirable experience

> which would otherwise be closed to them
> ... to learn, as many learn nowhere else, to
> live as responsible and contributory
> members of groups which they have joined
> voluntarily.

The Albemarle balance sheet

For all its pretensions to encouraging radical and innovative approaches to the 'new' 1960s teenager, Albemarle represented considerable philosophical continuity with the youth service's past. The report's commitment to individualistic educational values and aspirations was apparent throughout its analysis of young people's condition as well as in its prescriptions for practice. This was most clearly encapsulated in its strong commendation of the Maud definition of purpose which, it concluded, 'comprehensively expressed ... an educational purpose in a sense wider than that usually understood' and so, for the Committee, summed up what it believed the youth service should stand for.

As we have seen, to the report's explicitly expressed positions and recommendations must be added some important *unintended* consequences. Most telling here was its (albeit tentative) challenge to youth work's traditional values and aspirations. This opened up fissures in the service's value system into which some more liberationist perspectives and practices were in due course able to insert themselves.

However, the 'revolution' which Albemarle actually *intended* to set in motion remained sharply circumscribed – and not only by the limited expectations of its chair. Even though – perhaps because – it was part of an emergent progressive consensus on social policy, what it did not attempt to do was to radicalise or politicise the outcomes of youth work for young people. By ensuring that what they could expect to take away from their contacts with the service was very little different from what had been on offer since youth work was first conceived, the report ensured that the service's essentially conservative ideological instincts remained largely undisturbed. In an age where cultural differences within Britain were daily being highlighted by its development into a multi-racial society, this was perhaps revealed most starkly by its uncritical acceptance of the highly individualistic Maud definition of purpose for the service.

This of course is very far from saying that the report had no significant impact. This certainly was variable across the country and was not as enduring as has often been assumed. Some of it, as we shall see in later chapters, was negative as well as positive, and again unintended as well as intended. Nonetheless it did much to shift the service's structures and methodologies and to increase the volume and raise the quality of some of its material and human resources. Even more significantly, it tipped key balances of power within the service: from volunteer to paid worker and manager; from untrained lay person to 'expert' professional; and, most importantly, from charitable to state

sponsorship. Indeed, it simply assumed that, if its prescriptions were to be achieved, a clearer and stronger role for the state was essential and, directly and indirectly, made recommendations to bring this about.

The Albemarle Report also created a political consensus on the service which – sometimes to its own disadvantage – remained in place throughout the 1960s. Thus, both shortly before Albemarle was published and in the months immediately afterwards, each of the major parties went out of their way to make positive public statements on youth, youth policy and the need for a youth service. A Labour Party Youth Commission, completing its work while Albemarle was still sitting, anticipated a number of its key financial, organisational and staffing recommendations. In a tradition which continued well into the 1970s, the Conservative Party was even more proactive in exploring the service's needs and potential. In the 18 months after Albemarle appeared, its political centre produced four pamphlets which all had something supportive to say about the youth service. The one from the left-wing Bow Group, though not doubting the need for the service to be strengthened, did question its now given identification with public welfare and education (see Chapter 4). Two of the others, however, one written by the Young Conservatives and one by a committee of Conservative MPs, implicitly or explicitly endorsed the main thrust of the Albemarle thesis. In the fourth, the collection of Oxford Lectures, Home Secretary RAB Butler specifically included the Albemarle Report as one of a number of key state papers on education which, he believed, 'may amount in course of time to a Youth Charter for the sixties'.

While in government both the Conservatives and – if in some ways less energetically – the Labour Party continued to express their firm commitment to the youth service. To the extent that, at least for two decades, the report banished the 1950s debates on whether a youth service could be afforded or was needed, Albemarle was thus unmistakably 'a good thing'.

Main references

Albemarle Report, *Youth Service in England and Wales*, HMSO, 1960

Ashridge Conference Report, *Youth Service Tomorrow*, King George Jubilee Trust, 1951

Bow Group, *Responsibility for Youth*, Conservative Political Centre, 1961

Conservative Political Centre, *The Rising Tide: Report by a committee of Conservative MPs*, 1961

Conservative Political Centre, *Accent on Youth: Six Oxford Lectures*, 1961

C. A. R. Crosland, *The Future of Socialism*, Jonathan Cape, 1956

Bernard Davies, 'Non-swinging Youth', *New Society*, 3.7.68

Richard Hoggart, *An Imagined Life*, Oxford University Press, 1992

Anthony Jeffs, *Young People and the Youth Service*, Routledge and Kegan Paul, 1979

Peter Keunstler, *Youth Work in England*, University of London Press, 1954

King George Jubilee Trust, *Citizens of Tomorrow*, 1955 (Part IV)

Labour Party Youth Commission, *The Younger Generation*, Labour Party, 1959

Colin MacInnes, *England, Half English*, MacGibbon & Kee, 1961

Don Potts, 'Some notes on the history of the National Association of Youth Leaders and Organisers', NAYLO, 1961

Bryan Reed, *Eighty Thousand Adolescents*, George Allen & Unwin, 1950

David Smith, 'The eternal triangle – youth work, the youth problem and social policy', in Ian Ledgerwood and Neil Kendra, *The Challenge of the Future: Towards the New Millennium for the Youth Service*, Russell House Publishing, 1997

Pauline Wharton, 'An Examination of the Conceptual Foundations of the Youth Service in England', unpublished Masters thesis, Department of Social Administration, University of Birmingham, 1979

Young Conservatives, *The Young Idea*, Conservative Political Centre, 1961

3   Implementing Albemarle

Good times are here at last

If the youth service ever had a golden age, then the 1960s was certainly it. Some allowance has to be made for the spin-doctoring of those giving out the information, particularly the Ministry of Education: even then, governments wanted to deliver only good news. Nonetheless, over the decade the service really did experience steady and sometimes heady expansion – more money, buildings and equipment, increased support for the voluntary sector, extra staff and training opportunities, better flows of information and publicity.

Not that the youth service was picked out for special favours. As a proportion of gross national product, education spending overall increased from 3.2 per cent in the mid-1950s to 5 per cent in 1965 and to 6 per cent by 1969. In 1963 the Robbins report decreed that higher education, for so long the privilege of a social elite, must become much more of a mass medium for personal and occupational advancement. In the same year the Newsom report gave the secondary education of 'pupils of average and less than average ability' its charter for growth and reform. Four years later the Plowden report, unabashedly child-centred in its orientation, did the same for

primary education. Liberal and experimental approaches were also consistently promoted throughout the decade by the flow of innovatory projects, research studies and publications coming out of the government-funded Schools Council. To keep pace on the ground with the demands and expectations thrown up by this stream of new developments, both school building and teacher training expanded rapidly and very substantially.

What is more, the optimism of the decade was more than just economic. It was rooted, too, in a confidence that, through education in particular, it was possible to engineer significant egalitarian solutions. These, it is true, only envisaged an equality of opportunity rather than equality *per se*. Nonetheless, they led to major national policy initiatives. Eleven-plus selection was widely replaced by comprehensive schooling designed finally to make real the war-time commitment to secondary education for all. Educational priority areas were created for the 'deprived' and the 'disadvantaged'. By the end of the decade uncertainty, if not actual pessimism, had crept back in, particularly over whether it was really possible to change radically some deep-seated social patterns and entrenched institutions. Even so, Albemarle was launched into a climate which was sympathetic to its ideals and prepared to be generous in its responses.

Initially, the growth in service financial resources was very rapid. The Ministry's own direct spending on the service went from £229,000 in 1959–60 to £560,000 in 1960–61 and then to £775,000 for 1961–62. In the five years after Albemarle to June 1965 the annual revenue expenditure on the service nationally rose from £2.25 million to £8 million while its total committed capital expenditure, which in 1960–61 stood at a mere £200,000, had by then become £17 million.

Nor was this growth marked only by central government activity. For 1961–62 Essex's youth service estimates were £430,000 – up from £250,000 in the year Albemarle was published. Leicestershire's revenue expenditure rose in the five years from 1960–61 from £19,000 to nearly £50,000, while in Warwickshire between 1959–60 and 1964–65 spending increased from £30,000 to £129,000. By 1964–65, LEAs – over and above their capital expenditure – had more than doubled their youth service budgets to some £6.5 million.

Too rosy a view of the decade would be misleading. Many local authorities responded to Albemarle only very slowly. Economic ups and downs – sterling crises, balance of payments crises, pre-Thatcherite rumbles about levels of public spending being unsustainable – generated anxiety and in due course inflicted real pain. Denis Howell, as so-called 'minister for youth', was a member of the new Labour administration which, even then, had come to power in 1964 on a promise to modernise Britain after the '13 wasted years' of Conservative government. Yet one of his very early tasks was to warn

that the economic situation which Labour had inherited was 'extremely serious' and so was 'bound to affect … the youth service. The nation cannot spend (its money),' he asserted, again in a phrase which was to reverberate strongly two decades later, 'until it has earned it.' For one contemporary commentator, this was 'disappointing', especially 'given the material needs of the youth service'. Nevertheless, Howell's suggestion that 'we should begin now to plan an order of priorities for the time … when the economic situation improves' was uncritically accepted.

What these national economic crises did not produce was a political crisis of faith in the state's welfare role and responsibilities. David Smith has argued that the Conservatives, in government up to 1964, tackled the implementation of the Albemarle proposals much more energetically than their Labour successors: initially, for example, the Youth Service Development Council (YSDC) which Albemarle had recommended was chaired by the Minister of Education himself rather than, as happened under Labour, by a junior education minister. Nonetheless, the essential political consensus which Albemarle did so much to construct survived the decade's economic downturns, with key figures from across the political spectrum taking up positions on the service which were all but indistinguishable.

Junior or not, for six years from 1964 Denis Howell, the minister with responsibility for the youth service, actively chaired the YSDC. From a position of genuine personal commitment to the service which has never since been matched by any government minister, he kept up a sometimes contentious and provocative commentary on its work and development.

The Conservative opposition, too, offered broad support with its education spokesperson, Sir Edward Boyle, publicly regretting in 1965 that the Albemarle Report had never been debated in the House of Commons. Boyle also acknowledged that 'of course the youth service could well do with far more money than it now receives'. Over three years later, in more threatening economic circumstances, Charles Morrison, for the Conservatives, regretted the cut then being made in the capital building programme as 'a severe blow'. Both he and his Liberal counterpart also unquestioningly endorsed the advances ushered in by Albemarle and, eight years into the service's 10-year development plan, accepted that a further review was justified.

The one political intervention which in a quite prescient way did break the consensus came from the Bow Group, the progressive voice of the Conservative Party which at the time counted among its membership a future youth service minister, Christopher Chataway. While commending Albemarle for having 'inspired so much new thinking on the youth service', it nonetheless distanced itself firmly from some of what it saw as the report's patronising assumptions. It, for example, rejected the view that youth clubs must be justified either as welfare or as educational facilities, contending that this produced a compact between providers and users which was 'funda-

mentally unsound'. Instead it preferred that clubs should simply cater for social and recreational needs.

The Bow Group was also one of the few significant voices of the time to question the growth of state involvement:

> The state may intervene by providing money and machinery to complement or to replace existing services. If the community is concerned to harness young people's idealism behind specific objectives, then the state (in our free society) must not intervene directly, but must be concerned merely with creating the conditions in which the desired developments are likely to occur.

This, however, was very much an exception, even marginal, viewpoint which left the overall political agreement on the youth service intact. Despite the economic pressures of the decade, in financial terms too, this survived surprisingly well. 'Cuts' then often meant something very different from what they had meant previously and what they came increasingly to mean in later decades: not absolute reductions in expenditure but a slow down in planned rates of expansion. When in April 1969 a Conservative MP accused some LEAs of making 'such drastic cuts in the youth service budget … as to seriously damage the whole fabric of the youth service', the minister was able to claim that 'the amount reallocated this year for the youth service and adult education was considerably above the 3.5 per cent for education as a whole'. For that same financial year, this figure apparently included an increase in the amount allocated for youth service buildings – from the £3.8 million available in 1968 to £4.5 million.

Against this background of growth and optimism, it is perhaps hardly surprising that concerns about the adequacy of the service's legislative basis rarely surfaced. Within weeks of Albemarle's publication two of NAYLO's officers did question whether the report had given this issue enough attention:

> It must be remembered that the 1944 (Education) Act made it the duty of the LEAs to provide leisure-time facilities for those who have left school. The report shows quite clearly that many authorities have evaded their duty almost completely … Others have interpreted it in a very inadequate way … And yet the report never once does more than recommend the minister to urge local authorities that they should do certain things. Surely the minister must at times tell local authorities what they must do, and especially how much they must spend and what at least they must build.

This was followed up later in the year by a statement in NAYLO's journal *The Youth Leader* which stressed that 'the powers placed on the LEAs by the 1944 Act were mandatory, not permissive'.

Though in the post-Albemarle euphoria such criticisms amounted to little more than background noise, echoes of them did reverberate from time to time. In 1964 Lady Albemarle herself noted that, among the LEAs, 'in general the picture that emerges is still one of random growth'. In 1965, Sir Edmund Boyle also acknowledged that 'the standard of LEA provision varies a good deal'. And a year later Andrew Fairbairn, Leicestershire's Deputy Director of Education and an increasingly influential member of the YSDC, saw 'the comparative vagueness and the width of description of the relevant sections of the 1944 Education Act' as a 'pitfall' since 'the wording is open equally to an interpretation of passivity as to one of activity'.

Overall, however, the 1960s deserves its reputation as a period of youth service growth. At the time, especially for the survivors of the dismal post-war years, this was most visibly exemplified in both concrete and human terms: by the contemporary buildings for social and recreational use which were springing up all over the country, in rural as well as urban areas; by the new sports, outdoor pursuits and residential training facilities; and by the influx of newly trained and (sometimes over) enthusiastic full-time staff. As we shall see in a later chapter, within each of these major developments were embedded some of Albemarle's more negative unintended consequences. Nonetheless, during the 1960s such developments were invariably greeted as self-evidently benign, not least because they offered such clear evidence that youth work and the youth service had finally found a secure place within the post-war welfare state.

Bricks and mortar – plastic and Formica

As Albemarle certainly intended, premises sparkled particularly brightly on this newly energised youth service scene. If the Committee's vision was to be realised of much more accessible and welcoming facilities, the service had to establish a physical presence which was 'bright and gay'. Moreover, the report stressed, the need was 'not for a simple provision of more, and more expensive premises'. Rather, it was:

> ... primarily ... for a change of heart among many in or concerned with the youth service, for a more liberal attitude towards what is suitable and possible in physical provision.

In calling for a building programme which was imaginative, it therefore proposed that 'the needs of users ... be studied and buildings designed to house the type of activities and interests of an evolving service'. It recommended that the Ministry of Education's Architects and Buildings Branch should advise on 'the design of premises for youth work' and suggested that 'standards ... be raised in better furniture, lighting, decoration and equipment'. It also drew some unfamiliar, and for the youth service unflattering, comparisons with the union facilities of university students whose poorer and already less privileged non-academic contemporaries, they urged, should be treated at least as imaginatively and generously.

For most of the decade the youth service came to regard its own building programme as an entirely 'given' element of its development: indeed, as we have seen, it even survived the overall cuts in public expenditure. With the limit for individual projects of £5,000 having been removed, within months of the Albemarle Report's publication the (Conservative)

government announced allocations for 1960–62 of £3 million. Another £4 million was provided for 1962–63 plus an extra £0.5 million in the summer of 1962 specifically for sports facilities. By 1964–65, the annual total figure for new youth service building projects had been increased by a further £0.5 million to £4.5 million. In addition, the rules governing bids for small voluntary sector project bids were relaxed and from April 1965 the grant limit raised from £2,000 to £2,500.

As a result, by the end of 1962, 429 new projects had been started and another 99 approved. The total value of projects already up and running by March 1964 was £6.1 million with others valued at £1.9 million under construction. Final plans had also been submitted for others worth £1.6 million and a further £1.8 million-worth had had sketch plans approved. Three years later the total sum authorised over the whole post-Albemarle period had risen to £23 million and had generated nearly 3,000 projects. Two 'crash' programmes had also been added to help areas of high unemployment like Merseyside and the North East, providing further evidence of pressures towards the selectivity buried within youth service policy-making which became increasingly explicit and dominant from the 1970s onwards.

Within this programme, voluntary bodies were able to get grants for half the cost of a new building or for buying and adapting older premises. At first, they submitted their bids directly to the Ministry along-side those of all LEAs. However, by early in 1962, with expectations running high, bids were beginning to go way beyond what the government could approve. (By 1965–66, barely one-third of submissions totalling over £12.5 million could be met.)

At this point the Ministry distanced itself from the nasty business of choosing between bidders. A local consultation process was introduced to agree local priorities which placed the LEAs in what one commentator called the King Solomon role. This not only further emphasised the growing power of the local state in youth service decision-making. It also provided an early post-Albemarle test of the effectiveness – even, in some cases, the reality – of the much vaunted statutory-voluntary partnership.

However, the status accorded to buildings in this period was not just proclaimed by money allocated and projects approved. Also within months of Albemarle's appearance, and again entirely in line with its thinking, a sustained publicity campaign got under way to persuade youth work providers to think premises – and to do so in imaginative, youth-cultural ways. In September 1961, the Ministry of Education devoted one of its regular Building Bulletins (number 20) to *Youth Service Buildings: General Mixed Clubs*, choosing this focus because, it asserted, 'the general mixed club is likely to be the type most frequently in demand' by both statutory and voluntary providers.

Though Building Bulletin 20 made 'no claim to be either final or comprehensive', it did suggest 'new principles of planning which seem likely to prove generally acceptable (and which) might be applied

to local needs'. It also invited comment and suggestions from the field. After being strenuously hyped by the Ministry, within two months of publication 5,000 copies had been sold. Over a six-month period in 1961–62, the Ministry's monthly broadsheet *Youth Service* – itself an early product of the service's raised profile post-Albemarle – carried three substantial pieces on the Bulletin itself and the 'model' project based on it being built at Withywood in Bristol. This *Youth Service* described in late 1960 as 'an up-to-date "post-Albemarle" youth centre' and 'an experiment which will be watched with interest and confidence'.

Building Bulletin 22, issued in August 1963 as a follow-up to Bulletin 20, in effect used the Withywood project as a case study, giving a detailed account of its purposes and planning. The centre also attracted a full-page article in the *Times Educational Supplement*, complete with photograph, sketches and floor plans. The result was a rapid spread of Withywood clones across the country. Indeed Bulletin 22, in summarising the assumptions which had guided the Withywood development, all but created a national blueprint for 1960s youth club buildings. This laid down that:

- the main function of the mixed youth club should be seen as social: 'to provide a meeting place where interests and activities may arise spontaneously from the corporate life of the group';
- this social function should be supported by social, practical, physical and cultural activities, with a balance being maintained between these;

- the plan of the building 'should ensure close physical and visual relationship between activities';
- 'in general the club should not try to compete either in facilities or level of activities with specialist clubs'; and
- the building should be compact and as flexible as possible.

Across the country buildings thus uncannily reproduced themselves – according to Andrew Fairbairn 'lock, stock and barrel'. All seemed to have open-plan social areas, often on two levels and designed for simultaneous use by drinkers and chatters, dancers and even, it was claimed, weight lifters (who were said to need only limited space) and the irrepressible table tennis players. At one end or in one corner was the obligatory coffee bar, complete with high counter, high stools and perhaps gurgling drink machines. Leading off directly from this would be small meeting or activity rooms (often with doors without windows for checking what was happening within!) and a leader's office usually doubling as the centre's general administrative hub.

The design and furnishing of these premises continued to get detailed attention at least until mid-decade, above all because a sophisticated physical environment was seen as essential to opening the service up to a wider and previously sceptical clientele. The November 1962 issue of *Youth Service* and issues of the professional associations' journal *Youth Review* (in late 1965 and early 1966) ran special features on youth service building and on furniture and equipment for clubs and centres. As late as

November 1967 the weekly periodical *Education*, the trade journal of the LEAs, also carried a three-page supplement on *Buildings for Social Education*.

Though in September 1969 an architect declared the Withywood model successful in all but small details, over time its limitations revealed themselves to those required to use – and control – the new palaces. In some (perhaps many) places, a combination of unrealistic diagnosis of need and function and rock-bottom initial costings produced small rooms and offices without adequate sound-proofing against the liveliness of teenage activity outside. In due course, too, highly constrained repair and refurbishing budgets often led to deterioration into shabbiness (even into an unfitness for purpose) of materials and fittings used originally with an eye to creating a 'commercial' ethos.

In the longer term, the taken-for-granted equation of state-of-the-art premises, equipment and furnishings with imaginative youth work had another unintended consequence. In order to keep the new network of buildings open and secure, large proportions of the youth service's still far-from-generous revenue budgets had to be locked into a limited number of geographical locations. In any particular season or over longer time periods, youth service planners and practitioners were thus unable to follow young people's often restless movement to a newly fashionable meeting point or leisure activity. In combination with the professional rigidities which developed within the workforce, the fixation with physical amenities greatly constrained the service's responsiveness to a population group which all but defined itself by its ebbing and flowing demands for novelty and a change of scenery.

Much of this, however, is hindsight. During much of the 1960s, the youth service building boom was greeted by workers, managers and politicians as a great opportunity and major advance. Though many of the new buildings had been located on school campuses, often as youth wings, it was only towards the end of the decade that shifting priorities began to stem this growth in physical plant. In March 1967, in the same House of Commons statement in which he anticipated a £0.5 million increase in the youth service annual building programme, Denis Howell urged 'the fuller use of capital resources by the community'. This was a theme to which he (and indeed others) returned repeatedly in the later 1960s, as part of a developing campaign to get youth work to transform itself into a version of youth and community work.

In a Commons exchange of April 1968, not only was Howell much more direct about the shift of commitment from specialist youth premises to community facilities. He also revealed how far this new community orientation was budget and especially premises-driven:

> One effect of the reduction in the Youth Service Building Programme for the coming year ... might be to stimulate an interest in multi-use buildings and a search for greater value for money.

Three months later he insisted that, as one of the two central strands of his

philosophy, he wanted future school buildings to be planned as community facilities, including 'possibly also the youth centre where there is one'.

Between the powerful, and shifting, pressures of economy and ideology the youth service's precious building programme was clearly beginning to get badly squeezed.

Finding and training the full-time leaders

A 10-year 'emergency'

Some years after the Albemarle Report was published, Howell admitted that he and his fellow Committee members knew that their proposed five-year increase in the youth service's full-time staffing, from 700 to 1,300, was 'absolutely too small ... but the most we (could) get out of the Government'. Nonetheless, this near doubling of the workforce at least promised to tackle the immediate staffing crisis. At first sight, too, and as a short-term response, the Albemarle proposal for delivering on that promise – an 'emergency' college offering a one-year course – appeared simple and realistic.

The simplicity and realism seemed to be confirmed when within a year the National College for the Training of Youth Leaders welcomed its first 90 students to its adapted civil defence premises in Leicester. The other four training institutions which had survived the years of run-down also expanded their intakes, particularly the two-year course at Westhill College in Birmingham. As a result, by the end of 1965 the Albemarle target had all but been met with 1,287 full-time leaders on the Ministry of Education's register, nearly 30 per cent of whom were National College graduates. By the middle of 1968 the total number of full-timers had reached 1,500.

Yet even this apparently straightforward tale hides some serious limitations and complications. 'Woefully' few women came forward for training because, it was claimed, they found teaching a much more attractive option. At the time this was regretted mainly because 'feminine leadership' was seen as essential. However, in the longer term it had much more serious consequences. Interacting with the newly fashionable philosophy in favour of mixed provision, this male domination of the workforce contributed to the growing perception of girls and young women as 'problems' and to the marginalisation of work with them – both features of the 1960s service. Though less obviously, as these workers rose up the youth service's career ladder (such as it was) it was mainly their male attitudes, especially to handling people, which shaped the expressions of managerialism which took root in the service during the later 1970s.

Some of the deficiencies in the training arrangements were much more immediate, however. At a time when the service was struggling to make the intellectual and psychological leap from voluntary to full-time paid, the one year's training which most of the new entrants were getting was proving barely adequate for running mainly single-worker clubs and projects. Under its first principal, Ted Sidebottom, the National College strove self-consciously to respond to these pressures. Though its assessment processes could be mystifyingly authoritarian, it strove to apply the most up-to-date thinking and research on how adults learn. Largely avoiding didactic forms of teaching, it preferred active experiential and small group methods which could nurture the autonomy and self-reliance which future practice would demand. Like the other courses, it also invested considerable resource in long placements under the supervision of one of its own tutors as well as, wherever they were available, an experienced full-time worker.

Ultimately, however, the training institutions had limited scope for protecting the new workers from a field which was itself struggling to come to terms with Albemarle and its impact. The service's material advances alone were making some testing new demands on everyone involved: putting together applications for revenue and capital grants, overseeing the construction of new buildings, managing and maintaining these and finding and recruiting and supporting the extra staff needed to run them – to say nothing of negotiating the burgeoning mysteries of local authority bureaucracies.

And then there was the contagion of the new permissive philosophy and style which, it was said, the new recruits were determined to spread, often abrasively, into even the most traditional niches of the service. This was constantly traced back to the 'line' in which all National College students were said – especially by service managers – to have been indoctrinated. Its main features were defined as a disdain for activities and a constant mystifying evocation in their stead of the jargon of relationships and group work and even counselling. One LEA, Derbyshire, went very public on its impatience with what Leicester was producing. In a widely read report on professional youth leadership it recommended that the college 'should take urgent steps to ensure that students do not approach their professional lives with a false impression of their own importance'.

Throughout much of the 1960s, reservations – even deep scepticism – persisted about this new breed of leader, the quality of their work and the appropriateness and effectiveness of their training. One positive effect of this debate was an increasing emphasis on providing in-service support and post-qualifying training for newly appointed staff and those who supervised them, on the grounds that initial training could never produce the complete practitioner. Efforts – not always successful – were made to make the new arrangements for a probationary year for full-timers work more effectively. As a way of helping newly-appointed workers internalise and build on their initial training, staff supervision was also given a higher profile and its special skills explored – for example, in a London-based training project run by Joan Tash of the YWCA between 1964 and 1966. On the suggestion of the YSDC, in 1966 and then again in

1968–69 'experimental' courses for youth officers were also organised which together recruited nearly 120 participants – and were still over-subscribed.

Valuable though they were in their own right, such 'solutions' nonetheless masked the urgency of resolving another question which, not for the first time, had been ducked in 1965 when the life of the National College was extended for a further five years: what permanent routes to training and qualification did the youth service require? 'Teacher, social worker – or community worker?'

For many in the youth service this question induced a strong sense of *deja vu*. From the 1940s onwards, government departments and private trusts had produced a series of reports on the supply and training of youth leaders – McNair in 1944, Jackson in 1949, Younghusband and Fletcher in 1951. None had led to decisive action, mainly because no consensus existed, least of all within the youth service, on how to answer even the basic questions:

- *Was full-time youth work a "career for life" or did the demands of "youth", to say nothing of the unsocial hours, mean that as they got older those working face-to-face needed to be eased into a related occupation?*
- *If full-time youth work was to be regarded as a long-term career and so as an independent "profession", what training did its practitioners need, how long should this last, leading to what qualification?*
- *If it was not a career for life, did this mean that full-time youth work should be linked into another profession via training,*

qualifications, salary scales, pension arrangements and other conditions of service – and if so, which one(s)?

Though social work training and/or a social science degree were sometimes seen as the appropriate professional links, including in 1947 by NAYLO, most of the solutions floated before Albemarle favoured integration with teaching. Albemarle itself recommended this as the main source of recruitment – an outcome which seemed to be coming closer to fruition via the youth work options which 11 teacher training colleges had inserted into their courses by the early 1960s. However, during this period, far from developing into substantive routes into full-time youth work, these were justified mainly as ways of training more sensitised and innovative teachers, some of whom might also take up part-time youth work.

Moreover, Albemarle had also endorsed social work training as a potential route to youth work qualification as well as advocating one or two-year specialist courses for 'mature students'. By covering all the possible options, the Committee thus excused itself from making a decision on this 20-plus year youth service dilemma. More importantly, the service's support (at least in principle) for the two five-year phases of 'emergency' arrangements which were youth work-specific, and the priority given to these by government, allowed events once again to overtake all alternative proposals.

The late 1960s did see versions of the old solutions re-emerging. In 1968, for example, the autumn issue of *Youth Review*

noted that a confidential Ministry letter was recommending a 'closer integration of training and career prospects for youth and community workers (sic) with teachers and social workers'. Clearly representing the position of the professional associations which sponsored it, the journal went on to assert a need 'for specialisation of youth workers into educators and social workers'. Interwoven with such propositions was an emerging consensus within the service – which, it seemed, the DES supported – that 'a one-year course was too short … and that a three-year course should be considered'.

However, as with the youth service's building programme, these ageing prescriptions were by this stage needing to be tarted up to fit with the emergent proposals to divide the service into school-based and community-related. By March 1967 the minister was committing himself, through a YSDC review of the service, to 'a fundamental examination of the needs of training'. The service thus had to wait until 1969 for this review to be completed before it got what it had been seeking for at least a quarter of a century: a lasting solution to its problem of how to provide training and qualifications which would underpin the professional tag which its full-time workers were claiming.

From full-timer to professional

This claim was of course far from new. As early as 1951, *Citizens of Tomorrow* was welcoming 'the emergence of a recognisable profession' while the Albemarle Committee used the term in a wholly taken for granted way. Its report actually offered some, at least implicit, definitions which, by emphasising exclusivity, again produced influential unintended consequences. This particularly had repercussions for the longer-term relationship between full-timer and part-timer and volunteer.

Albemarle, for example, described the new full-time workforce it was advocating as 'a corps' which would 'bring a trained mind to bear on the needs and problems of the young worker'; 'experiment with new techniques and new modes of youth work' and therefore have 'an influence far beyond (their) own club'. As these workers were regarded as 'indispensable if the standards of the service (were) to be raised', the report concluded that:

> ... the service needs a sufficient body of full-time leaders, trained for the job, deployed in the right spots, and given conditions of service which make the best use of their professional skill.

Subsequent comments, for example, by Howell soon after he took over as Minister of Youth, reinforced the emphasis on trained social science workers and 'university people as youth leaders'.

Albemarle was also instrumental in ensuring that machinery was established to guarantee the salaries and conditions of these professionals. Here a long pre-history was marked by recurrent divisions among key youth service interests and by, at the very least, official lethargy. NAYLO had been pressing for some recognised codification of youth leaders' pay and conditions since at least the mid-1940s. By the early 1950s, when the Ministry seemed

to be warming to the idea, NAYLO's own membership was so low that it would probably have been excluded from any negotiating machinery. Nothing came of this initiative: indeed according to Peter Keunstler, a research fellow in youth work at Bristol University, it was far from clear that the Ministry was in earnest. In December 1952, after challenging the minister responsible on the issue, he concluded that the idea of setting up machinery to negotiate youth leaders' salaries 'had been quietly put to sleep before its birth!'.

Despite this, though still fragmented, the professional associations continued to struggle for more coordinated action. During the 1950s approaches were made first to the National Union of Teachers (NUT) and then to the National Association of Local Government Officers (NALGO) for help in getting the appropriate structures in place, either within the teachers' Burnham Committee or within the local government Whitely Council. Neither of these initiatives was successful. However, at its annual conference in May 1957, NAYLO was at least able to record that, despite the disunity among so many different types of youth workers and employers:

> ... encouraging ... progress ... has been made in the past few years in establishing agreement between the various bodies that make up the Joint Negotiating Committee.

Two years later, this committee was still meeting quarterly with the explicit goal of creating a negotiating body on salaries and conditions of service.

In due course Albemarle put its full weight behind the creation of a committee 'to negotiate scales of salaries and to review superannuation arrangements', pointing to the body responsible for agreeing the salaries of staff in teacher training colleges as a possible model. The Committee conceded that staff who had been working full-time for five years or longer should be recognised as qualified by experience. However, it also proposed that a date be agreed after which 'no new entrant to full-time youth leadership shall be able to claim qualification by experience alone'. Between 1963 and 1966 three- and six-month courses were organised to qualify workers who had been practising full-time for between two and five years.

By early 1961 a Joint Negotiating Committee had been established, representing employers in the statutory and voluntary sectors and the main professional associations and unions. Within six months – in July 1961 – it had published its first report. For the first time recognised qualifications for youth work were laid down – specifically the certificates awarded by the courses run by the National College and at Westhill, at University College Swansea and by the National Association of Boys' Clubs (NABC) in Liverpool and by the YMCA in London. A salary scale for a qualified leader with nine annual increments was also established.

Equally significant, full-time workers' employment conditions were specified. 'Normally' no more than 11 sessions a week were to be worked, of which in any fortnight no more than nine were to be evening sessions. An entitlement to six weeks holiday a year was laid down, to be seen as 'strictly personal leave', distinct from time for training or for running club events. Sick leave remained at the discretion of the employer while super-annuation arrangements were only to be put in place 'where possible'. Though Albemarle had recommended that LEAs increase the number of paid part-time leaders they employed, train them and give them payment which would 'match the quality of the job', it seems to have been taken as self-evident that the new contracts would apply only to full-time leaders.

Given the decline in their numbers and their exploitation in the name of dedication and service throughout the 1950s, this preoccupation with the full-timers was hardly surprising. Improving their morale and their staying power, as well as making sure they got a fair deal personally, had to be high priorities.

However, in its (albeit brief) consideration of the place of part-timers, Albemarle also acknowledged that they made up 'the great majority of leaders' and thereby, by implication, that even then they were doing most of the face-to-face work with young people. It also noted that, though about 4,600 part-timers were paid by the LEAs, most of those involved in youth work were volunteers. Finally, it accepted that, where posts 'do not warrant a full-time appointment', there was often a need for 'a part-time leader with professional experience of working with adolescents and a professional understanding of their needs'.

The Committee assumed that in the main these posts would be filled by qualified teachers. However, the combined effects of its rather elitist conception of the full-timer's role, the 'professional' label it almost casually attached to this and the eventual institutionalisation of this superior status in salary, training and qualification structures produced a deep rift in the youth service's workforce. Over the next four decades significant efforts were made to bridge this gap, especially through improved training and trade union organising. For most of that time, however, part-timers were in effect treated as a different breed of worker – mere lay people to be overseen and guided by a professional workforce.

Part-timers and volunteers in an era of professionalisation

Though this institutionalisation of the full-time/part-time division was undoubtedly one of Albemarle's most influential, if again unintended, negative consequences, it did not invent it. Doubts about the very need for paid full-time leadership had emerged long before the Committee reported. A decade earlier, for example, *Citizens of Tomorrow* had pointed to the 'strictly "amateur" attitude' within the service which even disapproved of paying volunteers out-of-pocket expenses. It had also noted the 'embarrassments (which) arise when a paid instructor is working with one group and an unpaid volunteer with another, even in the same subject in the same building'. Macalister Brew, too, writing in 1957, picked up on the 'petty jealousies and friction … when some helpers are paid and others are not'.

Underlying much of the 'regret (about) the professionalisation of youth work', it would seem, was a fear that this was acting as the carrier of secularised state values and aims which would undermine youth work's core charitable mission. Echoes of such worries can he detected in Jack Longland's description, quoted in the last chapter, of the 'servants' hall' culture and approaches which came with the LEAs entry into the direct sponsorship of youth work in the 1940s. They would seem to reverberate too in Alicia Percival's history of the voluntary youth organisations, *Youth Will Be Led*, published in the same year (1951) as Longland's address at Ashridge. Somewhat defensively, she acknowledged that 'it would … be most unfair to say of many local education authority youth officers and organisers that they were lacking in ideals or spirituality'. Even so, she concluded:

> The difficulties … are bound to be considerable, when the authority responsible for the club cannot of its very nature be distinctly committed to a religious, let alone a denominational, outlook.

This, however, was not just a cultural debate over whose values should prevail. It also contained the more practical fear that the new professionalism would so subvert voluntary leadership that it would eventually disappear altogether. In his highly influential report on *The Needs of Youth*, A. E. Morgan had acknowledged in 1939 that 'a certain romantic attraction in slumming' had played its part in bringing many privileged young men and women into youth leadership via universities, colleges and public schools! More seriously, he pointed too to the steep decline in their sense of *noblesse oblige* – the tradition which in previous generations had been their main motivation for taking up such work. He thus noted that:

> ... *in many clubs which bear the name of a public school, and are supported by subscriptions from the boys and old boys, there are few or no old boys giving their services.*

Despite in effect recording the death of the personalised nature of the 'gift', even in youth work, Morgan did not quite abandon the hope that the younger members of the more privileged classes might still be encouraged 'in the spirit of service'. To sustain this, his thoughts turned to other potential sources of volunteers – from the professions, business and those involved in running factories. He also indicated that some leadership was beginning to emerge from within young people's own communities – in the official designated special areas hit hardest by the 1930s depression, for example, where some of the unemployed were coming forward. However, he remained deeply pessimistic about what the new housing estates might produce from amid their 'inchoate masses of strangers' which had left 'the community spirit and the idea of service ... unformed'. Nor did he have much confidence in the 'less well educated leader': these, he judged to be 'as incapable of inspiring and organising a real club as of being headmaster of a school'.

With the 1948 PEP review of the youth service still concluding that volunteers were 'of vital importance', Sir John Maud,

in his address to the Ashridge Conference, continued to look to the boarding schools as a source of voluntary leadership as well as to 'distinguished people'. In contrast, *Citizens of Tomorrow* preferred to grasp what it obviously saw as an extremely prickly nettle. It recommended that, in order to recruit and hold onto less affluent and leisured volunteers, youth organisations should at least pay their travelling expenses.

The most substantive and authoritative statement on volunteers, however, came in 1953 from Peter Keunstler. His *Voluntary Youth Leaders* examined a wide range of evidence on volunteering as well as reporting on his own original research. It concluded that, with at least 250,000 volunteers operating alongside, at most, 1,800 full-time and 4,500 part-time paid leaders, 'the youth service has little to fear from numerical domination by the professionals'.

Keunstler did, however, note that – as throughout the history of youth work – 'the demand for voluntary leaders still exceeds the supply'. To solve the problem, he warned the voluntary organisations that some hard thinking and 'a ruthless courage in putting ... reforms into practice' were going to be needed. Given the traditions of most of the organisations he had in mind, this was certainly true. For, among the reforms he advocated was a radical shift in perceptions of volunteering. No longer, he argued, could this be treated simply as the prerogative of the upper classes. Instead there needed, for example, to be a recognition of:

> *the magnificent "self-help" record of the trade unions and friendly societies (which)*

showed that the "lower orders" were indeed capable of high standards of social organisation and leadership.

In general terms this was a view supported by Macalister Brew when she pointed to 'leadership (which) has been shown to be a quality which emerges in unexpected places and in all walks of life'. Moreover, at least in the Jewish community, the changes to which she was pointing seemed already to be well under way. From its earliest days its club movement had been dominated by anglicised aristocrats like Sir Basil Henriques. By the late 1940s, however, in the 'newer' Jewish areas to which the children and grandchildren of the original 19th century immigrants were moving, the development of innovative and successful clubs like the Clapton Jewish Youth Centre depended on the emergence of a much more indigenous leadership. The ethnic minority populations whose numbers were by then growing significantly were also setting off on a similar process.

Though Albemarle reached broadly similar conclusions to Keunstler's, its prescriptions were far less radical. It backed *Citizens of Tomorrow's* proposals that volunteers should be paid out-of-pocket expenses. It also called for publicity campaigns via the media so that 'ordinary citizens will be made aware of the help they can give' – particularly 'professional men and women, technicians, workers and gifted amateurs'. Buried away in these paragraphs, too, were sentiments which, by specifically endorsing 'a basic kindliness, a simple commonsense and unlimited patience (as) the most important

qualities', drew the line even more sharply between the volunteer and the report's new corps of full-time professional experts.

Beyond all this, however – and beyond, too, the usual rhetorical gestures in favour of volunteering – probably the most substantial contribution Albemarle made to sustaining the volunteer contribution was its emphasis on the need for more and better training for all part-timers. Much was already going on. The voluntary organisations had long provided training for their own leaders, some of it supported in the post-1939 period by some of the charitable trusts. So too had some LEAs.

However, Albemarle identified that 'in some areas painfully little (training) is provided'. It also commented on the considerable duplication of effort and the absence of opportunities for genuine progression even where training was available. It saw 'the purposes and techniques of youth leadership' as key focuses for such training which, significantly, it believed was 'particularly appropriate to the qualified teacher who is about to take up a part-time leader's post for the first time'. By insisting on cooperative provision by local authorities and voluntary organisations – 'there is no room for demarcation disputes' – it also laid the ground for some of the more ambitious and contentious 'partnership' developments of the 1960s.

The Albemarle challenge was taken up in July 1961 when, prompted by the YSDC, a Ministry of Education working party was appointed to advise on what training should be made available to part-timers and volunteers and how it should be arranged. It was chaired by Gordon Bessey, Director of Education for Cumberland and a YSDC member. It included strong representation from the voluntary sector and some high profile LEA youth officers.

Its report, published in September 1962, made passing reference to 'full use of modern teaching techniques and aids' which went beyond 'the well-tried method of lecture followed by questions and discussions'. However, it seemed mainly concerned, not to say obsessed, with the content of training, about which it was highly prescriptive. Its reference to 'the contribution of sociology, psychology and social group work' and its use of terms like 'academic' and 'theoretical' were widely taken as endorsements of highly formalised, trainer-led approaches. This interpretation was further reinforced by three appendices which in effect set out a national curriculum complete with a bibliography of 30 texts, some of which were very 'heavy'. Many local providers, either too intimidated by the report's authoritative tone or too unimaginative to override it, accepted what it had to offer 'as a precise blueprint without going very deeply into its implications'.

Perhaps the report's most enduring legacy – which was given added credibility by the breadth of the working party's membership – was its notion that, regardless of agency, target group or geographical area, all youth work contained a common element. This in itself was a novel enough idea. At least by

implication, it required some very disparate organisations to agree on what was the essence of youth work practice which all new recruits needed to be taught prior to individual organisations adding their specialised ingredient.

However, the report went even further. By what seems to have been an undetected collapse of two very different lines of argument, it called on 'local education authorities (to) take the initiative in calling conferences of all the interests concerned with a view to establishing *common training agencies*' (emphasis added). Heads, it seems, were to be firmly knocked together so that the training was *organised* jointly as well as based on a largely agreed common curriculum.

Despite this challenge, initial reactions to 'First Bessey' were generally favourable. It was followed, too, by some positive action by the Ministry of Education. In the February after the report was published it ran a training the trainers conference and in July 1963 issued a circular asking LEAs to report on local developments. By January 1964, 138 out of 146 local authorities had provided responses. These showed that 53 joint agencies had by then been set up to serve single LEA areas and 19 consortia agencies to service between them another 55 LEA areas. 'Existing satisfactory arrangements' meant that in most of the remaining 27 authorities no new joint agencies were seen as necessary. In England basic courses had by then been run in 75 areas, with one in a large county attracting over five hundred enrolments. In Wales, under the influence of the Welsh Joint Education Committee, eight training agencies eventually covered the whole of the country.

Yet on the ground progress seemed slow. One survey for 1963 showed that fewer paid part-timers were in post than in 1957–58 – 4,058 as against 4,414. (At the time the Ministry tentatively attributed the reduction to the conversion of some part-time posts to full-time.) At this stage comprehensive training programmes of taster, basic, advanced and specialist courses were being offered in only 49 areas while only 12 full-time training officers had been or were about to be appointed. Though extra youth officers were being taken on in some areas where the training responsibility was being spread, this latter figure clearly disappointed Bessey himself. The creation of specialist posts to develop and manage the new joint training agencies had been an important element of his report's proposals.

The ritual – and often, it seemed, self-deluding – incantations, particularly on the importance and success of local partnerships, nonetheless continued to be enunciated. In June 1965, for example, the secretary of SCNVYO, Brigadier Meynell, stated unequivocally that joint planning of 'Bessey training':

> In almost every case … has been a successful enterprise and has done a great deal towards bringing the statutory and voluntary organisations together and to like and respect each other.

The Ministry of Education, through *Youth Service*, echoed this confidence, suggesting that the Bessey report had 'stimulated wide interest'. While acknowledging that

even the progress which had been made might not be attributable to the report, it nonetheless concluded that 'in most of the country there are now facilities for the training of part-time leaders and assistants'.

Perhaps a more accurate assessment of the Bessey report's impact was at least implied by a key YSDC decision made later that same year (1965). In setting up a sub-committee to assess the youth service's progress half way through the 10-year Albemarle development plan, the Council specifically placed part-time leader training at the top of its agenda. What is more, this was seen to be sufficiently important to justify appointing a working group of HMIs and civil servants from what was by then the Department of Education and Science (DES) to provide the subcommittee with 'field' and other evidence.

Again a report was produced within the year. Though striving to remain balanced and tactful – 'we do not want to over-emphasise the problems. They are by no means universal and sincere attempts are being made to overcome them' – the subcommittee produced a pretty formidable list of 'circumstances which have so far hindered full cooperation in the planning of courses and participation in them'. This identified:

- joint agencies with representation only from club-based organisations;
- joint training agencies made up entirely of LEA officers;
- LEAs which assumed that they alone had responsibility actually for planning courses;

- the resultant fears of some voluntary organisations that LEAs might gradually 'take over' the service;
- varied interpretations of 'common element';
- voluntary organisations which were uncertain about how to reconcile the common element of the training with their own specialist training needs; and
- training facilities which had been set up before course requirements had been properly worked out.

In addition, using direct quotations from HMI reports, the subcommittee identified:

Certain attitudes in groups, and in individuals, which can militate against full partnership. Rivalries (real or imaginary), inadequacy of communication within and between voluntary organisations themselves, and between voluntary organisations and statutory bodies can all influence the opportunities for training and the quality of provision.

In responding to these problems this second report, though never openly critical of its predecessor, adopted a very different approach. Gone were the curriculum outlines and the book lists. In their place were detailed and insightful reflections on the development of multi-disciplinary training teams and on the training of staff for their roles. Stress was placed on the need to vary training methods according to what had to be learned; to think of participants as adult learners and take a lead from their needs; and to use small tutorial groups which actively drew on students' current practice experience. The second report also argued for a widened conception of youth work

and the youth work situations for which workers were being trained. And it proposed that each area should have a 'comprehensive plan'. This would provide initial training, training in activity skills and refresher training as well as opportunities for leaders to understand what was happening in other areas of education and social work.

On the ground, however, the enforced joint planning arrangements too often both played into and fed all the suspicions and even hostilities which had plagued relations between the statutory and voluntary sectors at least since the later 1930s. Two years after the second training report was completed, Howell was having to accept that cooperation on training between LEAs and the voluntary sector was 'patchy', with some authorities apparently working on the premise that 'we don't want any voluntary youth organisers and youth leaders, we'll try and have everybody full-time'.

Those much closer to the action on the ground strongly endorsed this conclusion. Angus McGill, the youth service training officer for Hertfordshire, reflected in 1967 that, though 'in some areas there was the fullest cooperation between local authorities and voluntary bodies ... in others (there was) no cooperation at all' – a situation which he described as 'a step back to the pre-(Bessey) 1962 era'. And at the end of the decade, the Reverend Roy Herbert, speaking to the annual conference of the Church of England Youth Council, offered his audience a list of 'enormous gaps' which even the 'welter of post-Bessey training' had failed to eradicate.

These included:

> An adherence to old methods which fails to make the most of new educational approaches; a failure to recruit new blood; a patchy picture of full partnership in real, as opposed to nominal, joint training agencies; (and) a failure to face the need for some nationally accepted yardstick by which to judge standards.

Indeed, throughout the 1960s and beyond, the service continued to struggle with its historic dilemmas over recruiting, holding and upskilling part-timers, especially volunteers. Particularly in the statutory sector, it also had yet to work out properly how to integrate this crucial section of the workforce into increasingly professionalised forms of direct delivery and of managerial supervision and accountability.

A professional discipline for youth work

For a service intent on professionalising itself, improved staff recruitment, training and supervision was seen to be essential but not sufficient. Rigorous intellectual activity was also regarded as essential. In April 1963 Ted Sidebottom made this the core of his message to the first annual conference of the Youth Service Association (formed out of a merger of NAYLO and the National Association of LEA Youth Leaders). Taking as his title *Making the best use of professional skill*, he used the language of Albemarle to argue that this required 'a corps of carefully selected and substantially trained full-time workers' with a responsibility to spread their 'multiple and substantial' skills. For

Sidebottom such dissemination was important partly because 'ideally a part-time leader should be as skilled ... as a full-time leader'. However, Sidebottom also had broader aspirations. At a time when, as he saw it, 'occupations are growing into professions':

> ... no group becomes professional by making claims. (As) status is earned ... ultimately the youth workers' status will depend on their solid intellectual effort and self-discipline; devotion to high standards of practice; and competent and responsible organisation.

Indeed discipline became a watchword for the new professionalism. Sidebottom, for example, was clear that the youth service's 'disciplines of practice should be at a high level'. A similar line was taken by two other National College staff members, Bernard Davies and Alan Gibson. In *The Social Education of the Adolescent*, published in 1967 as a text for the post-Albemarle service, they called for a professional discipline which was 'deeper and more conscious than that derived from an intuitive response to everyday events'. This would be 'enriched ... by the accumulated experience of practitioners and by the work of the human scientists'.

Over the decade the service experienced something of an upsurge of analytical and theoretical writing. George Goetschius, the YWCA's research and training consultant on detached work projects, was given considerable space in three consecutive issues of *Youth Service* to provide club workers with an easy-to-read guide to recording and analysing their practice. Joan Matthews, another National College lecturer, pressed the case for social group work to be adapted from its social work origins so that it constituted the youth worker's core discipline and method. She developed her ideas in a widely read book, *Working with Youth Groups* published in 1966, and also in a pamphlet for the National Association of Mixed Clubs and Girls' Clubs, *Professional Skill*. In this, like Sidebottom, she pressed the new breed of full-time workers to spread their skills to their part-timer colleagues, including volunteers.

Fred Milson, senior tutor in youth work at Westhill College, in a book aimed at committed Christians, also identified social group work as key to post-Albemarle youth work practice. The Department of Youth Work at Manchester University, founded by Cyril Smith, brought a distinctive sociological perspective to youth policy issues and introduced systematic action research methods into the detached work projects which it ran in conjunction with the Youth Development Trust. By the end of the decade, too, Leslie Button was starting to publish the results of the developmental group work approaches which he was pioneering out of University College, Swansea.

The Ministry's monthly broadsheet *Youth Service* was one early post-Albemarle attempt to encourage practitioners to write up their work and make its lessons more widely available to colleagues. However, by design, its scope and depth were limited. Over the decade attention turned to creating a structure capable of disseminating the service's accumulating experience in more systematic and analytical ways.

Lady Albemarle first talked of a 'centre' which would do this when she opened the National College in 1961. In his address to the YSA, Ted Sidebottom took up the theme, emphasising the need for practice-focused research and suggesting that 'information from such enquiries, and on a variety of work in the youth service, should be made widely available, especially for all leaders to study'. However, it was the Bessey committee which examined part-timers' training which first proposed – with, it claimed, wide support in the field – 'an intelligence unit to serve the new youth service'. To make its argument the committee not only highlighted 'the shortage of highly skilled staff'. It also pointed to 'the need to ensure that all schemes of training … are up to date and reflect the spirit and purpose of the post-Albemarle youth service'.

External pressure combined with influential backing from the YSDC produced the Youth Service Information Centre which, located in the premises of the National College, opened in April 1964. As Alan Gibson, its first head, explained at the time:

> This new arm of the service should be of great benefit to leaders, management, organisers, administrators, trainers, students and members alike by acting as a clearing house for the quicker transmission of knowledge and the fruits of experience.

By 1969, the centre had six full-time staff and had generated a range of publications of its own. These included an annotated youth work book list covering 400 titles which sold over 3,000 copies; a list of youth work training films; a monthly

Digest of information; a series of summaries of experimental projects; a guide to counselling services for young people; and surveys of more specialised initiatives – for example, for working with 'young immigrants'. It also published a periodic listing of forthcoming conferences and courses and had just appointed a specialist to develop the training materials emerging from full and part-time courses. To meet the individual enquiries, especially 'for references to the current frontiers of thought and practice', the centre had accumulated 3,000 'significant documents' for loan.

Before he left his post in 1969, Alan Gibson was beginning to see the centre's mainly reactive role as unnecessarily limiting – 'a tool whose value as a means towards sound practice has by no means yet been fully exploited'. He, for example, believed that it should start to evaluate some of the materials it received as part of a 'maturing dialogue with practitioners and researchers', and that interpretations and conclusions on specific topics might then be offered through the publication of occasional papers.

Significantly, by this stage Gibson was also quietly raising the possibility of something even more ambitious – 'a permanent national institution concerned with in-service training and advanced courses for full-time and part-time workers'. Anticipating that 'the phrase "youth service" may soon be thought unduly restrictive', he was pondering, too, whether an agency developed from YSIC might 'make a substantial contribution to the growth of whatever

educational, social or social educational services it covers'. According to John Ewen, Gibson's successor as director of YSIC, by the time he took over in 1969 there thus existed 'a grand design for a central research, information and training services agency' – 'a central think tank'. The notion was also beginning to attract wider support in the service and eventually materialised in 1973 as the National Youth Bureau.

Partnership in the era of a state-led youth service

We have already seen how key post-Albemarle developments – for example, requirements that they agree on local capital bids to the Ministry and on common element training structures and curricula for part-timers – helped to consummate a pre-war shot-gun marriage between local statutory and voluntary providers. The bluff of participating agencies about partnership was, it seemed, finally being called.

Other pressures during the 1960s helped to turn the rhetoric of cooperative working into reality – in particular a grants system on which the voluntary organisations came to rely more and more heavily and which therefore gave the state increasing leverage. Between 1959–60 and 1965–66 central government grants to voluntary organisations made under the Social and Physical Training Regulations rose six-fold – from £299,000 to £1.8 million. Much of this increase was spent on local voluntary capital projects though a substantial proportion, too, went to support the organisations' headquarters administration. In 1959–60 the Ministry made headquarters grants to 23 voluntary organisations. By 1963–64 the number had risen to 38.

In the following years, the level of support to voluntary organisations for capital works was affected by the wider economic crisis, falling from nearly £1.5 million in 1965–66 to just over £1 million in 1966–67. However, it recovered impressively the following year to almost £1.35 million while grants towards headquarters expenses continued to increase, from £299,250 in 1965–66 to £330,000 by 1967–68. So too in the same three-year period did special grants for 'experimental work', from £27,111 to £31,564.

In 1966 the Ministry asserted – though without providing any detailed evidence to support its claim – that over the decade most LEAs had also increased their financial assistance to local voluntary groups. Though, as we saw earlier in this chapter, some clearly did so, this did not necessarily teach the voluntary sector to love its statutory benefactors. On the contrary, as the evidence on organising common element training for part-timers showed, the field reality of partnership was often at serious odds with the PR image. As one commentator noted:

> Certainly since the revision of (local youth) committees following the Albemarle Report, the influence of the voluntary bodies has diminished ... leaving decisions about young people to be influenced by petty political motives.

Andrew Fairbairn, whose powerful role in the YSDC was making his statements on youth service matters increasingly authoritative, bluntly reminded his LEA colleagues that 'the law (was) quite clear' on their responsibility to the voluntary organisations. This, he insisted, required them:

> ... to foster a genuine partnership based on a mutual respect for, and full knowledge of, their aims and tasks ... all members of education committees ought to be made aware of the partnership.

The following year Gordon Ette, also an LEA officer whose involvement dated back to the formative days of the service of youth, displayed a similar scepticism about the current state of statutory-voluntary relations. In a *Youth Review* article which provoked considerable debate, he called partnership 'an ideal with few ideas and little power (whose) effectiveness as the best instrument to tackle the job is open to question'.

Not that the blame for this failure of partnership was seen to rest solely with the LEAs. One experienced voluntary sector practitioner dismissed local SCVYOs as 'moribund' while, from a statutory perspective, Fairbairn was clear that the voluntary organisations needed to be educated in the idea of partnership since 'there is still too much lip service paid (to it)'. A Scout leader who described himself as a 'representative engaged in liaison work with the local authority' added his doubting voice. He particularly castigated the voluntary organisations for their 'parochialism (and) their self-pride which had resulted in the LEAs saying:

"Let us get on with the business ourselves, in spite of them"'.

As this last comment shows, it took very little for these critiques of the voluntary sector's engagement in partnership to tip over into sceptical appraisals, including self- appraisals, of the voluntary organisations themselves. It is true that their ranks had been extended and to some extent refreshed in the years since a state youth service had been created. The British Youth Council emerged from a committee set up after the Second World War to enable British young people to get into international affairs. Reconstituted in 1966, it sought too to give young people a voice on domestic issues which affected them and from 1969 was helping to establish local youth councils. Two other new organisations with closely intertwined roots, Outward Bound and The Duke of Edinburgh's Award scheme, saw themselves as opening up a wider range of leisure opportunities, especially for working-class young people. The former began to take shape during the war years and was formalised as an independent trust in 1946 with the primary purpose of using the great outdoors as a vehicle for young people's personal development. The award scheme, launched by the Duke personally in 1956, aimed to challenge 'average and sub-average boys and girls' to greater individual achievement by taking them through a four-element programme which put a strong emphasis on outdoor and adventure activities.

Both organisations drew heavily on the elitist and romantic ideas and approaches of Kurt Hahn, the head of Gordonstoun in Scotland, the highly idiosyncratic private school which the Duke himself had attended. (As we shall see later, Hahn and Gordonstoun were also important influences on efforts to sell community service to the youth of the nation.) However, the appeal of both organisations remained limited, not least because in their early years they were restricted to boys.

Indeed over the decade the role and impact of the voluntary organisations in general came under considerable critical scrutiny. Those coming from the political left, perhaps not surprisingly, were often particularly sceptical, seeing such organisations as an anachronistic residue of an outdated class system. In its response to the Albemarle Report, *New Left Review,* for example, saw the 'paternalistic approach which these established organisations have towards youth today (as) one of the most detrimental legacies the youth service inherited'. For the writer, Peter Massie, tougher solutions than the creation of a YSDC were needed 'if the voluntary organisations are ever going to be pulled into the 20th century'.

Similar criticisms came from much closer to home. As we saw in the last chapter, there is evidence that doubts about the capacity of the voluntary organisations to adapt eventually helped convince Ministry of Education officials that they should risk a fundamental review of the service. In due course the Albemarle Committee itself openly expressed its reservations, reminding 'the pioneering voluntary organisations' that their original 'strong ethical feelings … (can) lose their immediacy and drive'. This could lead young people to 'turn away from many good enterprises especially designed for them'.

Later judgments – many also from insiders – were if anything harsher, questioning not just language and presentation but the very substance of what the organisations were doing. Gordon Ette, in his 1967 *Youth Review* article, started from the proposition that 'the national voluntary organisations need to re-form and reorganise' since, he contended, 'their claims to offering variety within the total range of youth service provision had little substance'. This critique led him to the radical conclusion that what was required was 'the graceful and honourable retirement of some organisations and the launching of new ones'. In the same year Alec Oxford, who had previously worked for NABC for many years, warned such providers that, if they were to have any continuing usefulness at a time of rapid social and educational change, they needed to 'change … or else'.

'Graceful and honourable retirement' was, it seemed, something which on behalf of the Methodist Youth Department its general secretary, the Reverend Donald Hubery, was actually ready to consider:

> *Youth associations, whatever their history, do not exist for themselves. The Methodist Association of Youth Clubs certainly does not exist for its own sake, nor even for the sake of Methodism. It exists for youth, and if modern youth can only be served by a new, ambitious programme, made possible by the pooling resources of money, manpower and premises, MAYC is prepared to "lose itself" to that end.*

For him, losing the organisation's identity was an acceptable price to pay for 'a more comprehensive and adventurous approach … to those to whom the youth service seems unable to make any lasting appeal'.

Few in the voluntary sector were prepared to go this far. Indeed some not only fended off the more fundamental criticisms but were convinced that they remained the service's pioneering arm. They included Denis Howell who, no doubt reflecting on his years as chair of Birmingham Association of Youth Clubs, described the voluntary youth organisations as 'the great stimulators and the great originators of ideas … You get … more new thinking out of them than you get out of the best intentioned statutory body'.

Though, especially locally, such assurance about their role was common, even dominant, many of the voluntary youth organisations saw the need – indeed the urgency – to at least look again at what they were doing and how they were doing it. Shrewdly reading the times through the Albemarle lens, they agreed with Alec Oxford that they must change to survive. According to a SCNVYO account of their work published in 1965, in the five years after its publication, the report's 'impact was akin to a shock-wave through the service'. The voluntary organisations, it claimed, had 'seized particularly on two aspects of Albemarle: the need to experiment and the need to build'. Individual organisations like NABC specifically saw the report as having created 'an appropriate time for assessing the application of the principles by which the boys' club movement regulates its policy'.

This mood was strongly reinforced by an awareness that new commercially oriented organisations were emerging or being planned. Youth Ventures, for example, initiated by Lord Stonham, described itself as providing 'informal youth centres throughout the country'. Its starting point was 'the sense of frustration among some voluntary youth workers' and doubts about 'the usefulness of the work done in many orthodox youth clubs'. The detail of what was proposed – attractive decor and furnishings, coffee bar, dance hall, gym, work and study facilities and provision for a wide diversity of pursuits – did not in itself break many new barriers. However, the whole was clearly intended to be much greater than the sum of its parts with particular emphasis being placed on members electing their own officers, being responsible for the programme and enforcing agreed rules of conduct. The rhetoric was certainly challenging for the 'conventional' clubs and organisations which were being urged 'to adapt themselves to the changed social climate if they (were) to achieve more'.

A similar challenge was coming from some out-and-out commercial organisations which were showing a growing interest in catering for young people. This was illuminated by a special *Youth Review* feature on 'the new providers' which appeared in the autumn of 1967. Three of the biggest commercial operators spotlighted – Butlins, Rank and Mecca – were unapologetic about profit being the bottom line of their activities. However, according to a senior executive from Butlins (who was also an ex-youth worker), they were able, it appeared:

> ... to succeed more quickly with young people than a "social service" hamstrung by committees, lacking finance, and bedevilled by those who create a "do-gooder" image in the eyes of young people ... Our motive must be commercial but we know we ensure better holidays by helping people to "improve" themselves.

What seemed even more immediately threatening were some of the proposals of the Newsom Report. Published in 1963, this, as one commentator put it at the time, generated fears among the voluntary organisations that:

> ... the schools will be usurping some of their functions, that some of the traditional youth activities will become extra-curricular school activities.

This perceived threat was registered by a number of organisations whose vulnerability seemed to be all the greater because they were operating from outside the magic circle of the local state – and because so many of their users were the 'non-academic' 13 to 16-year-olds on whom the proposed Newsom develop-ments were to be focused.

In response to these changes, real, predicted or imagined, some of the most traditional of the organisations undertook very searching self-evaluations. The Haynes Committee report on the Boys' Brigade, published in 1964, took three years to produce and at least as long to implement. Two years later a 'Commission' report on the Methodist Association of Youth Clubs (MAYC) was completed. An 'Advance Party' report on the Scouts (also two years in the making) was used as well by the Sea Cadets as a prompt for some of its internal rethinking.

Other organisations carried out more modest, though often very prompt, internal review exercises. The Church of England Youth Council published a policy statement in 1961. In the same year, in *Boys' Clubs in the Sixties*, NABC restated the core principles of the boys' club movement (and, in 1967 also published *Newsom and Boys' Clubs* which reflected on the Newsom report's implications for its work). Some of the decade's new thinking on work with girls initiated by NAYC and its affiliated associations and by the YWCA (to be considered in the next chapter) stemmed from the same concern to remain responsive to the changing times.

The voluntary organisations' publicity literature of the time contained common, and repeating, themes. Following some, usually token, reference to Albemarle, nods of recognition were often made to 'the affluent (or at least better off) society' in which young people were growing up. The new model teenager, it was recognised, had more leisure and a wider range of recreational outlets than earlier generations and a life style distinguished by 'bicycles and scooters, transistor sets and record players (and a) variety of clothes'.

It was accepted that all this meant that most young people gave up the uniformed organisations as soon as they entered their teens or, even where the youth work was more 'open', very soon after. In addition, there was sometimes frank admission – for example, by the Scouts and the Guides – that their programmes could actually

result in young people experiencing failure rather than achievement. As the Guides put it at the time:

We had broken an educational principle by creating a system in which failure could flourish … Had we created a special class for the select few while the majority, though probably benefiting from the movement's principles, were leaving as second class citizens?

To combat these trends and deficiencies, conscious efforts were made to modernise programmes, decision-making and staffing structures, sometimes radically. The Scouts, for example, dropped the requirement to obey from its oath and set up Venture units for older young people which were given considerable freedom to organise their own affairs. The National Association of Mixed Clubs and Girls' Clubs re-created itself in 1961 (for the fourth time in its history) as the NAYC. In the process – and in the spirit of the times – it finally removed from its mission any political focus on young women's working lives and conditions in order to reposition itself as a provider of personal and social education delivered through leisure facilities. Perhaps as a further sign of the diminishing place of distinctive work with girls, in June 1964 the Girls' Life Brigade, the Girls' Guildry and the Girls' Brigade of Ireland amalgamated to become the Girls' Brigade.

Less radically, some local, regional and national structures and approved programmes were loosened up to allow leaders on the ground to be more responsive to young people's local, and changing, demands. The Association for

Jewish Youth (AJY) appointed two development officers and (later) the Church of England Youth Council made a similar appointment, particularly with a view to initiating forms of work which would connect with the unattached.

Images too often came in for a remake. Where uniforms were worn, considerable effort, attracting considerable media comment, was devoted to making them more fashionable – or at least less dowdy. More substantively, new commitments were made to recruiting and training volunteers ('of the right kind') and to increasing the voluntary organisations' leverage on the statutory youth service's developing power centres. Links were also to be strengthened with wider, especially Newsom-inspired, educational develop-ments and international contacts extended.

Above all organisations publicly touted their, at least for them, innovatory credentials – as when, for example, the Guides pointed to its encouragement of 'group dynamics and discussion techniques'. The non-club based approaches they were pioneering for reaching and working with unattached young people were particularly highlighted with the reports of the best known of these experimental projects – those sponsored by the NAYC and the YWCA – being published by two of the most respected publishers of the day, Penguin and Routledge and Kegan Paul. NAYC also initiated a young-people-to young-people project (the Weekenders) which was aimed at defusing bank holiday tensions at seaside resorts between mods and rockers. MAYC opened up Call-

in Cafe and Coffee Corner clubs in provincial centres while, through LOOT (London Out Of Towners) AJY sought to provide a haven for the Jewish young people from small outlying communities who were being sucked towards the bright lights of the capital.

Increasingly the prospectuses of the established organisations highlighted the progressive elements of their provision and programmes, especially where the unattached were seen as a special target. Most commonly these sought to show how they had taken in 'popular modern interests'. Motor cycling and motor car maintenance in addition, at that stage, to less familiar outdoor activities such as canoeing, sailing, gliding, rock-climbing were frequently quoted as exemplars of how the hearts as well as the minds of the new teenager were going to be won.

Perhaps most strikingly, however, were the approving gestures which were increasingly being made – by the Boys' Brigade, the Scouts, the Guides and NABC no less than NAYC and MAYC – towards 'mixing'. Often, it is true, only certain activities were seen as appropriately co-ed. Sometimes too the presence of girls seemed to be justified mainly on the grounds that they would help to attract in and then civilise the uncouth males who apparently patronised most single-sex youth facilities. Nonetheless the meeting of the sexes within a club or unit seemed gradually to come to be regarded by many single-sex organisations as the missing magic ingredient. Once injected into their programmes, older teenagers would, it seemed, be instantly and fully integrated into styles of operation and philosophies which at their core were to remain sacrosanct.

Indeed, on this, most of the organisations were clear and often deliberately assertive. Their stalls, they agreed, needed to be set out in ways which were more appealing to young people of the 1960s. However, certain dominants remained – core values and principles – and the essentials of their historic approaches and methods were not open to fundamental review. Here, the Boys' Brigade's Haynes Report was particularly honest and unambiguous:

> We would strongly deprecate a toning down of the Brigade's purpose so that it might fit more congenially into prevailing attitudes in order to attract larger numbers.

For some organisations these commitments included nurturing young men's masculinity through 'virile pursuits' and preparing young women for their roles of homemaker and mother. Firm stances were taken, too, on the need to encourage all young people 'to belong to some religious body and to carry into daily practice what he professes' or at least to have leaders who were 'aware of their own need for a religious faith … (and) constantly seeking to find and to strengthen it'. Such principles were enunciated as openly by ostensibly secular organisations like the Scouts and NABC as they were by the Boys' Brigade.

Despite – or, as many would have claimed, because of – this firmness of will, in the post- Albemarle period the voluntary youth organisations displayed that

familiar characteristic of so many British establishment institutions: a capacity to ride the white waters of the rapid cultural flows with some skill. In fact they often did more than just survive these threatening currents: they redirected some of them to their advantage. The warnings of the Alec Oxfords and Gordon Ettes thus came to seem superfluous. Over the decade, despite many a distinct shift in their membership towards the younger age groups, the traditional voluntary organisations fended off the threatened take-overs of the schools and social work agencies and maintained their structural place within the youth service.

In one crucial respect, however, their position did change. Without in any way seeking to strengthen or even review the legislative base of youth work, explicitly as well as implicitly the Albemarle Report had dispensed with the notion of the role of the state as mere gap-filler. Instead, it proceeded on the premise that, for high quality and effective youth work to be delivered to young people, the state's role both centrally and locally must be active and pro-active – that is, *interventionist*. The report thus helped significantly to alter the underpinning beliefs and assumptions of youth work's constituent organisation (voluntary as well as statutory) about who should resource and therefore who should manage and ultimately shape the work. Clearly this transaction had shifted the balance of power within the service to the disadvantage of the voluntary organisations.

Sometimes these changing power relations were signalled very clearly, even brutally.

According to Fairbairn, LEA youth committees and officers could end up 'adopting too precipitately a hectoring attitude (or) a go-it-alone attitude'. Though most immediately such reactions might be prompted by frustration with the voluntary sector's perceived lethargy or complacency, beneath them lay some more far-reaching realities:

> Voluntary bodies must realise that authorities are willy-nilly going to be the main pace-makers because of their increasing number of full-time professionals and the size of their financial outlay.

If Fairbairn's embrace of statutory leadership appears somewhat over-enthusiastic when viewed through the anti-statist lens of the 1990s, albeit for very different reasons it would have jarred even more with many of his 1960s youth service contemporaries. Their memories, still often vivid, would have been of state function-aries needing to seek permission even to advise the 'real' providers, the voluntary youth organisations. The assertion that it was for the statutory sector rather than for them to set the pace would have provided a barely palatable reminder of just how fast and how far power in the service had slipped away from them in the previous 10 years.

Yet, notwithstanding the Bow Group's early warning on too interventionist a state role, Fairbairn's view was widely shared – and across the political spectrum. As Denis Howell's very active and often apparently decisive role within the YSDC suggests, the Labour governments of the later 1960s simply took it as given – as did the other main political parties – they the state should be at the heart of decision-making and resourcing within the youth service. They also assumed that this was true too of the LEAs whose duty it was to use and manage these resources and to raise and disburse their own.

On the back of the Albemarle Report, a national youth service had thus by the end of the decade come into being. This was embodied most concretely in specific and, it was assumed, permanent, state policies, facilities and resources. It had made the provision of youth work much less reliant on a loose network of independent (some might say maverick) organisations and entrepreneurial (and also perhaps maverick) paid and unpaid workers. Though the changes were still in process, what were replacing these arrangements by the end of the 1960s were increasingly bureaucratic structures created to manage provision increasingly being paid for out of national and local taxation. These structures contained within them the seeds of much more stringent processes of accountability, including expectations that face-to-face work itself should be subject to tighter controls. Indeed, one of the YSDC's newer members, Eric Bourne, who was himself a county youth officer, was by 1967 explicitly defining youth work professionalism as synonymous with improved management skills.

Clearly these changes represented both gain and loss – or at least strain. On the one hand they promised greater coherence and security of provision, on the other, increased rigidity and impersonality. Increasingly in fact the state-led youth service would be required to reconcile two powerful and often contradictory imperatives. The one from below still required responsive and flexible forms of service delivery which, at young people's pace and often on their ground, could develop a curriculum which in significant ways they had helped to shape. The other, emanating from above, required the greater accountability which all welfare state provision was demanding and which increasingly assumed 'managerialist' methods and styles of organisation.

Main references

Albemarle Report, *Youth Service in England and Wales*, HMSO, 1960

Eric Bourne, 'The Unprofessional Youth Service', *New Society*, 7.12.67

Bow Group, *Responsibility for Youth*, Conservative Political Centre, 1961

Derbyshire Education Committee, 'Professional Youth Leadership', 1965

John Eggleston, *Adolescence and Community: The Youth Service in Britain*, Edward Arnold, 1975

W. M. Evans, *Young People in Society*, Basil Blackwell, 1965

King George Jubilee Trust, *Citizens of Tomorrow*, 1955 (Part IV)

J. Macalister Brew, *Youth and Youth Groups*, Faber and Faber, 1957

Ministry of Education, *Training of Part-time Youth Leaders and Assistants* (Bessey Report), HMSO, 1962

Ministry of Education, *A Second Report on the Training of Part-time Youth Leaders and Assistants*, HMSO, 1966

Roy Herbert, 'Youth Service – has it a future?', Church of England Youth Council, 1969

Peter Keunstler, *Voluntary Youth Leaders*, University of London Press, 1953

James Leicester and James Farndale (eds), *Trends in the Services for Youth*, Pergamon Press, 1967

Peter Massie, 'Lady Albemarle's Modest Proposals', *New Left Review*, May/June 1960

Ministry of Education, *Youth Service Buildings: General Mixed Clubs* Building Bulletin 20), Ministry of Education, 1961

Ministry of Education, *Youth Club: Withywood Bristol* (Building Bulletin 22), Ministry of Education, 1963

A. E. Morgan, *The Needs of Youth*, Oxford University Press, 1939

National Organisation for Work with Girls and Young Women, *Background and History*, undated

Alicia Percival, *Youth Will Be Led*, Collins, 1951

Political and Economic Planning (PEP), *The Service of Youth Today*, PEP, 1948

Don Potts, 'Some notes on the history of the National Association of Youth Leaders and Organisers', NAYLO, 1961

H. Rohrs and H. Tunstall-Behrens (eds), *Kurt Hahn*, Routledge and Kegan Paul, 1970

Celia Rose, *Touching Lives*, Youth Work Press, 1998

Joan Tash, *Supervision in Youth Work*, National Council of Social Service, 1967

4 Post-Albemarle Aspirations – and Realities

Take-up and targeting

How many users?

As the evidence of the last chapter shows, over the Albemarle 10-year development period the youth service experienced real growth. With increased revenue and capital budgets, locally and nationally, it acquired many more purpose-built premises, it more than doubled its full-time workforce and it extended training for its part-timers. Through a major shift of sponsorship from the voluntary to the statutory sector, it also gained greater leverage on governmental decision-making.

Nonetheless, the service's soul-searching continued. In particular it went on anguishing over its primary mission as defined by Albemarle and constantly reiterated thereafter: was it turning the one million who were said to have used it in the past into two million? Rather glib Ministry progress reports offered statistics first in 1963 and again, unaltered, in 1966 claiming to show that in most areas there had been 'an increase – varying from less than 5 to as much as 150 per cent – in the number of young people using the facilities'. Figures for 1960–61 and 1962–63 also suggested that among 14 to 20-year-olds membership of the main national

voluntary youth organisations, though showing significant variations, had overall risen by some 23 per cent.

These statistics were presumably based on returns from the LEAs and voluntary organisations themselves and gathered at a time when systematic monitoring was not one of the service's greatest strengths. Their reliability is therefore open to some doubt. Moreover, with the number of 15 to 20-year-olds rising year on year from three million to over four million – between 1961 and 1966, from 13.5 to 14.3 per cent of the population – they hardly provide an accurate before-and-after picture of proportionate levels of take-up.

Throughout the decade, the interplay of conventional wisdom, anecdotal evidence and a limited amount of formal research painted a rather different picture. One study of young school leavers carried out in 1966 did find that between 42 and 47 per cent of the 15-year-olds interviewed were members and that two-thirds had attended in the previous seven days. However, this used a definition of 'youth club or organisation' which went beyond youth service provision. Other studies – for example, one by Cyril Smith in Bury in Lancashire in 1963 and Pearl Jephcott's in Scotland carried out between 1964 and 1966 – suggested that young people's overall use of specifically youth service facilities had at best stuck obstinately at around one-third of the age group.

This was also the finding of a major study carried out for the DES by the Office of Population Censuses and Surveys (OPCS) in 1969 (though not published until 1972). Two of its conclusions were that 'the prevalence of attachment among young people has not changed markedly since at least the later 1940s' and that (though with some relevant organisations not covered) the overall attendance figure may have fallen to 26 per cent.

The researchers' generalised statements also contained some important shades. The OPCS study, for example, revealed that 68 per cent of 14 to 20-year-olds had passed through a youth group of some sort before they were 21 while 57 per cent of Smith's Bury sample had belonged for a minimum of three months since they were aged 14. Class and gender also compli-cated the broad findings: the early leaver report, for example, showed that usage was slightly lower among 'the less able' and those with fathers in semi and unskilled jobs and that girls were much less likely than boys to stay involved beyond the age of 15.

The unattached – or do we mean the delinquent?

Given the overall findings of these studies, it was perhaps not surprising that throughout the decade anxious attention continued to be paid to the unattached. Both Denis Howell and his Conservative shadow Edward Boyle, using almost identical language, acknowledged in 1965 that 'in all that has been done in the five years (since Albemarle) we have really not made much inroad' into reducing the numbers of those outside the service's sphere of influence. In Boyle's view 'the youth service as constituted today is inadequate to serve (their) needs … Even the best youth clubs cannot hold them'. Three years later Howell was justifying a major initiative for extending community service opportunities for young people (examined in detail later in this chapter) as 'a tremendous approach to the unattached youngster'.

Much opinion in the field seemed to share this preoccupation. A constant flow of features on detached and coffee bar projects aimed at the unattached appeared in *Youth Service* while most of the very limited number of books on youth work published over the decade had a similar focus. One professional commentator's end-of-decade assessment of the service's record in tackling this key Albemarle target was blunt: 'the vision of a great influx of the unattached … has not been realised'.

Such generalisations masked a more complex situation, however. The term 'the unattached' – which anyway meant some very different things to different people – was one of the issues which carried the service's version of a much wider welfare state debate: at what point should its responsibility to serve all-comers give way to its need to focus limited resources on identified priority groups? This was not of course a new dilemma – youth work since its earliest days had set its sights quite explicitly on disaffected sections of working-class youth. In the context of significantly expanded state provision, however, the tensions between these universalist and selective principles became much sharper.

Immediately post-Albemarle, a commitment to universalism was sometimes articulated. In *Lady Albemarle's Boys*, for example, Ray Gosling stressed the need for the service to attract 'the ordinary consumer'. At about the same time Peter Massie in his *New Left Review* article described the key target group as 'the more independent youth of today'. A more negative defence of the universalist principle was embodied, too, in the service's widespread resistance to providing 'intermediate treatment' as proposed by the 1968 White Paper *Children in Trouble* and as ultimately embodied in modified form in the 1969 Children and Young Person Act. For many practitioners and managers, participation in these diversionary programmes for 'labelled' young offenders was seen as undermining the service's core commitment to open-door and non-stigmatising facilities as well as young people's voluntary attendance.

Yet, as in the past, this defence of principle was never total. Some outsiders – and not just social workers – continued to explore the youth service potential for tackling juvenile offending. In 1965 the Medical Research Council Social Psychiatric Unit funded a survey to tease out the correlation between delinquency rates and youth service provision in 22 towns and cities in England. At about the same time, Cyril Smith, who as Director of Youth Studies at Manchester University was much more of an insider, was writing in the *Howard*

Journal on the youth service's role in delinquency prevention. And in more commonsense terms, one architectural expert was expressing the view that the open-plan premises then being built throughout the service might ensure that less trustworthy youth club members were not left on the periphery of events 'to hatch his (sic) dark delinquent designs'.

However, it was the service's specialist and experimental work with the unattached which revealed the extent to which selectivist ideas were being further refined and embedded in the service's collective psyche. Increasingly such programmes were directed at much narrower target groups – particularly those most at risk of breaking the law or in other ways revealing their disaffection from the wider society. Significantly, in reviewing relevant previous studies, the Medical Research Council's researcher used detached youth work projects as examplars of 'youth service schemes designed to reduce delinquency'.

In common with the dominant perspectives on social policy generally, key political explanations of unattachment emphasised personal pathology and cultural deviance. For Edward Boyle influential factors in creating unattachment included family breakdown and educational failure. According to HMI Simpson, an important reason for developing detached youth work was to tackle:

> ... the alienation of broad sections of young people – (and) their sense of being ... out of touch and out of sympathy with the values which we would like to see prevail.

A similar analysis underpinned Denis Howell's comments on the NAYC report *The Unattached* – though, unlike Simpson, he seemed to regard such disaffection within the younger generation as no more than an exception to the consensual and affluent rule:

> It reveals a degree of alienation amongst a growing number of young people … Even though those described remain a minority group they represent a challenge to anybody who cares that we should build a happy and healthy society.

Even when they aspired to a wider focus, such projects often in practice ended up prioritising young offenders or those most at risk of breaking the law – and in doing so implicitly adopted definitions of delinquency which brought working-class young people most sharply within their sights. The NAYC workers who produced *The Unattached*, for example, narrowed down their target group to 'those who do not belong to a youth organisation and are unhappy and/or delinquent'. Though most of the contacts made by the parallel YWCA project were categorised as the 'simply disorganised', the line between this group and the 'seriously disorganised' was far from clear-cut. Moreover, though the latter group was the smallest numerically, it 'needed the most intensive guidance and support on a long-term basis and … made up the bulk of the serious probation, court work, and boy/girl problem cases'.

Other projects with similar emphases included Avenues Unlimited in east London, the Youth Development Trust's Wincroft Project in Manchester, the Freebooters Club in Cambridge (run for 'troublemakers' by a university student, John Ewen, who was later to become head of the Youth Service Information Centre) and the Double Zero Club in Birmingham. The latter, the focus of considerable media interest, illustrated the selective approach in action in somewhat sensational terms. Founded and led by a minister, his highly populist paperback account of its work described the scene for the club's activities as 'murder, sex, drugs, death on the road, thieving, malicious damage, and all the turbulence of ignorant and indisciplined youth'. Its main target group was 'unclubbable Rockers, Hells Angels and Mods' who lived in a 'difficult area' characterised by unemployment and short-time working.

Separate or mixed – what shall we do with the girls?

The choice of so many – probably most – detached youth work projects during the 1960s to target delinquent working-class young people ensured that they advanced one particular form of selectivity within the service: they gave *young men* a special priority. Young women did get considerable attention within the NAYC and YWCA project while right at the end of the decade the Manchester Youth Development Trust mounted a detached work project with girls as its specific target. Overall, however, as one cafe project put it at the time, girls took 'an inactive part in the proceedings'. The centre of gravity of much of this early detached work thus settled itself around disruptive, which most commonly meant delinquent, male behaviour and activity.

This, however, was no more than a particular example of a much more general phenomenon. In its view of girls and their needs, Albemarle had little new to offer – indeed, it clearly did not regard them as requiring any very special consideration or recommendation. On the contrary, with the proposed ending of national service, it identified 'the young men of military age previously lost to them' as a priority for clubs. The subsequent failure to recruit more than a handful of full-time women workers helped to entrench further the hold of male priorities within the service.

Yet even by the late 1950s the rapid if sometimes contentious emergence of mixed work had left both young women and women workers and organisers in increasingly marginalised positions. According to one assessment for 1963, though nearly 2,000 boys' clubs had survived this trend, only 216 girls' clubs had done so – a mere 8.5 per cent of the 2,555 mixed clubs operating by then.

As the shift to what some called a more liberated and others a more permissive society relaxed public constraints on male-female relationships (and not just among young people), the state in its many forms played its part in rendering girls and young women within the service increasingly invisible. Secondary schools, for example, encouraged too by the capital investment in large comprehensive schools, swung more and more to co-education.

As was so often the case, Albemarle was quick to spot these trends and to make their implications for the youth service explicit. It did make a token gesture to the special value of each type of club, including those 'for one sex only'. It also denied that it had any intention of proposing 'a uniform pattern'. Nonetheless it thought it important:

> ... to emphasise the value of mixed activities in our kind of society. More and more schools and colleges are becoming co-educational, and the working and meeting together of the sexes from childhood is now so much part of the social scene that adolescents do not always take kindly to segregation in their clubs.

Its advocacy of 'association' as a key element of youth work also seemed to carry at least implicit messages about the 'real' work being aimed at both sexes.

Subsequently other influential political and professional opinion formers contributed to the creation of this new 'progressive' conventional wisdom and thereby, albeit unintentionally, to the reduced opportunities for young women. In 1967 Denis Howell, for example, told Parliament of his 'personal preference for mixed clubs', adding:

> Bringing boys and girls together in a wholesome atmosphere seems to me to be one of the great needs of our society and one of the tasks of a relevant youth service.

In a provocative article in *Youth Service*, HMI Simpson also took mixed work for granted when, among other key questions about 'the social side of their clubs', he asked leaders to consider whether:

> ... there are (young people) who show increased readiness to consort with members of the opposite sex in a

relationship other than one of the forms of courtship.

The Ministry of Education's *Building Bulletins* were equally matter of fact in their assumption that the future of the youth service belonged to 'the general mixed club'.

Paradoxically, however, it was NAYC which most vigorously led this charge towards mixed facilities. It continued to offer opportunities for girls only – for example, through its MacAlister Brew Courses, first run in 1952. On the other hand though, not only did it in this period finally remove 'girls' from its title, it also reissued a statement in praise of mixed clubs first produced by one of its predecessor associations 'in the early years of the youth service'. This, it noted with obvious pride both in 1965 and again in 1967, had helped stimulate the early growth of mixed work and 'still sets out with clarity and emphasis some of the special assets of the mixed youth club'. According to Lesley Sewell, NAYC's general secretary through much of the 1960s, mixed provision enabled:

> ... *boys and girls to meet in circumstances and against a background in which they can learn good manners, where they will learn to make and can be guided towards an intelligent choice of companions; where they can meet each other as acquaintances on the firm common ground of membership.*

At times, the mixed club enthusiasts were provoked into such an uncritical stance by the assertiveness of those determined to maintain the pre-eminent position of boys in youth work – which most powerfully at that time meant NABC and its affiliated bodies. In their turn, the advocates of boys' clubs often responded to the perceived threat of mixed work as if they were engaged in a desperate rearguard struggle. In the early 1960s, for example, NABC issued a policy statement which – in contrast to other voluntary and statutory providers – made no mention of Sections 41 and 53 of the 1944 Education Act as providing the statutory basis of the youth service. Instead it put its faith in Section 76 of the Act which dealt with the education of pupils 'in accordance with the wishes of their parents'. Because, NABC argued, the youth service was part of further education, 'it follows that ... all concerned have an obligation to have a regard to the wishes of parents to no less a degree than in primary and secondary education' – and therefore to support them when they wished their sons to attend a segregated leisure-time club.

NABC in fact seemed determined to carry the fight in favour of separate provision for boys to its opponents. It continued to highlight boys' 'instinctive sense of comradeship' as 'the germ of citizenship' as well as, as we have seen, their need for 'virile pursuits'. The London Federation of Boys' Clubs added its support, emphasising, for example, that it was part of a boy's intrinsic nature to take part in sports 'because he must pit his strength and his skill against other boys, or try to master a skill "for its own sake"'.

At the same time, supporters of boys' clubs seemed ready to play both ends of the argument – for example, by accepting, especially for its weekend programmes, that 'by invitation ... girls can be welcomed either as individuals or as a group'. To its credit, the London Federation chose to confront this issue head on, appointing a special subcommittee to examine the involvement of girls in its clubs. Its report, published in 1963, acknowledged that a quarter of the Federation's affiliated clubs were boys sections of mixed clubs – a label which in practice could mean little more than that a mixed youth club had a (boys) football team. The report also accepted that 'boys' club leaders are often "marked" as being too one-sided and specialised in their approach'.

Underpinning its main conclusions, however, were some well established stereotypes of the sexes – especially in their teens. It was clear, for example, that because 'at the age of 16 (a girl) ... may already be thinking about marriage', she:

> ... often appears lost until she meets up quite happily with her boy friend in the canteen towards the end of the evening. Her club desires are often primarily social, or the means of finding a boyfriend.

The report also saw it as 'clearly recognisable' that:

> ... the boy upon arrival at the club asks "What's on?" (while) the girl wants to know "Who's here?" ... The girl depends on her personal relationships ...

Unsurprisingly the Federation sub-committee concluded that, though opportunities should be provided in boys' clubs for boys over 16 to meet girls in 'constructive activities' rather than just on the dance floor, *'we do not advocate that more boys' clubs ought to become mixed clubs'.*

(Italics in original.) Indeed it reiterated its conviction that:

> Boys' clubs have a particular responsibility for boys and great care must be taken to ensure that the too rapid development of mixed activities does not seriously hinder the normal boys' activities.

At the time it seemed urgent for NABC to be making this case. Though conceding that 'the boys clubs particularly ... will find a response in the lower age ranges', in 1968 Denis Howell made public his view that their contribution to work with the most under-represented group in the service, those over 17, was likely to be limited.

By then, however, other doubts were stirring – about the consequences for young women of the apparently unstoppable rise and rise of mixed work within the service. A decade before MacAlister Brew had noted that:

> The experience and figures would lead one to suppose that far from being more attractive to girls, the mixed club tends to attract more boys than girls. The history of random samples of such clubs, which have changed over from being girls only to become mixed clubs, would seem to show that, if there is a fall-off of membership after the club becomes a mixed one, it is on the girls' side.

By the 1960s even boys' club advocates were seeking to exploit these worries. The London Federation report on boys' clubs and girls, for example, asserted that 'we do not believe that youth clubs (mixed clubs) are the answer to all the needs of girls'. It also recognised that, where girls were allowed into boys' clubs, 'provision should be made for a room exclusively for girls, i.e. not only a powder room but also a lounge for the use of girls only'.

The element of special pleading within such arguments drew a sharp riposte at the time from Joan Tash of the YWCA who, in a barely disguised sideswipe at the NABC and the London Federation, commented acidly on the practice of some organisations of 'using ... one sex to attract the other without equal membership rights' and even seeing girls 'apparently as an activity for the boys'. Nonetheless, the concerns about the service's record in catering for young women were very real. By 1967, even the Minister, self-confessed devotee of mixed clubs though he was, was deploring its 'lack of comparable interest in providing for girls'. As Tash's intervention demonstrates, reappraisal by this stage was starting within organisations which had been at the forefront of the drive to mixed work. By the middle of the decade, NAYC, the London Union of Youth Clubs and the London branch of the YWCA had commissioned and published pamphlets on the interests and needs of young women and the role of the service in responding.

These analyses located themselves in wider critical perspectives as they had by then developed. *Girls at Leisure*, for example, a research report produced by Jalna Hamner for the YWCA and the London Union of Youth Clubs, noted that deep-seated societal attitudes to women were at the heart of the youth service's 'problem' with girls. As a result, she concluded, girls are seen as 'extras'. Mary Robinson, too, in an NAYC pamphlet *Girls*

in the Sixties pointed to the effects on the youth work with girls of the double standards more generally applied to men and women:

> *Men are excused up to late middle-age for the little boy that remains in their nature. No middle-aged women is excused for the little girl that remains in her ... every attempt to make girls aware of their responsibilities as setters of standards must be matched by a concern that boys too shall accept their responsibilities.*

Other stereotypes were also challenged – for example, the assumption that 'it is only girls for whom relationships are important' and 'the underestimation among ... adults ... of those gentler and more sensitive qualities which in our society are normally associated with women'. Girls' need for space to escape from the boys was recognised, as on occasions was an overall goal of helping to make girls 'more complete women' and 'to develop as a woman'. Finally all this was underpinned by calls for more women workers as well as for more favourable conditions for their work:

> *If youth clubs are to offer a really helpful service to girls, there must be an increase of women in the service ... The woman youth leader is ... frequently expected to run the girls' part (of the club) very much as the poor relation of the boys'.*

Each of these newly progressive analyses of work with girls – for that certainly was what they were at the time – had its own distinctive features. None, however, was radical in its perspectives on women's role and position or in its prescriptions for future action. The commentator who acknowledged girls' need for 'a sitting room and powder room', justified this on the grounds that 'there is nothing girls like to do more than to share their secrets in a quiet corner'. Similarly, when girls were not seen as 'notoriously unclubbable as regards activities', their interests and those of boys were usually assumed to be quite distinct:

> It would not be wise to include provision for any of the more delicate womanly pursuits in any room where vehicle maintenance was being carried on.

Even the commitment to girls' 'development as a woman' was explained in terms of their future need to take on the roles of 'budgeter, buyer, dressmaker, cook, interior decorator, nurse, hostess, voter, partner and mother'. One imaginative experimental project in Bristol operationalised this interpretation of woman's destiny by arranging for the girls on its school leaver courses to 'shadow' middle-class housewives as they went through their daily homemaking routines.

In particular, the new focus on girls' needs reflected the then dominant individualistic conceptions of social policy and of the professional practices seen as necessary for implementing it. Thus, according to Mary Robinson:

> Girls' activities … need to be geared to help the girl to become herself, to widen her interests and to develop her talents.

The Social Education of the Adolescent, which by the end of the decade was increasingly appearing on full-time and even some part-time youth work course reading lists, was even more explicit in focusing on the girl as individual:

> The fundamental error that adults make may well be to think of young people as girls (or boys) first and only afterwards as individual human beings, and therefore to allow their hypersensitivity to any client's sex to determine their approach.

By the end of the decade, the insufficiently inventive and proactive nature of youth work with girls was thus clearly beginning to be recognised. Nonetheless this critique was still being conceived as a specific example of a more general problem: that public provision like the youth service was still not succeeding in creating the conditions in which all young people could release and develop their personal abilities. Approaches which started from presumptions about girls' distinctive collective needs and possibilities as young women, and therefore as requiring separate provision designed to get them to explore and assert these, had to await the re-emergence of feminist thinking and organising during the 1970s.

Separate or integrated – what shall we do about the immigrants?

Some very similar 1960s perspectives underpinned the youth service's debate on how to target another of its emerging 'problem' groups – the children of the expanding Black and Asian communities. Crucial to the wider historical and contemporary context here were still-influential voluntary youth organisations which, created at a time when British imperial fever was at its height, had taken into their youth work philosophies and purposes notions of the 'white man's burden' and the superiority of the British 'race'. Baden-Powell, for example, looked to 'Britons who are now growing up to be the men of the Empire' and saw the Scout movement in particular as helping to create 'a new race of boys in England when the Scouts of today have little Scouts of their own'. As in the wider society, such implicitly or openly racist notions remained within most 20th century youth work developments, including those eventually sponsored by the state, to re-emerge most directly when the demand came that the youth service respond to new concentrations of Black and Asian populations in British cities.

Here, Albemarle's nose for social change as it might impact on youth let it down. Though called together only months after the Nottingham and Notting Hill 'race riots', the committee seemed not to have noticed how rapidly this shift to a multiracial and multi-cultural society was occurring, nor did it reflect much on how severely this would test the youth service's vision, to say nothing of its nerve.

In due course, 'the immigration issue' thrust itself into the heart of political life – as when in 1964–65 blatantly racist election campaigns in the West Midlands' constituency of Smethwick and in Leyton in London defeated a former Labour cabinet minister. It also produced the notorious 'rivers of blood' speech by Enoch Powell which in 1968 fundamentally shifted the parameters for debating race within British politics. In response, the new Labour government controversially pursued a dual policy, introducing a race relations act aimed at

constraining racism while placing much tighter controls on immigration itself.

Denis Howell was no stranger to these pressures. He too represented a West Midlands constituency with a substantial ethnic minority population. He also carried responsibility within government for 'immigrant education'. As minister of youth, he sought to seize the initiative towards the end of 1965 by requesting the YSDC to set up a subcommittee 'to consider the part the youth service might play in meeting the needs of young immigrants in England and Wales'. As Howell explained later, in 'making policy on a vitally important matter', this was ahead of its time.

The committee was chaired by Lord Hunt (of Everest fame). Its other members included one of the service's few qualified full-time Black leaders, Paul Stevenson, and Stuart Hall who later became Professor of Sociology at the Open University and was to provide some of the sharpest critiques of British society and of social policy from a Black perspective. Its report, *Immigrants and the Youth Service*, was published in July 1967, sold out quickly and had to be reprinted. Whatever its limitations – and, as we shall see below, it had many – it thus seemed to strike a chord, perhaps even touch a raw nerve, within the service.

Indeed, over a year before it reported, the voice of professional youth work as relayed through the journal *Youth Review* had flagged up a range of anxieties and even fears about 'the race problem'. Significantly, however, it saw as an exception the 'whites only' stance of a

POST-ALBEMARLE ASPIRATIONS – AND REALITIES

youth club in Smethwick where, in the run-up to the 1964 by-election, children were reported to have been roaming the streets chanting the slogan: 'If you want a nigger for your neighbour, vote Labour.' At the same time, subtly and sometimes not so subtly, it also managed to locate within the immigrants themselves and within their communities a number of the causes of racial tension. It, for example, conjectured that 'it might well be that there is more colour exclusiveness shown by Indian and Pakistani groups'. And it went on:

> There is some evidence that coloured parents discourage their children from joining existing clubs ... Quite under-standably, some of the coloured youngsters have quite a chip on their shoulders.

The Hunt report displayed some similar ambivalences (at the very least). While noting, for example, that 'coloured immigrants constitute less than 2 per cent of the total population', it nonetheless expressed concern at 'the sheer size of this latest wave of migration', calculating that the percentage in the youth service was likely to rise by a third in the near future. In various ways it urged the host community to stay open minded in its relations with the new arrivals – while at the same time reinforcing some well entrenched and limiting stereotypes of young Black and Asian people by pointing to their special prowess in sport and music.

Though detecting the host community's tendency 'to ascribe faults to immigrants which are really the consequence of the social and economic conditions prevailing in the United Kingdom', it nonetheless at times fell back on 'blaming the victim' models of Black and Asian communities and their problems. It thus drew on then fashionable theories about restricted language codes among 'underprivileged (that is working-class) children' to support its conclusion that:

> ... immigrant children ... often do not use words very precisely; their poor vocabulary and inadequate command of complex sentences lead to an inability to express any great variety of abstract ideas.

At times the Hunt report even came close to suggesting that a significant cause of the prejudice and discrimination encountered by Black and Asian groups was their assertion of their distinctiveness:

> There is a need for the immigrant also to accept the idea of integration, to keep an open mind about the people around him and to make the effort involved in achieving better communication. The more he remains apart, the more likely is it that he will develop a sense of rejection, attributing the intolerance of a few with whom he has come into contact to the majority he does not know. This could lead to a pattern of prejudice where the bigotry of one side is matched by the resentment of the other.

The report did recognise the often harsh material realities – poverty, competition for jobs, bad housing, too few hospitals beds – which could at least fuel such responses. However, as this passage illustrates, for the Hunt Committee the root of the problem lay in prejudicial attitudes, reactions and interactions – that is, in the way, one after another, individuals laid their hostile personal feelings on Black and Asian people and in the way the latter responded.

When 'solutions' came to be considered therefore, the Hunt committee concluded that:

> It (was) <u>only</u> through ... (personal) relationships that we can hope to establish the channels of communication and understanding which a healthy, integrated society needs. (Emphasis added.)

Nor in this context was integration merely a throw-away term: indeed, in this period it was seen as the essential aspiration for every Briton, Black or white, as the Home Secretary himself, Roy Jenkins, had made clear while the committee was still at work. In a widely reported speech at the Commonwealth Institute, Jenkins asserted that 'to maintain any sort of world reputation for civilised living and social cohesion', Britain must aim to achieve 'the final and necessary stage towards integration between all groups resident in Britain'. Setting this as 'the goal', he went on to define integration as:

> Equal opportunity, accompanied by cultural diversity, in an atmosphere of mutual tolerance.

In the context of race relations, the 1960s' confidence in Britain as a fundamentally consensual society meant that Jenkins – and indeed the Hunt committee following him – could assume that what was shared and agreed by the different ethnic communities was far greater and more significant than what separated them. Moreover, this confidence held up even when many of its citizens were not Christian, had lived for much of their lives in very different societies and continued to see these religious and cultural differences as at the heart of their personal and collective identities.

Though acknowledging that an overnight solution was not possible, the Hunt committee used Jenkins' definition of integration as its template. Specifically it recommended that the youth service's aim needed to be 'full integration between immigrants and the host community, and between the various immigrant communities'. As applied to young people, this meant that they should be able:

> To settle happily in this country without prejudice and in close relationship with the indigenous population ... to enjoy the social and recreational amenities they prefer ...

The Hunt committee was prepared to be patient. Quoting from the 1966 *Youth Review* leader, it conceded that 'it is pretty natural for the young folk to group themselves first with their compatriots'. It therefore accepted that 'the integration of coloured clubs within local groups and federations' and 'joint activity and cooperation with white youngsters' may need to be seen as longer-term goals. Nonetheless, it pointed firmly to 'the dangers of differentiation' and in effect labelled separate provision – other than for Asian girls – as 'inauthentic'. To support this position, it quoted from an article in *Youth Service* which had savaged separatist approaches:

> If one were to accept that the youth service should provide separate facilities for each racial group then one might just as logically accept that racial groups should live in separate communities of their own – and if one accepts this the road to apartheid is wide open.

Ethnic minority communities, it seemed, could not be permitted a positive and strategic choice to preserve distinct cultural identities – or even simply to seek respite and reaffirmation in the midst of everyday racist pressure and discrimination.

In contrast to the 'piecemeal attempts and *laissez-faire* attitudes in some areas', the report described the positive, planned approach adopted in two cities – Bristol and Sheffield. In Bristol the result was a number of substantially multi-racial initiatives. In choosing Sheffield as its other case study, however, the report, albeit inadvertently, gave national prominence to a more separatist strategy which had resulted in a youth club 'aimed primarily, but not exclusively, at attracting West Indians'. While commending 'the Sheffield venture … (for its) willingness to listen to the wishes of the immigrants themselves', the committee all but acknowledged its mistake in highlighting this work by warning that it carried within it 'a danger of permanent segregation'.

That the committee had good reason to hedge its bets on the Sheffield initiative was illustrated by an account of the work in progress provided at the time by Sheffield's own youth adviser, Joan Bennett. Writing in *Youth Service* in June 1966 – that is, over a year before *Immigrants and the Youth Service* was published – she did concede that what was happening in Sheffield was seen 'as a first positive step towards the integration of the West Indians within the community and in no way as a segregationalist move'. Nonetheless, she was forthright about the need to 'face up to the situation, honestly and realistically, accepting that it is was no good propounding idealistic and

impractical solutions'. For her and her colleagues this meant that they:

> … came down very strongly in favour of the idea that, before the West Indians as a whole could start to play a full part in the social life of the community, it is necessary that they should have … their own youth club. (This) would cater primarily for West Indians and would be organised and controlled by West Indians themselves. They badly need a place where they can be among their own people.

With Denis Howell and the YSDC remaining committed to the Hunt report, the DES asked every LEA a year after publication to account for what they had done to adopt its recommendations. Nonetheless scepticism about its single-minded adherence to integration as the way forward remained – and deepened. A report of a NAYSO subcommittee, released in the summer of 1969, stated bluntly that 'attempts to develop multi-racial youth groups had failed'. Its explanations for this included both 'the resistance and prejudices of indigenous young people' and 'the strong ties of the separate ethnic groups which create a substantial demand for separate provision'. The NAYSO group also saw youth workers as 'making disproportionate and unrealistic efforts to integrate immigrants' – especially in the case of young Asian girls where religious and cultural restrictions virtually ruled out any traditional youth service contribution. Though still refusing to let go completely of the aspiration of multi-racial youth work, the NAYSO committee recommended that:

> The most important immediate necessity was ensuring that there was equal provision for all young people. This may

mean setting out with a deliberate policy to provide special facilities to cater for the immediate needs of young immigrants.

It also offered examples of good practice across England, some of which were based on this policy.

If further support for such a position were needed, it was provided in 1969 by Bryan Hartley, NAYC's Community Development Officer (Young Immigrants). Giving written evidence to the House of Commons Select Committee on Race Relations and Immigration, he traced the 'limited success' of youth service's multi-racial goal to the deprivation and disturbance experienced by both Black and white in the communities where it most often needed to be achieved:

The youth clubs usually match the rest of the amenities in these areas: few are purpose built, they are run usually by part-time leaders with little equipment or they are entirely non-existent.

He then described in some detail what happened on the ground to multi-racial youth work, highlighting the tensions and hostility which sometimes 'erupts into violence' and which meant that few clubs survived as multi-racial – if they survived at all. His conclusion was unambiguous:

The youth service is in a genuine dilemma over whether its goal is to promote integration or to meet the needs of coloured teenagers because the two do not necessarily always coincide.

Hartley also talked of 'a somewhat ominous portent for the future' when a national youth service conference on

young immigrants had to be cancelled through lack of interest. His concerns were further underlined by one of the YSIC's publications in the early 1970s. This quoted the uniquely poor response to a survey of provision for young immigrants it had undertaken as evidence of how unready the service was to address multi-racial issues. Even so, the material which YSIC did manage to gather, while identifying some multi-racial successes, painted a discouraging picture, noting, for example, the patronising attitudes of the national voluntary youth organisations to young immigrants and their families and their *laisse-faire* approach to recruiting Black and Asian young people. Against this background it asked:

What about the coloured youngsters who either don't want or for various reasons feel they can't join multi-racial provision? Does the youth service stick to its (integrationist) principle, or does it aim to meet the expressed needs of groups of coloured young people by assisting and sometimes offering separate provision?

The YSIC also noted how 'a growing number of second generation coloured young people are making vociferous demands for what they see as equal treatment in grant-aid procedures' and suggested that:

Separate provision (not perhaps just for months but for years) is the only way in which some groups and individuals will be able to find sufficient security to step out into a multi-racial society.

And it confronted what was perhaps the most testing, and usually neglected, of all issues faced by the service – white racism:

If ... good community relations founder not on the attitudes of immigrants but on the attitudes of the indigenous populations, what is the youth service doing in this respect, regardless of whether there are few or no immigrants living in the county or city?

Overwhelmingly, however, throughout the decade policies continued to be made and implemented by politicians, officials and practitioners from these white indigenous populations. This was true even though immigrants, including young people, were sometimes surveyed and even consulted and despite the tokenistic involvement of some high-profile Black personalities in the official decision-making processes. It was in this context that Black and Asian groups and organisations began to generate their own analysis of their situation and to define their own prescriptions for action which usually contrasted, indeed conflicted sharply, with the Hunt report's integrationist solutions. As one of the few Black historians of the youth service, Lincoln Williams, noted later: 'The principal recommendation of integration by the Hunt Report was ... completely against the dominant trends taking place in the Black and white communities' and was therefore, he concluded, 'doomed to failure'.

Pauline Crabbe, a Black member of the Race Relations Board speaking in February 1969 at a conference organised jointly by the Community Relations Commission and NAYSO, pointed to factors within Black and Asian families which were helping to produce this resistance to integration among African-Caribbean

young people. From a more specifically youth service perspective, Black youth worker Gus John expounded similar views. The final chapter of *Because They're Black*, which he co-authored with Derek Humphry, openly queried: 'Why Black Power in Britain?' and pointed to the attempt of Black young people 'to find an identity, one which can only be Black, not Asian, West Indian or British by nature'. On the grounds that 'it is futile to talk of integration when so little concern is expressed about inequality', the book homed in on 'the futility of flogging the integrationist horse'. Instead it proposed 'the strategy for Black people lies in working towards Black consciousness'.

As by the end of the decade these perspectives became more explicit and more assertive, slowly and against great resistance they began to force themselves into the youth service's discourse on race. If the service was to have any chance of targeting Black and Asian young people, it was thus clearly going to have to take on board some of their and their communities' definitions of need and of appropriate responses.

All of which suggested that the shelf life of the Hunt Report was likely to be even shorter than most such official documents.

Young people in rural areas

Whether the target group was working-class young men, young women or Black and Asian young people, implicitly at least the focus of most of the reported youth service practice, research and comment in the post-Albemarle period was on the urban young. The needs of rural young people did, however, get some consideration, though invariably from a marginalised position. As in general it was assumed that young farmers' clubs were catering for the more motivated and socially skilled young people, here too the need to reach and engage the unattached provided much of whatever impetus to action existed.

On the advice of the YSDC, a working group was set up in November 1963 'to consider whether … there are special problems – identifiable on a national scale – in youth work in rural areas and, if so, whether the existing methods of dealing with these problems are adequate'. Chaired by R. D. Salter Davies, the chief youth service HMI at the time, it drew only on the personal experience of its members. Its report, published in March 1965, concluded that the basic needs of young people were the same whether they lived in town or country and that on the whole at that stage these were being adequately met. It did, however, identify some key changes in rural life and a number of practical obstacles to carrying out effective youth work. It concluded that the 'social pattern of village life' should be the prime focus of the youth work response and made recommendations on field support staff, the role and recruitment of leaders (paid and voluntary), training and information, premises, transport and the involvement of 'adult bodies'.

Some youth service development in rural areas did occur during this period. Somerset reported some careful analysis and extra provision on the ground while Cumbria, Cambridgeshire and Leicester-

shire extended their facilities based on community schools. However, given that these were authorities with an established track record of providing for rural young people, evidence of the impact on the ground of the working party's report is hard to find. With urban, especially inner city, youth remaining the most consistent preoccupation throughout the 1960s, questions about gaps in rural provision, leading to similar conclusions and equally slow responses, reappeared in each subsequent decade of the youth service's history.

Providing for disabled young people

Some specialist and innovative work with disabled young people also developed in this period. Much of it was dependent on the self-help efforts of parents and the commitment and flair of determined individuals, including teachers working with the young people during the day. By the mid-1960s it had generated new voluntary sector organisations, particularly for 'backward', 'educationally sub-normal' or 'mentally handicapped' young people. The Elfrida Rathbone Association was formed in 1963. With the National Society for Mentally Handicapped Children taking the initiative, this was followed in 1966 by the conversion of an Advisory Committee on Youth Clubs for the Handicapped into a Federation of Gateway Clubs.

Though separate clubs were usually still seen as the most realistic way forward, some of this work was specifically aimed at integrating disabled young people into mainstream youth facilities. Here Mary Robinson, who was responsible for senior member training at NAYC during the 1960s, undertook initiatives which for the time were genuinely pioneering. These sought to define all participants as equal contributors to the programmes on offer and so to avoid placing the disabled young person in a merely dependent relationship with those without a disability. Originating in 1957, by the mid-1970s this work had produced a nation-wide network of some 60 PHAB (Physically Handicapped and Able-Bodied) clubs.

In 1961 a DES grant was made to the Royal Association in Aid of the Deaf and Dumb so that, as a start, they could provide a youth work service in the Metropolitan area. It was followed in 1965 by one to the Elfrida Rathbone Association. None of this, however, amounted to a concerted effort with consistent state support to recognise the social educational needs of disabled young people, to make youth work provision for them or to incorporate them into mainstream facilities.

Most disabled young people thus remained largely invisible – often literally so, hidden away in institutions, special schools and even, in their leisure time, in their own homes. As they were clearly not perceived by policy-makers as a 'problem' in the way that, for example, inner city unattached young people were, they gained only limited attention and even less priority in the allocation of resources.

Gay and lesbian young people

One group which remained completely hidden – and which demonstrates the need in any historical account to think 'absences' as well as 'presences' – were gay and lesbian young people: indeed, in this period, they seem to have been significant *only* by their absence. At the time Albemarle reported, male homo-sexuality itself had yet to be decriminal-ised while lesbian relationships, though usually less overtly persecuted, still remained largely in the closet. Perhaps not surprisingly therefore, 1960s youth service policy-makers seem not even to have considered that gay and lesbian young people might have some specific needs or require some targeted responses. These had to await pressure exerted by their own liberation movements of the 1970s even to begin to force themselves into a wider public consciousness and on to public policy agendas.

Community service by young people

One particularly fashionable way of targeting unattached (if not necessarily alienated) young people during the 1960s was voluntary community service: indeed for a time the service was all but claiming some exclusive promotional rights to it as a form of youth work. The idea had a long youth work pedigree. According to one interpretation its origins were to be found in that sense of *noblesse oblige* which had carried the young and privileged into the city slums. Over time, it had become embedded in youth work programmes themselves – for example, in some of the uniformed organisations' training schemes – and had also helped to attract young people into bodies like the Red Cross and the St John's Ambulance Brigade.

By the time a state-sponsored service of youth came to be constructed, the emerging premise was: 'Lady Bountiful is out. Service by young people is in.' Increasingly youth clubs were being urged to provide 'service corps' and opportunities for 'being useful'. One practical workers' handbook in 1942 asserted: 'To serve is to possess the world. To live for others is the way of adventure'. When the Duke of Edinburgh made training for public service one of the core elements of his newly-established award scheme in 1956, he was thus building on a long tradition.

Yet the youth service could hardly claim exclusive ownership of community service as a way of working with and informally educating young people. As a product of Gordonstoun School, the Duke of Edinburgh had been greatly influenced by its head, Kurt Hahn. Hahn, according to one biographer, was 'obsessed with rescue and with other kinds of service less dramatic, but more available in an urban civilisation'. The same period also saw the creation in Britain of Voluntary Service Oversees as well as, abroad, President Kennedy's attempt to tap the idealism of American youth via an American Peace Corps of volunteers.

The Albemarle Report did offer some support to activities aimed at getting young people 'to make a significant contribution to society'. However, it explicitly distanced itself from the more 'picturesque and dramatic' versions of

community service then being promoted. It somewhat bleakly reminded enthusiasts that its 'true challenge … lies in the more humble forms in which need presents itself' and that as 'the old and sick can be demanding, most forms of help … have all the tedium of repetition'.

Nonetheless, far from stalling, the community service bandwagon gathered pace throughout the 1960s, acquiring a charismatic and energetic national advocate in Alec Dickson. After his success in helping to set up the VSO, Dickson founded the Community Service Volunteers in 1962 with the aim of creating a domestic vehicle for promoting and coordinating community service opportunities for young people. In 1963 this was given further national credence by the Newsom Committee which suggested that it might become part of the school curriculum and by a follow-up publication five years later in the form of a Schools Council working paper, *Community Service and the Curriculum*. By the end of the decade it was, according to Bernard Davies, 'one of the "in" things of our times' which, as with the royal family, made 'any attempt at objective analysis … seem petty and indeed even traitorous':

> *Voluntary service thus now bids fair to do for the second half of the 20th century what … the playing fields of Eton are said to have done for our predecessors.*

On the ground, local organisations and networks acting as clearing houses for voluntary service opportunities for young people thus began to appear, many with strong youth service connections. (A guide published in 1967 identified 14 of these in

England, Wales and Scotland though, if the features carried by *Youth Service* are any guide, this list was certainly incomplete.) The National Council of Social Service (NCSS) made community service by young people its annual conference theme for 1964, pointing to 'a remarkable growth' which had led to a 'wide and imaginative range of service' being offered. This, it said, was 'a boon to the hard-pressed social services and an adventure for the young people'.

Some voluntary organisations like the Association for Jewish Youth took strong initiatives of their own as did some LEA youth services. A local councillor from Portsmouth, also a YSDC member, got government support for a two-year clearing house 'experiment' whose final report in 1964 brought together experience and conclusions on both organisational and practice issues. Often the aims of these local projects were modest: as one LEA youth officer put it, such service should be a 'self-effacing part of responsible citizenship'. Often, too, they emphasised the good being done *by* rather than *for* young people – though many of the projects insisted that as far as possible young people should run them themselves.

Task Force in London attracted particularly favourable media coverage. Its founder and first director Anthony Steen, a young barrister who a decade later was to become a Conservative MP, established himself as another of its powerful public voices. As it became increasingly fashionable, early political recognition arrived, both for the organisation and for community service itself. In June 1964

Christopher Chataway, then an Under Secretary at the DES, announced in the Commons that Task Force was to get government 'seed' money of £3,000.

Though the Conservative Party resisted pressure to make support for community service official party policy, leading politicians from both the main parties publicly associated themselves with what one MP called 'the revolutionary change in emphasis from service *to* youth to service *by* youth'. They included Denis Howell who, within months of coming into government, set up a YSDC subcommittee (to be chaired once again by Gordon Bessey). Its brief was to consider 'whether there should be facilities for the coordination of community service by young people in England and Wales and to make recommendations'.

By the time it reported in December 1965 the value of service to the community as 'part of the social training of young people' was so taken for granted that the committee was able to state baldly that the desirability of such provision 'is not an issue'. Though unable to undertake any systematic research, the evidence it collected from 42 organisations revealed 'discontent with the present lack of facilities for the development of community service', with the majority urging greater coordination. This, the committee unanimously agreed, was essential. It proposed it should be provided locally by clearing houses run either by the LEA or by a voluntary organisation or by a partnership between them. These bodies were to be advised by committees which as far as possible represented young people and would have a remit which included both extending volunteer opportunities and placing young people in them.

The committee also envisaged 'a national council for service by young people', to promote the idea, disseminate information and advise on grants to support it. It proposed that NCSS should be invited to administer the new body though not to run schemes. It also stressed 'most emphatically' that these were 'not intended to detract in any way from the work already being done by a number of voluntary organisations on a national basis'.

The committee's concern to avoid any suggestion of government empire-building proved well founded. Within the field, its own proposal for a national council was very coolly received. One young organiser of a local youth volunteer agency not only doubted NCSS's commitment to young people and its readiness to let them into its decision-making, she also suggested that any such national body 'might well damp enthusiasm'. Least welcoming of all, however, was Denis Howell. He, like his Secretary of State, Edward Short, continued to throw their full weight behind community service, hoping that it would 'become part of the life of every youth centre and school in Britain'. However, the idea of a national council was rejected and by July 1967 Howell was making mysterious noises to the effect that 'the Government had proposals afoot'. Eventually, in November 1967 he announced that he intended to set up a new national organisation to be called the Young Volunteer Force Foundation (YVFF).

The 'professional jealousies' stirred up by this decision made reactions to the Bessey committee's recommendation seem like enthusiastic support. Hostility resulted in part from the 'cloak of secrecy' which, it was felt, had preceded his announcement – though Howell himself forcefully rejected accusations of inadequate consultation. In itself, however, his move had left some influential – and very territorial – voluntary organisations feeling seriously threatened and unfairly excluded. When Howell appointed Anthony Steen as YVFF's first director, the worst suspicions of CSV (and indeed many others) were merely confirmed. What he was intent on doing, they concluded, was, at their expense, creating a 'nationalised Task Force' by the backdoor.

Certainly such an interpretation could be read into the substance of Howell's proposal. YVFF, for example, was mandated to go way beyond the primarily hands-off informational and promotional role of the national council envisaged by the Bessey report. Its remit was to select and train its own central unit of 30 young people who, by local authority or voluntary organisation invitation, would intervene directly in selected areas. Working in pairs or threes, they would set up local volunteer clearing houses, win local organisational and financial backing for these (including from local businesses) and then move on to other localities. For some organisations this approach threatened their own local (often hard-won) role and fundraising capacity. As one analysis at the time put it, it smacked of 'a Whitehall blueprint' to be imposed by 'whiz kids with no experience of local conditions' and with only minimal training. In the words of Elisabeth Hoodless, CSV's deputy director:

> A lot of people have spent a lot of time building it (community service) up, and one boob can undo a great deal.

A second major shift from the Bessey proposals, and indeed from most of the approaches which had been developed on the ground, was the way YVFF was sold as yet another instant remedy for solving the 'problem' of the unattached. At the press conference to launch the new organisation, this rationale was made explicit:

> Clearly the youth service has to change its emphasis if it is to provide a useful service, and it must be tailored to the needs of the later 1960s and '70s if it is to attract a greater number of young people.

Subsequently, in an apparent effort to scale down expectations, Steen claimed that if the Foundation managed to attract only 25 per cent of unattached youth it would be doing a good job. For CSV, however, such claims suggested a serious confusion of aims:

> Is it (YVFF) meant to reform the youth service, using the community service bandwagon, or is it a genuine effort to involve youth in community service?

In many localities, often for pragmatic reasons, YVFF quickly gained allies and supporters: by June 1968, as well as setting up its own advisory council, it had recruited 19 staff, its first field team was due to start its training, key central government departments had issued a

joint circular urging local authorities to cooperate with it and a Downing Street reception was about to mark the start of projects in Newport in Monmouth-shire, Newcastle, Derbyshire and Gloucestershire.

Nonetheless, some national organisations remained irreconcilably hostile. In the spring of 1968 Steen was still sufficiently concerned to go on the offensive. He commented on the rivalry and backbiting afflicting voluntary organisations generally and talked of 'a party of people (who) are intent on completely destroying it (community service)'. 'Their attitude,' he concluded, 'could wreck the whole spirit of voluntary service ... It could wreck us all.'

In one somewhat contradictory sense, Steen turned out to be right. Within a decade YVFF had metamorphosed into the Community Projects Foundation which itself in due course became the Community Development Foundation. What is more, as these changes of name suggest, its focus over the years shifted from operating as a youth work organisation using community service as its core method to sponsoring and supporting (often radicalised) forms of community work.

In a broader sense, however, Steen's worries proved entirely groundless. Voluntary service by young people proved to be one of the great survivors in the youth work – though not necessarily the youth service's – portfolio, making impressive comebacks in each of the next three decades.

Plotting a direction for the youth service

Even before the half-way point had been reached in Albemarle's 10-year development period, the 'where is the youth service going?' debate restarted, internally and in government circles. In part this fresh burst of navel gazing was politically driven. As the first Labour government for 13 years took power in October 1964, Denis Howell, a former Albemarle Committee member, set about making his mark on an area of provision which he felt he knew something about. Economic factors also exerted their influence, especially the £500 million deflation package of July 1966 which, as Howell reminded the service, was bound to have 'extremely serious' consequences.

Pressures within the service were also building. Concern over take-up rates never went away, especially as it became clear that the Albemarle expansion had failed to produce the expected miracle. Increasingly, however, a more fundamental debate developed: what – if anything – did the service stand for? As early as October 1964 a visiting American caused something of a stir in professional circles with an article in *Youth Review* which he chose to call *Looking for the Youth Service*. In 1968 Howell himself admitted: 'I'm still trying to find out after three-and-a-half years in this job what the youth service is.' Conference addresses, articles and pamphlets appeared regularly in the second half of the decade bearing such angst-ridden titles as *The Future of the*

Youth Service and even *The Youth Service: Has it a Future?*.

Some, it seemed, were still in search of the holy grail, looking to the minister not just to clarify what 'the service' was but to offer some 'hard' solutions to its problems:

> Mr Howell, what the youth service needs now is a proper plan – authoritative guidance – a directive. We have been too long listening to too many commentators, each with his own pet angle, his own special axe to grind.

The divisions which needed to be reconciled were, however, real ones, rooted in some genuine value conflicts and demanding difficult policy choices. Debates on them initially seemed to revolve around (and around and around) the somewhat simplistic question: is youth work education or is it social work? As the decade progressed, the question was increasingly reconceptualised into: should the youth service ally itself with the schools and/or is it part of 'the community'?

A school take-over?

In the process of pursuing these debates, the service's long-established educational commitment and philosophy were strongly reaffirmed. Though one full-time worker at the start of the decade could not see 'what the relationship is between what a teacher does and the work of a youth leader', throughout the 1960s wider developments pulled – or, as some who have had it, pushed – the service into a much closer embrace with the schools.

Albemarle had anticipated and sought to encourage this – for example, by proposing that the youth service age range be lowered to 14 so that it overlapped with what was then the final year at school. As we have already seen, notwithstanding the economic and educational facts of life in the late 1960s, youth service debates proceeded on the premise that the Newsom Report (published in 1963) would radically recast secondary education for 'the less able' – that is, for a key youth service target group. In the process, it was assumed, the schools' approach and curricula would become much more informal, less academic and more 'social educational'. The expansion of extra-curricular activities which was also anticipated would increasingly overlap, if not actually overwhelm, traditional youth service programmes.

Throughout the decade the proposed raising of the school leaving age from 15 to 16 also cast its shadow over the service. Originally envisaged in the 1944 Education Act, in 1959 the Crowther Report on the education of 15 to 18-year-olds had urged that it be implemented sometime between 1966 and 1969. Newsom also threw its weight behind announcing a definite target date, opting for 1969–70. Following a 1964 manifesto pledge, the Labour government first set this as 1970–71 and then, when this became a casualty of the 1968 economic crisis, postponed it to 1972–73.

However, the mere prospect of all young people remaining at school until they were at least 16 set youth service minds racing. What programmes then would the service

be able to offer which were genuinely different from those developed by the schools? And how would it appeal to the older, better educated and more sophisticated teenager who in increasing numbers would, it was expected, be tempted to stay on at school voluntarily until they were 17 or 18?

Over the decade many responded to such questions by adopting a tactic of: if you can't beat 'em, join 'em. In long unsigned articles in its June and July 1963 issue, *Youth Service* openly identified much that the schools and further education colleges had in common with the youth service and suggested how the youth service could develop much closer working relationships with them. One of the leading thinkers on Youth Service buildings, starting from a similar proposition, explored some possible wider policy and financial implications:

> *Schools should operate clubs for young people in full-time secondary education and for this purpose schools should be given more generous access to the physical and financial procedures at present available to the youth service.*

Such rhetoric was converted into reality on the ground by the steady growth in full-time teacher-leader and youth tutor posts. Though often producing some confusing lines of accountability for the post-holders, these gave more and more youth workers an official foothold across the schools-youth service boundary. By mid-decade, it was estimated that such posts constituted 20 per cent of all youth service appointments, with LEAs apparently offering them increasingly to qualified teachers.

This trend lead *Youth Review* to conclude as early as 1965 that 'many authorities must be regarding this type of appointment as past the experimental stage – something which would certainly not have been said at that stage of (for example) detached work which still largely retained its marginalised 'experimental' label.

The growth of joint appointments of this kind was to some extent fuelled by the expansion of youth work courses within teaching training, from the original 11 immediately post-Albemarle (involving some 250 students) to at least 27 by the early 1970s. By 1965 about 60 per cent of students who had taken this option were said to be attracted to applying for teacher-leader posts.

Such developments were underpinned, and the boundaries between schools and youth service blurred further, by the construction on school sites of youth wings or youth annexes. Often these were used for teaching or as a social and recreational base for older pupils during the day and for youth work activities in the evenings and at weekends. Some of these initiatives (as at Egremont in Cumbria and Countesthorpe in Leicestershire) gained a national profile. At Minsthorpe near Doncaster an experiment labelled 'Pattern for the Future?' sought to erase the 'dividing line between "educational" and "leisure-time" activities'.

For some groups – particularly Asian parents who looked to youth work to offer well organised and clearly educational activities for their children – this linking of school and youth service was welcome.

However, the relationship was not stress free. As early as 1965 a national survey of youth service buildings was highlighting the possible negative effects of placing these on school sites. These were seen as including:

A high leaving rate of the older members, presumably reflecting their opinion that the club is too much a part of the school ...

and

... the headmaster (who) feels chagrined that a part of his building – and usually a central part – is not under his control; neither has he the power to control the behaviour in it.

For the youth service itself, Alec Oxford suggested in 1967, the challenge could be fundamental. He saw the service as 'well and truly launched on the task of developing a partnership with schools and colleges of further education'. The result, he projected, could be that 'before too long ... (the service will) be faced with a similar choice vis-à-vis the schools etc, as now faces the voluntary partner in the youth service itself' – that is, presumably, whether it was going to be able to preserve its distinctive organisational identity.

Nonetheless, under growing political and economic pressure, more and more youth workers were having to learn to love their teaching colleagues and to work with, and often under, them. Roy Herbert of the Church of England Youth Council might still fear that the mere mention of schools in youth service circles would 'cause the hackles to rise'. For Denis Howell, however, it was axiomatic that, especially in catering for the younger age group, 'the youth service … and formal education have got to come closer together'. Nor was there any comfort from him for voluntary organisations feeling threatened by what Newsom might bring:

> The more you get Newsom-type projects and thinking, and the more you get the appointment of teachers part-time in the schools, part-time in the youth service, the more the schools (and certainly when the school leaving age has gone up) will be doing a job, and will have greater resources at its disposal than many voluntary bodies.

Well before the YSDC formally got to grips with the issues, the basic policy question had been settled, nationally and in many places locally too: if it wanted a future, then the youth service had better make its peace with the secondary schools and indeed with further education, too.

Youth work in the community

According to one influential interpretation, this alliance of youth work and formal education would also be the key to another of the proposed panaceas for saving the youth service: ensuring that it had a clearer community orientation. This view could be dated back at least to the 1920s when Cambridgeshire began to provide for a widely dispersed and often isolated rural population by developing large community colleges. These were designed from the start to incorporate both schooling and all-age further education and recreational facilities, including youth work.

This policy was taken up later by other LEAs such as, from the 1950s, Leicestershire where one of the most influential

figures within the YSDC, Andrew Fairbairn, was deputy director and later director of education. It was also given increasing central government endorsement: an article in the April 1967 issue of the HMSO periodical *Trends in Education*, for example, looked in some detail at the model of community schooling practised by Lawrence Weston School in Bristol.

As the Labour government's drive to turn the secondary schools into comprehensives gathered pace from 1964 onwards, urban as well as rural schools – in some places including primary schools – opened up their sporting, cultural, technical and social facilities to the community. Many began to call themselves community schools and bid strongly for a lead role in community education initiatives being introduced by local authorities. In Scotland this acquired a broad developmental meaning and eventually became the setting for all youth work. In England and Wales, different educational and organisational cultures emerged, resulting in programmes which were much more task-focused and provider-led – 'we offer the service, you take advantage of it'.

Other traditions of community work were starting to impinge on youth work, however. These were revived or strengthened by a school of sociological enquiry which was highlighting the spirit of community in areas like the east end of London which had been destroyed by rehousing policies. Some of these were closer to the 'rescue' mission of social work than to schooling. Others had roots in the pre-war colonial forms of community organisation and community development which had been adapted for work on new housing estates and in the new towns built within Britain itself after the war.

During the 1960s these forms of community work experienced a major resurgence: indeed by 1974, one influential community work practitioner was talking of 'politicians and professionals … using it (community) as a kind of "aerosol" word to be sprayed onto deteriorating institutions to deodorise and humanise them'. Under the influence of Derek Morrell, a civil servant who has been described as 'a gifted and inspirational maker of progressive social policy', the DES became increasingly enamoured with the term. It developed a 'special areas' analysis of individual and social breakdown which it used to justify its targeting of extra resources on educational priority areas (EPAs). This then became the key strategy of the Labour governments of the 1960s for tackling low levels of working-class educational achievement.

With Morrell transferred to the Home Office, this same analysis re-emerged in the 1968 White Paper's proposals for intermediate treatment for young offenders – seen by many youth workers as the social work equivalent of Newsom-inspired intrusion by the schools into their territory. At the same time, again inspired by Morrell, the Home Office initiated 12 community development projects explicitly designed as a neighbourhood-based experiment. These aimed to find new ways of 'meeting the needs of people living in areas of high social deprivation'.

Similar assumptions about the need to intervene purposefully in disorganised urban communities influenced the social worker-dominated Seebohm Committee. Its proposals for reorganising local social services, published in 1968, assumed the existence of special areas within local authority boundaries which, it concluded, called for 'a community approach'. At least one unsigned paper circulating shortly after Seebohm appeared not only questioned whether the schools really were an appropriate setting for youth work. It also argued that, with their proposed 'anti-institutionalised approach to the community', the new local authority social services departments would offer a much more congenial home for local youth services than the school-dominated education departments.

Extra currency and credibility were given to community-oriented thinking and policies by other official and semi-official documents. In 1967, for example, the Ministry of Housing and Local Government and the Welsh Office jointly published *The Needs of New Communities*. Their report focused on 'social provision in new and expanding communities' – that is, in the new towns and the (mainly council) housing estates which had grown up in the post-war period. It was followed two years later by the Skeffington report, *People and Planning*. Its remit – in part a response to growing community activism against contentious planning proposals – was to identify ways 'of securing the participation of the public at the formative stage in the making of development plans for their area'. All this coincided with the appearance of a widely publicised study of community work sponsored by the Gulbenkian Foundation and with, even then, emerging and ambitious plans to rejuvenate local participatory democracy by radically shaking up local government.

At first sight, this new flirtation by social policy-makers with community seemed to start from a more structural analysis of social problems and to assume more collective solutions to these than had been entertained previously. The reality, however, fell well short of this. Fresh initiatives were certainly being sought which offered the prospect of tackling 'social problems' – poverty, juvenile delinquency, family breakdown, rejection of schooling – which seemed obstinately resistant to the benevolence of the post-war opportunity society. In their rationale and design, however, these could not by themselves incorporate any radical social, and especially economic, change. In practice, the new policy orientation involved little more than laying on top of the long-established explanations of defective individual and defective family a guarded notion of 'defective community' as a cause of the problems.

The strategy was also as ever run through with contradictions. This after all was the period when some clearly identifiable communities (especially those which were Black or Asian) were demanding that their distinctiveness and inner strengths be recognised. In return the message they were getting (including from the youth service) was: *integrate* with the host society. Only 'official' definitions of community, it seems, were acceptable.

Nonetheless, across the country a limited number of 'flawed' inner-city neighbourhoods and council estates were identified whose residents were provided with some limited and short-term help from outside experts. This, it was assumed, would equip them with the personal and inter-personal skills needed to root out their 'under-privilege' for themselves. Implicitly, if not explicitly, such solutions thus again largely located the causes both of the communities' own difficulties and of the problems they were creating for the wider society within the residents themselves.

This analysis did not go unchallenged. Some of the Home Office's community development projects, for example, pointed to major structural problems such as the impact of multi-national companies on their target communities. To enable local residents to take on these big guns, some of the projects proposed, somewhat optimistically, that political structures be reformed and local allocations of power shifted. One result was that most of them were wound up, sometimes early.

It was in this climate that the youth service of the 1960s moved steadily towards its own destiny with community. Occasionally, a token warning about what this could bring might be issued. *Youth Review*, for example, cautioned against 'a lowest common factor on which to base our oneness', stressing that the service needed to ensure that:

> ... *we are not left with a dull and insipid splodge of community service, sound but uninspired, tidily organised, but unimaginative.*

The youth service's educational and developmental traditions also made it rather less preoccupied with pathological versions of the concept than some other services.

None of this held back the tide however. Over the decade policy-makers, locally as well as nationally, more and more used the notion of community as a peg on which to hang solutions to their most worrying and high-profile failures – the disinterest of the unattached, the unruliness of so many young men, the rejection of the service by so many young women and older teenagers.

As was so often the case in youth service policy development in this period, Denis Howell presented his own position vigorously and uncompromisingly. From his early days in office he recognised that the service needed to get greater access to other local authority facilities such as schools and public parks. Only later did he put a community label on such resource sharing, in the process broadening – though not necessarily sharpening – his analysis of how the service needed to change:

> Young people don't want to commit themselves to formal membership of a club week in, week out. This is why the army of the unattached is growing ... (who) want to use facilities of a community character ... The youth services from age 17 onwards, which are really youth services in relationship to community and leisure ... will have to rejig to take account of this change ... Current thinking, which I share, is that there should be much greater emphasis on community work ... even if it has to be at the expense of youth work. It is

> the place of the individual in the community which I think is important.

Other contributions to the debate, while perhaps making a more coherent case for a community orientation within youth work, nonetheless only served to demonstrate just how differently the idea was understood by different, often very experienced, practitioners and policy-makers. Joe Benjamin, for example, pioneer of adventure playgrounds in Britain, reminded the YSDC in 1967 that, 'they are no longer the only people concerned with youth and community work'. The kinds of community play-schemes he was developing for the London Borough of Camden needed serious study 'if "youth and community service" is going to mean anything at all'.

Detached worker (and, later, HMI) John Leigh added a further gloss, drawing a distinction between two contrasting interpretations. One he described as the overlap of 'youth service and a more liberal approach to school education'; the other as 'youth work in the community (carried out) by detached workers using commercial facilities and cheap basic provision' and aimed particularly at those in greatest need. Meanwhile another former detached worker, in an article called The Youth Officer in the Community, based his interpretation on work carried out on an Essex housing estate. In this case, the main thrust was a community organisation approach designed to encourage inter-professional and inter-agency responses to young people's disruptive street behaviour, homelessness and drug-taking. Another key YSDC member, Fred Milson, advocating that 'we must rediscover community', agreed that the service must become 'more integrated in the whole pattern of the educational and social services'.

However, as doubts deepened about lost ways, unclear directions and uncompleted Albemarle agendas, there seemed little room for semantic or definitional quibbles. Few seemed to want endless debate on whether community youth work, youth work in the community and a youth and community (or community and youth) service were synonymous, still less on how they could be made compatible. Most youth service policy-makers as well as many managers and practitioners were more than ready to hitch their aspirations to the increasingly fashionable community bandwagon – almost whatever it might mean. This, it seemed, offered the best, even the only, way of giving the service a clear and politically acceptable steer.

A new review: By accident or design?

The issues which dominated the youth service's debates during the 1960s both influenced and were significantly influenced by the YSDC. Foreshadowed by a *Citizens of Tomorrow* proposal for a youth advisory council, the body brought into existence by the Albemarle Report acted as a (relatively) high powered and high-profile national group for the service capable of exerting continuing pressure for the evaluation and review of post-

Albemarle developments. Over the decade, the Council's membership changed at least four times. Some 'big names' were recruited – not just Lady Albemarle but also playwright Arnold Wesker and Baroness Birk, associate editor of *Nova*. So too were top academics including a professor of education, a senior lecturer from a college of domestic arts, a tutor in social work; as well as managers from the statutory and voluntary services. Some (like Gordon Bessey and Andrew Fairbairn) were very senior and, as we have seen, played very central roles in its work.

Efforts were also made to maintain a number of balances – for example, between Welsh and English interests and urban and rural. Influential youth service trainers were found places: Joan Tash of the YWCA, Joan Matthews of the National College, Josephine Klein who led the youth work qualifying course at Gold-smith College in London and her counterpart at Westhill College Birming-ham, Fred Milson. Not quite perhaps as an afterthought but always a small minority, youth work practitioners were also brought in. Perhaps the best known of these was Stanley Rowe, a long-established full-time leader who had kept youth work trade unionism alive in the 1950s and who came onto the Council in his capacity as chair of the employees' panel of the full-time youth workers' Joint Negotiating Committee.

The one interest group which, it appears, was never considered for membership was young people. In a very stark way this reflected a significant post-Albemarle gap:

between the report's rhetoric on 'self-programming' and 'the fourth partner' in running the service and the minimal movement made over the decade towards genuine user participation.

The Council conducted most of its public work through the subcommittees which considered part-time leader training, provision for 'young immigrants' and community service. Initially each of these pieces of work was presented as part of an overall review of the service triggered by arrival at the half way stage of implementing the 10-year Albemarle development plan. With Lady Albemarle herself as chair, this new review group was to re-examine ('with great urgency') the objectives which her report had set for the service and recommend on future development.

News of this new appraisal came from Denis Howell in a statement to the House of Commons early in 1965. In the somewhat cloak-and-dagger manner which came to dog the process for the rest of the decade, he announced that the sub-committee had already met several times – it had in fact been appointed in the previous December. He also disclosed that, in addition to looking again at the training of part-time leaders, it would focus on youth service buildings and on 'ways of approaching young people to whom the existing provision makes little appeal'. Though willing to receive papers from the field, he made it clear that the committee had no plans for taking formal evidence. Nor would it necessarily report 'in one go' or even, he implied, publish its findings at all: 'in the first instance' these

would simply be presented to the YSDC itself.

Precisely what happened to this second Albemarle committee remains something of a mystery. Though Howell was still making public reference to it as late as November 1966, by the spring of the following year *Youth Review* was complaining about the committee's 'lack of speed' in carrying out its work and surmising that in fact it had by then 'disappeared from the scene'. Lady Albemarle's name *was* attached to the second report on the training of part-time leaders, published in December 1965. However, the subsequent YSDC subcommittee's reports – those concerned with provision for 'immigrants' and young people's voluntary service – did not locate themselves in any wider review of the service or refer to Lady Albemarle's involvement even though she did not resign from the Council until late 1968.

The only formal acknowledgment that the original review process had run its course came in an official statement in early 1967. This announced that 'the Council will itself assume responsibility for reviewing the broad aspects of the youth service such as the training of youth leaders, hitherto undertaken by the Review Committee'. With its numbers now reduced from 24 to 18, the Council was initially to carry out this work via a series of new ad hoc committees. In the event, however, only two ever materialised. The first, chaired by Andrew Fairbairn, was given the remit of examining the youth service's relationship with the schools and further education. Once the Hunt committee on immigrants and the youth service had reported, the second under Fred Milson started its work, focusing on the service's relationship with 'the adult community'.

Over the next two-and-a-half years the work of these two subcommittees dominated the life of the YSDC – and increasingly of the youth service as a whole – to the point where, almost by absence of mind, the service found itself embroiled in 'a new Albemarle'. Howell made clear from the start that he was expecting the overall exercise to result in a fundamental look at the service, and particularly to take into account the different needs of its upper and lower age groups. Expectations thus ran high from very early on and were raised still further as organisations and individuals prepared written and verbal evidence and as Council members undertook the occasional consultative (and PR) regional roadshow.

Mystery surrounding the committees' activities and scepticism about the real motives behind the review were created by Howell's continuing insistence that their reports were not necessarily going to be made public. At least initially, they were to be received only by the YSDC which in due course, it was implied, might release a consolidated (and edited – expurgated?) version. A mood of hope mixed with uncertainty and distrust thus built up throughout 1968.

In July of that year the Fairbairn Committee finally delivered its report to the full Council, with completion of the Milson Report expected in the autumn. At

that stage, Howell told Parliament that the Council needed 'to consider how best to formulate its advice' to the Secretary of State for Education. With the Minister refusing to predict when the conclusions of the two committees might get a public airing, a further 12-month policy vacuum followed.

To some extent this was filled by a steady stream of leaks, especially in the weekly *New Society* though also (for example, on proposals for the training of full-time workers) in *Youth Review*. These gave the field some advance notice of what the two committees were thinking. In particular they revealed that some of their findings and recommendations were pulling in quite contradictory directions and that therefore a struggle was taking place within the Council over the content of the final report. In addition, occasional Parliamentary flurries such as a House of Lords' debate in February 1968 on 'the need for a more comprehensive policy towards the youth of the nation', gave some distant diversionary outlets for the developing frustration.

However, press speculation was no substitute for conclusive evidence on what was being proposed for the service's future. The insecurity and self-doubt which the review process itself had produced was thus greatly exacerbated, leaving the service ready, it seemed, to accept whatever the Council might decide was best for it. In the event, a consolidated version of the Fairbairn and Milson reports were delivered to Denis Howell in April 1969 and the long awaited *Youth and Community Work in the '70s*, finally published in July.

Beyond Albemarle

The Albemarle Report had delivered a great deal – and not just money – for the youth service. It major advances had included:

- the implementation of a 10-year development programme;
- constant monitoring, review and policy development through the work of a Youth Service Development Council (YSDC);
- a major building programme which had produced purpose-built premises across the country specifically designed with the 1960s teenager in mind;
- the establishment of emergency training at a National College which in 10 years more than doubled the full-time youth work force;
- the establishment of a committee to negotiate salaries and conditions of service for full-time workers in both the statutory and voluntary sectors;
- an increase in the number of paid part-time workers and the introduction of more systematic arrangements for their training which drew together both statutory and voluntary organisations;
- increased government grants to national voluntary organisations both for headquarters costs and for 'experimental' work; and
- the establishment of a Youth Service Information Centre committed to collecting, collating and disseminating information and research on young people, youth work policy and practice and relevant training.

Above all, however, Albemarle and its aftermath had tipped the balance of power within the service. By 1970 this had moved decisively in favour of state sponsored and state controlled forms of secular and professional youth work and, therefore, against the philanthropic and religious motivations which had created this form of practice with young people in the first place. If any doubt had existed before, by the end of the decade a service of youth had unmistakably become a youth service.

With these changes, another crucial balance had tipped, too – in favour of full-time workers and against part-timers and volunteers. As the former strove to establish their professional credentials, a deep gulf appeared within the service's staffing structure, stemming not just from salary differentials but also from the status attached to college-based training and qualifications.

Indeed, despite all the substantial, even radical, change which Albemarle had brought, some very basic issues remained unresolved. Levels of take-up had barely increased and may even have reduced. Though targeting (selectivity) continued to be a core guiding principle, it was still largely implicit and locally determined rather than overtly embodied and proclaimed in national public policy. Nonetheless, failure to bring in some of the more recalcitrant 'unclubbable' young people – now starkly retitled 'the unattached' as if to make clear that their outsider status was the service's and not their own fault – was still deeply felt. In spite of – even sometimes if unintentionally because of – all the modernising which the 1960s had brought, rigidities in the service's staffing, training and funding structures continued to limit its capacity even to get at these young people, never mind actually to engage them in any numbers.

Constraints remained, too, within the philosophy of the service. This continued to be preoccupied with individual development and so ignored or simply missed how this was constrained by the limitations of power and money in the lives of so many young people. As more and more facilities became mixed, the range and quality of work with girls and young women declined. Though the Hunt Report, a subcommittee of the YSDC, aimed to prompt more sensitive responses to young 'immigrants', its insistence on multi-racial (integrated) provision as the only way forward actually got in the way of local youth services responding to young Black and Asian people on the basis of their daily, especially racist, realities. Other marginalised groups – the young disabled, young people in rural areas – though receiving some specialised attention, remained on the fringes of mainstream youth service provision. Gay and lesbian young people were simply invisible and uncatered for in their own right.

Much therefore was riding on the latest national review of the service being carried out by the two YSDC sub-committees and on their prescriptions for how to update the youth service for changing economic and political times.

Main references

Albemarle Report, *Youth Service in England and Wales*, HMSO, 1960

John Benington, 'Strategies for change at the local level: some reflections', in David Jones and Majorie Mayo (eds), *Community Work One*, Routledge and Kegan Paul, 1974

Margaret Bone and Elizabeth Ross, *The Youth Service and Similar Provision for Young People*, HMSO, 1972

Leslie Button, 'A survey of youth leadership training in eleven training colleges', National Union of Teachers, 1965

David Collyer, *Double Zero*, Fontana, 1973

Bernard Davies, 'Voluntary service', *New Society*, 4.7.68

Bernard Davies and Alan Gibson, *The Social Education of the Adolescent*, University of London Press, 1967

Mora and Alec Dickson, *Count Us In*, Dobson, 1967

Paul Foot, *Immigration and Race in British Politics*, Penguin, 1965

George Goetchius and Joan Tash, *Working with Unattached Youth*, Routledge and Kegan Paul, 1967

Ray Gosling, *Lady Albemarle's Boys*, Fabian Society, 1962

Jalna Hamner, *Girls at Leisure*, London Union of Youth Clubs / London YWCA, 1964

H. M. Holden, *Hoxton Café Project*, Youth Service Information Centre, 1972

Derek Humphry and Gus John, *Because They're Black*, Penguin, 1971

Hunt Report, *Immigrants and the Youth Service*, HMSO, 1967

Tony Jeffs and Mark Smith, *Young People,*

Inequality and Youth Work, MacMillan, 1990

Pearl Jephcott, *Clubs for Girls*, Faber and Faber, 1943

Pearl Jephcott, *Time of One's Own*, Oliver & Boyd, 1967

London Federation of Boys' Clubs, *Boys' Clubs and Girls*, London Federation of Boys' Clubs, 1962

NABC, *Boys' Clubs in the Sixties*, NABC, 1962

NABC, *Newsom and Boys' Clubs*, NABC, 1967

NAYC, *Girls in Two Cities*, NAYC, 1967

Godfrey Pain, *Boys' Clubs*, Ludgate Circus House, 1943

Mary Robinson, *Girls in the Nineteen Sixties*, NAYC,

H. Rohrs and H. Tunstall-Behrens (eds), *Kurt Hahn*, Routledge and Kegan Paul, 1970

Cyril Smith, *Young People at Leisure*, Department of Youth Work, University of Manchester, 1966

John Springhall, *Youth, Empire and Society*, Croom Helm, 1977

Lincoln Williams, *Partial Surrender: Race and Resistance in the Youth Service*, The Falmer Press, 1988

Youth Service Information Centre, *Youth Service Provision for Young Immigrants*, YSIC, 1972

5 Youth – and Community?

Fairbairn-Milson: From compromise to confusion

When compared with the impact of its 1960s predecessor, *Youth and Community Work in the '70s* got a very low-key reception: most journalists, it seemed, could not get beyond its passing reference to the service helping young people 'chat up the birds'. Nonetheless, the product of a three-and-a-half year review, it was one of the youth service's landmark documents.

Certainly the YSDC set itself the task of producing an Albemarle for the 70s which would survey the youth work landscape at the turn of the decade and set the service on its way for the next 10 years. According to Denis Howell, the DES minister who chaired the Council from 1964 to 1970, its aim had been to 'produce proposals for a comprehensive youth service'.

In search of radical solutions

In one key respect *Youth and Community Work in the '70s* went much further than Albemarle. It dared explicitly to ask: 'What kind of *society* do we want?' On the premise that 'a "value free" approach is not feasible', it found its answer in the work of an American sociologist, Amitai Etzioni. Etzioni, and in particular his

concept of communitarianism, had to await the arrival of Blairite Britain in the late 1990s to achieve full political flavour-of-the-month status. A quarter of a century before, however, the YSDC seized on his notion of 'the *active* society' (emphasis added) – 'a society in which every member can be publicly active'. They did so because, they contended, in such a society 'all are encouraged and enabled to find public expression of their values, avoiding the extremes of indifference and alienation'. Through it, too, 'all individuals should grow towards maturity'.

The committee was clearly nervous about appearing over-ambitious. 'The sort of society we describe,' it warned, 'may be a long way off, perhaps unattainable in full.' Anticipating the pie-in-the-sky sneers which did indeed follow, it also felt the need to add: 'We are anxious to keep our feet on the ground'. What it was offering, it reassured the service, was 'a bearing to travel rather than an easily-reached destination'.

In search of community

The grounding in which it actually rooted its aspirations was 'evidence of work we have seen done in existing communities'. This, the committee claimed, provided 'proof that effective communities based on neighbourhoods or even other shared characteristics can flourish within the modern urban environment'. As a major part of its 'platform', it stressed the need to encourage such groups 'to expand themselves and their activities and placed 'learning by doing' and 'choice in the form and content of what is learnt' at the heart of its notion of social education. Again suggesting language which was to resurface two decades later, it interpreted this as meaning 'opportunities for learning, both formal and informal, (which) are needed throughout life'. In a hugely significant but unexplained confusion of arguments it also used evidence from NAYSO to advance a particular version of community which equated this kind of lifelong learning with an education service which needed to 'strive by its methods and approach *to bring together people of all ages*'. (Emphasis added.)

In the run-up to the publication of the report, the committee's most serious and most pressing challenge was to reconcile these libertarian social and educational values with the organisational structures for a rejuvenated youth service which it was assuming were essential. Particularly problematic in this context was its advocacy of a still closer partnership between youth work and formal schooling and further education.

Once again its discomfort showed through. Its preferred approach of community development implemented in non-directive ways was, it acknowledged, 'obviously more pertinent for the upper age group ... the "young adults" rather than "the young teenagers"'. It recognised, too, that 'while the concept of community

development is immediately relevant to the work of the educationalist, it has not always been observed'. In fact, it admitted, 'educational organisations as a class have greater degrees of authoritarian attitudes in their relationship to "out groups" than many other organisations'. Its proposed solution was for 'public organisations (to) become more responsive to the varying needs and views of those whom they effect' – with the statutory educational organisation particularly needing to face this challenge.

In struggling to negotiate such contra-dictions, the Fairbairn-Milson Report (certainly in comparison with Albemarle) failed to fulfil its own aspiration of providing the youth service with a viable structural as well as inspirational map for the 1970s. Albemarle was constructed by a relatively cohesive group. As the subsequent testimony of one of its most influential members, Richard Hoggart, showed, it was prepared to take a highly pragmatic view of what it could achieve. By contrast, *Youth and Community Work in the '70s* showed all the signs of being the compromised product of a complex 'political' negotiation, some of it over basic values and purposes.

The politics of Fairbairn-Milson

These compromises were largely forced on the Council because of the very different, even conflicting, departure points and ideological underpinnings of its two sub-groups and the reports each had agreed. The Fairbairn Committee, for example, strongly advocated more teacher-leader and youth tutor posts, more youth wings on schools and more community use of such facilities. In taking up this position it was not just driven by financial and practical pressures or a desire for organisational tidiness. Rather it was seeking the fullest possible integration of youth work into the institutional and cultural milieu of *schooling*.

Here, it seems, the role of its chair, Andrew Fairbairn, would have been critical. As deputy director of education, he had bigger fish to fry than merely reshaping the youth service. More pressing and difficult challenges for him would certainly have been the proposals of the Newsom Committee which in effect called for the secondary education of 'pupils of average and less than average ability' to take on a range of youth work-type approaches. He and others on his subcommittee would also have been very aware that, with the raising of the school leaving age to 16 in 1972, secondary school curricula and methods needed to become more responsive, especially to pupils who had been reluctant to stay on. A more strategic youth service infiltration into formal education was thus seen as having great potential benefits for the schools.

The enthusiasm of the Fairbairn sub-committee for such a cross-over led it, in its own report to the YSDC, to one of its starkest and most radical conclusions: that 'the concept of youth service as a separate system should be allowed to atrophy'. For the Milson subcommittee, however, this was wholly unacceptable. Though agreeing that community schools were increasing in number, it was clear that 'this does not warrant the attachment of all

community provision to the schools'. On the contrary, from its perspective it was no less blunt than the Fairbairn subcommittee: 'the school', it asserted, 'should be seen to be part of the community rather than that the community should gather round the school'. It wanted youth work facilities to move away as much as possible from being building and membership oriented, emphasising instead that they need to 'take many forms – only one of which should be organisations; and (that they) should be seen in many different places'.

Even in its final form, therefore, *Youth and Community Work in the '70s* represented something of a battleground on which strongly institutionalised and would-be de-institutionalised perspectives struggled to shape youth service aims and methods. Most damagingly, these differences between the two subcommittees compounded confusions already abroad in the service. With hindsight, it is possible to accept that, given the broader social policy climate of the time and notwithstanding the term's widespread lack of definition, little could have been done to divert youth service policy-makers and practitioners from 'going community' in some form or other. What left them floundering were the unclear and indeed internally contra-dictory ways in which this core concept was used within what they saw as the service's 'bible' document for the decade.

Youth and Community Work in the '70s did make some attempt to prevent or dispel these confusions. In advocating community development as the appropriate method for youth and community work, it explicitly and sharply distinguished this from two other community-oriented approaches. One was community provision – 'buildings, centres and facilities provided by institutions and organisations for people, into which they are expected to fit'. The other was community organisation – 'the coordination of the effort of existing groups rather than (as with community development) the direct involvement in stimulating groups to action'.

In its focus on work with older young people it also sought consistently, albeit in largely rhetorical ways, to spell out how its preferred approach might be applied.

> There can ... be no lasting answers to the dilemmas of youth work without a radical rethinking of the position of young people in society, and of adult attitudes to the young.
>
> Those who work with young adults should no longer see themselves as "providers", placing young people in the position of "receivers" who are sometimes to be given "shadow" responsibilities.
>
> It is no part of our aim to achieve a comfortable integration of the youth and adult populations, nor to attempt to 'socialise' the young so that they are reconciled with the status quo, and capitulate to its values ... The aim should be to establish a dialogue between the young and the rest of society; a dialectical, and not necessarily amicable, process ...
>
> There can no longer be an underlying consensus about all the issues which face our society. All who read this report should realise that its approach has considerable implications. Those who want nothing more than a quiet life should think again.

These, even in the context of the liberated 60s, were brave words – and words which

contrasted sharply with the nervous reassurances which the Albemarle Report had given in its discussion of youth work values. Then the line had been that, far from challenging the youth service's core concepts, it sought only to get youth workers to adjust some of their language.

Unfortunately, elsewhere in *Youth and Community Work in the '70s,* and especially in those passages contributed by the Fairbairn subcommittee, its radical messages were, implicitly and even sometimes explicitly, contradicted. The final published report, for example, all but dismissed self-programming for the younger age group as unrealistic, on the grounds that 'the facts of life of *school* programming mean that no one group can have completely free choice of activity' (emphasis added). Similarly, on 'valid self-government with real teeth', the report concluded: 'It is difficult to see how it could be made to work' – again because of the constraints of the school regime.

Throughout the Fairbairn-Milson discussion of youth work with younger teenagers, including its rather token consideration of the (still substantial) contribution of the voluntary organisations, its arguments were framed entirely within its self-imposed parameters. Almost all such future work, it presumed, should be located in schools and colleges. Notwith-standing its later unambiguous commit-ment to community development, in these major sections of its report the committee thus advanced a community facilities conception of delivery to be made mainly through large bureaucratic institutions whose prime function was *not* youth work.

In one other key respect the committee left its intentions blurred. As we have seen, with one of its voices it endorsed, even if without much elaboration, a 'youth *and* community' remit: that is, one which would increasingly turn the service into an all-age facility. With another often louder voice, however, again especially when dealing with older young people and young adults, it conveyed a very different message. This assumed that young people would continue to be seen as the primary clientele, though to be treated in the context of significant wider (including collective) identities, loyalties and involvements. In these passages therefore it in effect pressed for a 'youth *in* community' remit.

The Politics of Fairbairn-Milson

As we shall see later, the confusions arising from these small 'p' politics in the making of *Youth and Community Work in the '70s* had major long-term consequences for the youth service. But so too did the large 'P' Political processes which were particularly set in motion by Denis Howell's close association with the compilation and recommendations of the report. Though adding prestige and perhaps some clout to the committee's work, this also blurred some important boundaries. Most significantly, it prevented the committee from making choices – for example, about what it might wish to define as achievable objectives – which had been open to Albemarle.

From the start Howell's unashamedly hands-on role as chair of YSDC ensured that these parameters were very firmly set.

He, for example, publicly pressed for youth work with the under-16s to be done under the aegis of the schools. He also openly advocated for some of the report's more radical stances – though, once young people like the student radicals of the mid and late 1960s took the notion of active citizenship rather too seriously, he seemed unable to take the heat. (In one intervention run through with racist stereotypes, he seemed to suggest that protests at the London School of Economics happened only because so many overseas students were involved.)

With Fairbairn-Milson thus at least partially identified as 'party political', it was always in danger of weakening the cross party commitment to the youth service which had been such a feature of the service's advance after Albemarle. During a Lords debate in March 1970, for example, the Earl of Arran not only attacked the report for being wordy and impractical, he 'took particular exception to … a situation in which the voluntary organisations should take orders from a government-inspired and sponsored set-up'.

Moreover, the report was released at precisely the moment that the broader political consensus on social policy which had existed since the Second World War was coming under unfamiliar pressure. In 1969, for example, a group of right-wing academics, professionals and politicians published the first of a series of 'black papers' on education. These were vitriolic in their condemnation of just the kind of ideas by which Fairbairn-Milson set such store. Over the decade these collections of highly polemical essays helped to turn notions like non-directive teaching and learning-by-doing into despised epithets synonymous with 'woolly-liberal' and 'dangerously permissive'.

More soberly and with a much lower public profile, some commentators also began to question whether, economically, the post-war welfare consensus could be sustained. As early as 1967, for example, the *Times* correspondent Peter Jay was suggesting that:

> *Any substantial improvements in the social services will require unprecedentedly draconian treatment of privately financed personal consumption … otherwise economic progress will itself suffer.*

Youth and Community Work in the '70s was not of course unaware that wider social transformations constituted a crucial context for its recommendations. It described contemporary society as 'constantly in the process of change' and in particular as coping with 'a rapidly developing technology'. Like Albemarle, it was highly sensitive to new social and cultural threads which were being woven into the texture of British life. It, for example, noted that:

> *The normative structure is eroding; the behaviour of the individual is less and less defined by society; the authority and power of older people is questioned by the young who have more power economically and politically; there is no longer a belief system which receives general assent.*

The report pointed, too, to accentuated changes in the role of women; to 'the young's feelings of hopelessness in the face of a property-owning society in whose

values and priorities they do not fully share or indeed wish to share' and so, still, to 'some breakdown in communication between the generations'. Like Albemarle, and despite an initial tremble of doubt, it gave renewed endorsement to the notion of a distinct and separate youth culture – 'a way of life linked with dress, speech, art forms, patterns of relationships and entertainment which is commonly associated with the young … (and which) seems likely to maintain its position though its forms may change'. In contrast to Albemarle, the Fairbairn-Milson Report also recognised that the economic facts of life must impact on its recommendations: it, for example, offered its prescriptions for improvement 'knowing that there can be little increase in the public funds available to implement them'. It, therefore, treated as given the need to set priorities in public spending.

Yet the committee dealt with such matters as mere 'administrative implications'. In doing so it in effect categorised each of the financial crises of the 1960s as small one-off local difficulties rather than as increasingly powerful tremors which, cumulatively, were redefining the political and cultural as well as the economic terrain on which youth work was operating.

Inaction – and rejection

All this might have mattered less if action on the report had been taken quickly. However – as the Conservatives were subsequently to remind it – the Labour government continued to deal with the service at the same leisurely pace which had characterised the whole review process. It was anyway at best ambivalent in its public statements. Its spokesperson in the Lords debate, for example, presented the report as no more than a discussion document and mounted a distinctly milk-and-water defence of it.

Though his interpretation was disputed by his Conservative successor at the DES, Howell himself asserted after he left office that he had publicly accepted the report 'in principle' at a press conference. He also described a chain of events after its publication which sought to explain his own and the government's stuttering follow-up. These included 'a great degree of hostility from some senior civil servants who always regarded the youth service as a fringe activity'. Acting as a 'strenuous opposition' and as 'forces of obstruction (which) were very formidable', these officials had, he claimed, 'ganged up to prevent the report being put into operation, and possibly even to suppress it'. He even admitted to powerful political opposition from within the Cabinet, particularly from Richard Crossman. The then Secretary of State for Health and Social Security, he said, had 'had the gravest doubts about whether the report could be implemented'.

As a result, he had been forced, albeit reluctantly, to agree 'that the report would go to a working party of officials who would study the detailed implications'. Chaired by 'a distinguished civil servant', this, according to Howell, 'came to the conclusion that the concept of community service was something they could not

accept' because 'they could not see where you could draw the line on expenditure'. For Howell, however, the real roots of this opposition lay elsewhere. With some anger, he identified those who obstructed the Fairbairn-Milson proposals as 'people who have not the faintest knowledge of the youngsters we are talking about ... who send their children to Oxford and Cambridge or other universities'.

In crucial respects this analysis rang, and still rings, true. However, though Howell himself played this down, the implementation process was certainly not helped by his own move from the DES to housing very soon after the report appeared. Nor, as Crossman's reservations illustrated, by the fact that, unlike Albemarle, *Youth and Community Work in the '70s* promised few opportunities for rapid, high-profile and practical governmental action. In the eyes of a government looking for instant brownie points in the run-up to general election, its chances of rapid approval were thus never good.

In the event – and against all the odds – Labour lost this election and in May 1970 one Margaret Thatcher took over as Secretary of State of Education. She certainly was not unaware of the large 'P' Politics which had helped to shape *Youth and Community Work in the '70s* nor of the resistance to it among officials in her Department. As she came into office, she was anyway confronted with more pressing priorities. Within two years, the commitment to raising the school leaving age to 16 was due to be implemented. She also set about preparing a white paper which eventually appeared in 1972 and which, for the woman who as Prime Minister a decade later fiercely opposed any further growth in state provision, carried the striking title of *A Framework for Expansion*. Though covering the whole field of education including adult education, this made not a single mention of the youth service. It was therefore perhaps hardly surprising that she took her time pronouncing on a document which even insiders were saying was strong on rhetoric (much of it leftish leaning) and decidedly weak on pragmatic and achievable solutions to the continuing 'youth problem'.

The initial response to Fairbairn-Milson was therefore a 10-month silence. It was briefly interrupted only by the far from reassuring announcement in December 1970 that the youth service building programme for LEA projects was to be abolished. A substantive statement on the report itself did not come until March 1971. It took the form of a 400-word reply to a written Commons question and amounted to a comprehensive rejection of the whole Fairbairn-Milson doctrine and approach:

> *The Government do not think it would be right to change the nature of the service in England and Wales radically by setting up a youth and community service with not very clear responsibilities.*

Or, as Thatcher herself was to put it in a Commons debate in April: 'In the department I wish the emphasis to continue to be on youth work.'

Some minor reforms to the service were conceded: 'reasonable latitude' in applying the 14 to 20 age limits; further joint use of premises; local supervision of capital

building projects; the diversion of some capital funds to experimental work. Only in two respects did the new Secretary of State take any radical new steps, however. Firstly, in a move which anticipated her own and a wider right wing distaste for government-by-quango, she peremptorily dismissed the YSDC in favour of what she called 'the normal processes of consultation'. Secondly, she decreed that more resources were to be targeted on areas of high social need – on, for example, school leavers in 'deprived' areas and via the Urban Programme which was specifically intended to help such areas.

Needless to say the youth service was not best pleased at being relaunched into limbo. The Community and Youth Service Association (CYSA) – the professional youth workers' body which, in tune with the times, had recently metamorphosed out of the Youth Service Association – deplored the Secretary of State's rejection of the report and the abolition of the YSDC. It even compared the service's newly 'downgraded situation' to the neglect which it had experienced during the 1940s and 1950s. Fred Milson predicted that the decision to give local authorities more responsibility for funding would mean that 'bad will become worse'. Not surprisingly, he was also particularly pained by Thatcher's disdain for the strong community development orientation which his YSDC subcommittee had recommended:

> *To reject (this) central notion without replacing it with another suggests an approach to the youth service that is pedestrian, perfunctory, grudging and half-hearted.*

Writing in *New Society*, Bernard Davies concluded that 'only platitudes' were being offered as an alternative to the report, while a leader in *Youth Review*, the monthly periodical produced by the National Union of Teachers for CYSA and NAYSO, talked of the service's unresolved 'expectancy and uncertainty'.

In two Commons debates (in April and July 1971) and in an article in the autumn issue of *Youth Review*, Howell added a passionate, if sometimes strident, voice to this chorus of complaint. He too regretted the policy vacuum to which Thatcher had abandoned the service and her failure therefore to offer it any kind of alternative vision. He talked of the new Government's 'fundamental indifference of attitude' and the resultant 'tremendous lowering of morale' and reiterated that radical and even revolutionary changes were required in order to create two youth services:

> *... one following the traditional pattern, with the uniformed organisations ... which could properly be attached to the formal education service ... (and) a new young adult service.*

He also deplored the abolition of 'the one body which could do this job effectively' – the YSDC.

By some, the ministerial statement was seen as containing much more than a rather peevish rejection of a review report's unrealisable recommendations. *Youth Review*, for example, particularly noted its focus on deprived young people and its reference to Urban Aid, detecting in these 'a hint of ... a change in the position of the DES itself towards the youth service and an increasing interest and influence on the part of the Home Office'. It even wondered out loud whether the latter's community development projects might provide a more appropriate home for those wishing to nurture 'the spirit of the active society'. With the arrival on the policy scene of intermediate treatment for young offenders and of local social services departments with a proposed community remit, Bernard Davies also suggested that youth workers might reflect on whether it was 'now good enough ... to go on talking about youth work and the youth service as if they are completely synonymous'.

The wider policy climate had anyway already begun to shift with the introduction of Urban Aid programmes for 'deprived' areas and the Education Priority Area strategy for getting alienated young people to re-engage with schooling. In an effort to draw the youth service into such targeting initiatives, perhaps for the first time in relation to youth work, the state thus made its own selective expectations quite explicit. Going beyond vague homilies on the need for youth workers to win over the unattached or even the young delinquent, it had also made its own priorities much more specific and had set these out very firmly in a public policy paper.

The youth service as ping pong ball

At that stage *Youth Review* was right: what was being offered was no more than a vague hint of what national policy-makers might be looking for. On the ground, at least in England and Wales, the Thatcher statement therefore left local youth service planners, practitioners and trainers with only the inconsistencies and contradictions of the original report to guide them. With many local authorities planting their seeds even before the statement appeared, they proceeded to use their considerable freedom of action to let many, often limp, flowers bloom.

Some simply adopted the tactic described by John Benington as aerosol-spraying community onto otherwise unaltered provision. Others favoured the 'youth *and* community' solution , often it seemed because it held out the promise of bigger empires to oversee and – perhaps – more status for the service. And then there were those, including particularly professional trainers, who opted for the 'youth *in* community' position. For some this might be because they identified themselves primarily as community workers, for others because a focus on such community identities as ethnicity and sexual orientation helped to underpin their commitment to the issue-based work which was by then just starting to take shape.

This contrasted in significant ways with what happened in Scotland. There, too, an overall review of the service was carried out, by a committee of what was already called the Standing Consultative Council on Youth and Community Service. Completed almost a year before the Fairbairn-Milson Report appeared, its report, *Community of Interests*, was equally preoccupied with youth service-school and youth service-adult community links. By 1975 this had been followed by the

Alexander Committee report on adult education, *The Challenge of Change*. Just at the point that local government was being reorganised, this proposed that three separately developed traditions focused on providing for leisure – adult education, community work and youth work – be brought together. Most Scottish local authorities implemented this recommendation by creating community education departments. At the same time attempts were made to develop new forms of generic training for relevant practitioners and to introduce team approaches within the provision itself.

Though often under-prioritising young people, this comprehensive reshaping of services from the top did at least provide Scotland with a uniform local government structure and some direction for the new community orientation. In England by contrast the embrace of community was neither strategic nor coherent in either its intent or it impact. Most often, as Davies noted at the time, the results, where they were not crudely cosmetic, involved little more than tinkering with the machinery:

> *Many local authorities have renamed what they are doing "youth and community work", embodying the change not in forms of community development but in such relatively superficial modifications as building community centres rather than youth centres. Or they have opened some of their youth service buildings to pre-school playgroups and old people's welfare clubs. Because it is administratively and economically so acceptable, school-based youth work has taken root more firmly, although with very few schools being genuine "community schools".*

Over the following two decades, policy-making in this field seemed often to depend on the personal preconceptions, if not the idiosyncratic whims and prejudices, of a principal youth officer here, a director of education there, a council leader somewhere else. In consequence, much local youth service provision was dragged in, out of and then sometimes back into a youth and community service, or a community and youth service, a community education service, a community development service or even a community college system. In the process, that least popular and 'biddable' of all client groups, 'youth', increasingly lost its priority (including often its budgets), sometimes to the point where these disappeared from sight altogether. After travelling this route, one local authority concluded 25 years later that 'the strategic importance of services to youth … is not adequately profiled or resourced within (the community education) structure'.

Indeed, outside its training recommendations (to be examined in Chapter 8) and perhaps its emphasis on the needs of older young people, it is difficult to point to significant concrete outcomes of *Youth and Community Work in the '70s*. Its 'hard' proposals for change were few and were not adequately developed for effective operationalisation. Its challenging philosophical and methodological messages, when they did not simply confuse, lacked specificity or were internally contradictory, exposing the political and Political compromises which had produced them. Too often therefore the report, rather than building on the image and the achievements of Albemarle (as the YSDC had obviously hoped) proved to be distracting, diversionary and even debilitating for the service's work with young people.

Main references

Committee on the Youth Service and the Adult Community (Milson Committee), 'The relationship of the Youth Service with the adult community', YSDC/DES (unpublished), 1968

Bernard Davies, 'What Use for the Youth Service?', *New Society*, 1.7.71

Douglas Jay, 'Social services – a 70s crisis?', *Times*, 31.5.67

Milson-Fairbairn Report, *Youth and Community Work in the '70s*, HMSO, 1969

Fred Milson, 'Destiny of the Youth Service', *Times Educational Supplement*, 30.4.71

School and Further Education Committee (Fairbairn Committee), 'The relationship of the Youth Service with the schools and further education', YSDC/DES (unpublished), 1968

6   From Economic Downturn to Political Action

Rediscovering economic stringency

Not only did the hole at the heart of national youth service policy continue through much of the 1970s: it did so against a background of repeated economic and political crisis. On the back of the 1973 Israeli-Arab war and of huge price rises for imported oil, public spending for 1973–75 was cut by some £1,800 million. The 1976 sterling crisis was if anything even more serious, forcing the Labour Government which had been returned to power two years before to negotiate an International Monetary Fund loan of £39,000 million. As part of what was a very harsh package, it had to agree to even deeper cuts in public spending of £3,000 million for the following two years.

As both cause and effect of these economic pressures, political unrest in the widest sense also flared. It was most dramatically expressed in the two miners' strikes in 1972 and 1974, the second of which led directly to the fall of the Conservative Government. However, with union activism by no means confined to the miners, community activism, though usually out of the national media spotlight, also spread as local groups took up housing, planning and indeed welfare

rights, health and educational issues. By the early 1980s, too, a number of violent street disturbances in inner-city areas suggested, especially to the media, that Black young people were in outright revolt.

Though clearly important in their own right, cumulatively these events helped to shift the ways in which policy-makers thought about social policy. The 'welfare settlement' to which all the main political parties had been broadly committed over the previous 20 years started to unravel, revealing in particular how flawed two of its key underpinning assumptions were. One of these was that Britain was an affluent society which, self-evidently, could afford relatively generous educational and welfare provision. The other was that basic conflicts of values and interests had been eliminated and that therefore the prime tasks for the welfare state were to ensure equality of opportunity, promote maximum personal development for all its citizens – and win or coerce compliance from that residue of 'anti-social' citizens unreconciled to the new opportunity society (see Chapter 2).

As the nation's economic and political fissures widened, first Labour and then, very radically, Conservative politicians began to question these axioms of post-war social policy. Their reservations did not just focus on whether the cost of welfare state provision like the youth service was any longer sustainable at its existing level. They also doubted whether it – and especially other educational provision – was doing the job which the new national plight demanded. In an increasingly competitive world, that job was coming more and more to be (narrowly) defined as upskilling the nation's human capital – its workforce – to the standards required to boost its economic capital. So deep had these doubts become by 1973 that, largely with cross-party support, a specialised national agency was established, the Manpower Services Commission, whose primary task was 'manpower planning', including rejuvenating Britain's vocational training arrangements.

Youth service policy-makers and practitioners were of course only too aware of this changing, especially economic, context – of the pound's 'apparent kamikaze decline' in 1976 and the new 'perilous economic times' in which the service was operating. In struggling to fill the policy vacuum left by the vagueness of so much of the Fairbairn-Milson Report and then by the Thatcher response to it, at the start of the decade the youth service therefore had to contend with more than just reducing local and central government funding. It also had to learn to operate in an ideological climate which was less and less sympathetic to its core philosophy and approaches.

Even before the worst of the economic downturns, resources had often been scarce. One (albeit somewhat crude) survey carried out in 1972 showed that huge discrepancies remained in local authorities' spending on the service, with some allocating (much) less than £1 per head of its youth population. In addition, funding was apparently now actually starting to disappear – for example, as a result of changed administrative arrangements announced in August 1971 for grant-aiding voluntary sector building projects. By the time these worked their way through the system by June 1972 some rural areas were getting barely 10 per cent of what they had been led to expect.

Though not instant, the wider crises were in due course seen to have their inevitable effects. At the high profile North of England Education Conference in January 1975, the new Labour Secretary of State for Education, Reg Prentice, specifically included the youth service in a list of services for which in the immediate future there was going to be 'no scope for improvement'. When shortly afterwards the DES finally got round to considering the service specifically, its discussion paper, *Provision for Youth*, bluntly warned that 'in the present economic situation action in the short term must necessarily … be undertaken within existing resources'. It also made a somewhat forlorn attempt to reverse the drift of government policy towards targeting 'the deprived and the depraved' which the 1971 Thatcher statement had set in motion. The service and its resources, it said, were to be returned to a more specifically defined educational role, with the task of meeting other specific social needs being left to other government departments.

What all this was going to mean on the ground was spelt out by *Youth Scene*, the bimonthly publication of the National Youth Bureau (NYB) into which the Youth Service Information Centre had been absorbed in November 1973:

> There is a total standstill on development almost everywhere. In most places there are also to be substantial cuts on existing services ... not filling vacancies; ... a cutback in part-time paid workers; a pruning of activities; economies in maintenance; either a freeze or a cutback on grants to voluntary bodies; ... and a cutback in the number of opening nights of clubs.

And *Youth Service* warned: 'We are talking about real cuts.'

Under both Labour and Conservative governments, these generalisations produced a stream of headlines and press stories which built into a picture of decline by attrition. In 1975 these were highlighted in Leicestershire (always seen previously as a generous and pioneering authority), in Dudley, West Sussex, Hampshire, Cambridgeshire and Hereford and Worcester. When in early 1980 Cumbria budgeted to save £331,000 on its youth service expenditure, the jobs of 35 of its staff – 30 youth workers, three youth officers and two training officers – were put at risk.

More of a bird's eye view of the damage which was occurring was provided by a survey of LEA youth service expenditure between 1975 and 1980, published in October 1979. This was commissioned by four of the service's main national bodies which were just beginning to put pressure on jointly. One was the National Association of Youth and Community Education Officers (NAYCEO) into which the National Association of Youth Service

Officers (NAYSO) had converted itself in 1975. Another was the National Council for Voluntary Youth Services (NCVYS), the successor body to the Standing Conference of Voluntary Youth Organisations (SCNVYO). The other two were CYSA and NYB whose research officer Douglas Smith carried out the enquiry.

His findings showed that three-quarters of local authorities in England and Wales were planning to cut their services in 1979-80 by an average of 4.6 per cent. This perpetuated a trend which had started in 1976 and which by the time Smith's results appeared had led to a 17 per cent reduction in staffing. His report went on to warn that 'if the decline in youth service provision is allowed to continue then the ability of the service to function effectively will be in serious doubt'.

This warning seemed even to have the backing of two (now once again Conservative) DES ministers who claimed that 'we've done all in our power to tell local authorities that we don't want to see reductions in this important area of work'. However, with the Smith survey producing evidence of possible cuts by some local authorities for the next financial year ranging from 2.5 to 15 per cent (and perhaps overall of up to 30 per cent), their words seemed to be falling on deaf ears. According to Smith, reductions of well under 15 per cent would mean closed premises, fewer sessions and further reductions in staff levels. His conclusion was that the service was facing a bleak future.

The predicted overall trends seemed largely to be confirmed nine months later when a second report from the same four organisations – now formally allied as the Youth Service Partners – revealed 75 per cent of local authorities were planning to cut youth service spending in 1980–81. In 31 per cent of the authorities the proposed cuts were to be by more than a 'severe' 10 per cent.

Resistance was both local and national, and came not only from the unions. In September 1979, Peter Mandelson who, as chair of the British Youth Council, was constantly using his position to campaign on youth issues, wrote the first of two open letters to Neil MacFarlane, the new Conservative minister with youth service responsibility. In this he appealed 'in the strongest possible terms' for recognition of 'the effect of the sweeping financial cuts on provision for young people throughout the country'.

And yet all, it turned out, was not quite as desperate as it appeared – and certainly not as desperate as it was to become. When Douglas Smith returned in 1985 to re-examine the decade's actual youth service spending, he presented a rather more upbeat view:

> The pattern revealed is one of a real but declining rate of growth during the early 1970s and retrenchment or slight expansion during the mid-1970s, probably reflecting the then Labour Government's financial crisis and the IMF expenditure restrictions. There followed a period of recovery up to 1979 as public expenditure controls were eased. Over the course of the decade, in common with many other public services, expenditure on the youth service increased. By 1979 the youth service was receiving some 50 per cent more in real terms than it had in 1970.

Smith's retrospective research thus showed that it was only after 1979 when 'the political and financial climate changed' that the youth service experienced its first 'real cut' for ten years.

Even at the time evidence of continuing growth rather than cuts could still be found. This was the period, for example, when YSIC became NYB and when the Bureau's specialist units – to support youth social work, youth counselling, youth work and youth unemployment programmes – proliferated rapidly. It was also the period when a special DES-funded grants programme was created to promote experimental work.

Nonetheless, in comparison with the 1960s, during the 1970s the mood on the ground tipped from optimism to doubt and eventually to self-doubt and pessimism, uncertainty and insecurity. An unfamiliar struggle developed to hold on to what had been gained, especially after Albemarle. Regardless of retrospective and objective evidence, these feelings and readings of the situation at the time helped to shape, not just the motivation and morale of practitioners in those years and into the 1980s, but the policy and political tactics and strategies adopted within the service.

Voluntary organisations for a new age

In all this gloom, the voluntary youth organisations had reason to feel especially threatened. As early as August 1971 the

DES under Margaret Thatcher transferred responsibility for administering its 50 per cent contribution to voluntary sector capital projects to the LEAs. (They were at that stage required to add 25 per cent of their own funds to any grant.) In 1977 even this central government support was in effect withdrawn in a move which NCVYS described as 'losing' the DES's £3 million contribution in the overall rate support grant to local authorities.

This, however, was only a (small) beginning to the cuts to voluntary sector funding. By April 1976 *Youth Service* was identifying a number of local authorities which were making 'huge reductions' in revenue expenditure grants. By the time the 1980–81 figures were being analysed, the voluntary organisations were being cut by 13.8 per cent as compared with an overall 9.9 per cent for the statutory services.

Nonetheless, throughout the 1970s, the traditional voluntary sector maintained influential leverage on the service's thinking and action. This was confirmed by an in-depth DES-funded research project into the organisation and purpose of the service carried out by John Eggleston of the University of Keele. Commissioned in 1968 and completed in 1974, its findings pointed to 'the undoubted strength of the influential pressure groups which represented the voluntary organisations singly and collectively', including at the level of national politics and administration.

NCVYS's emergence in 1972 as a National Council out of what had for over 40 years been merely a Standing Conference in itself represented a significant effort by the voluntary sector to maintain and indeed extend this influential position. Its revised constitution and statement of aims, in addition to emphasising young people's aspirations as well as their needs, allowed it to respond more flexibly to changing conditions on behalf of its member organisations. In April 1980, spreading its wings even more riskily, it broke free of its parent body the National Council for Social Service and, without giving up any of its newfound independence, joined NYB in its premises in Leicester. Francis Cattermole's appointment as its new director in 1980 also added a more determined political perspective to its interpretation of its role.

For the voluntary youth sector, searching reappraisal in this period went much further. In the first half of the decade it was the focus of two national reviews both of which demonstrated how the service's wider preoccupations and policy shifts were lapping into its territory. The first of these was undertaken by an independent working party set up by the Department of the Environment in June 1972, with a remit to advise on 'the role of voluntary movements and youth in the environment'. It was chaired by Denis Stevenson, later to become chair of NAYC, who also associated himself with the efforts made by NYB's director, John Ewen, to persuade the Prime Minister Edward Heath to develop a more coherent youth policy. The report of the working party also had Black youth worker Gus John as one of its members.

In its chapters devoted specifically to the youth service, the report, which was published as *Fifty Million Volunteers*, identified the voluntary sector with the service's wider failure to take on key Fairbairn-Milson recommendations. It especially regretted that so little had been done to move away from 'the club is the youth service' approach and to make provision more community oriented. It also noted how statutory help was still largely given to 'more traditional movements rather than to some new developments' – by which it meant community service organisations and those 'concerned with the problems of young people, particularly in socially deprived environments'. It thus proposed that 'an independent funding agency' be created to allocate government grants to, and to raise additional funds for, voluntary youth organisations and to seed the development of more experimental projects.

Though gaining some immediate attention, *Fifty Million Volunteers* was by no means as wide-ranging as the second of the two 1970s reports on the voluntary sector, *The National Voluntary Youth Organisations*. This was carried out by PEP, the independent social science institute whose interest in the youth service dated back to the 1940s. Financed by the DES and supported by NCVYS and its Welsh equivalent, the specific brief of the review was 'to undertake an impartial study of the work and finances of youth organisations'. The wider context was a new Conservative Government which, in line with its historic commitment, was already looking to boost volunteering and the voluntary sector. Motivating it too,

however, were hopes and even expectations that wider use of voluntary organisations and their unpaid workers might help reduce costs in the public sector.

Most directly, the PEP enquiry arose out of Thatcher's 1971 statement on the youth service which asserted that 'the system of capital and recurrent grants made by the Department needs to be simplified'. For her, changes were clearly essential if she was to achieve two of her other key goals: to shift 'the balance of the programmes ... towards the provision of assistance to less prosperous areas' and 'to devote more resources to experimental work in the youth field'. This need for change was reinforced the following year by one of her junior ministers, Lord Belstead, who encouraged voluntary organisations to make 'a fundamental departure from the traditional activities (through) the promotion of promising new lines of approach'.

When it finally appeared in February 1975, the PEP report further fuelled the debate on the need for a national youth policy which, without ever quite catching fire, was by then slow-burning in youth service circles. It, for example, noted that 'the government does not have, and never has had, a coherent youth policy' and that 'even within the restricted ambit of the youth service, an overall policy has never been made clear'. As a result 'no set of criteria (for judging grant applications) was formally laid down in advance, nor was any formal system of criteria developed on the basis of precedent'. With grants therefore having to that point been made purely via 'a history of ad hoc departmental decisions', it recommended that a youth organisations grant committee be established. This was to operate independently of government but within an overall policy framework.

The PEP report focused on much more than funding, however. It had some tart comments to make about the concept of partnership, noting that it 'resulted in an undue emphasis by government depart-ments, the YSDC and the youth organisa-tions themselves on the idea that it was … necessary to present a united front to the world … This has led to a tendency to gloss over the disagreements, disparities and differences in approach and values'.

PEP also undertook a field survey in 50 LEA areas focusing on 733 local units affiliated to the 12 largest organisations. Notwithstanding the acknowledged limitations of its methods and sample, this produced what NCVYS subsequently called 'the most major survey of voluntary organisation economic need, sources and disposition that had been undertaken ever'. It concluded that 'troop-like' organisations such as the Scouts, Guides and the Boys' and Girls' Brigades were catering mainly for 10 to 14-year-olds and providing them with 'small, sex-exclusive, disciplined activities'. 'Club' organisations like NABC, NAYC and their Welsh equiva-lents on the other hand were attracting mainly 14 to 18-year-olds and were offering 'larger scale, sex-balanced, less disciplined activities'. The report also suggested that 'even small voluntary "clubs" have rather more working-class members than small voluntary "troops"'.

The report shied away from applying these findings in any rigid way on the grounds that 'it is not possible to impose narrow criteria onto so diverse a group as voluntary youth organisations'. It did, however, tentatively define some priority groups. These included early school leavers, girls (and) over 14s, thereby apparently tipping the balance in favour of the club organisations. In doing this it also helped to constrain further the voluntary organisations' freedom of action and reinforce the place of selectivity and targeting in the service's policy-making processes.

The PEP report's proposed system of allocating headquarters grants to voluntary organisations was in due course implemented by the DES. Nonetheless, it seemed to attract surprisingly little comment. This may have been because by the time it was published, it was being overtaken by events – particularly by the change of government from Conservative to Labour, by the efforts to get a youth service bill through Parliament, and, almost simultaneously, by the release of the DES's own discussion paper, *Provision for Youth*.

Both the Parliamentary Bill and the DES paper were in fact bland in the extreme in their references to the voluntary sector. *Provision for Youth*, for example, contained the usual ritualistic nods to its 'substantial and diversified contribution' and to 'the value of statutory/voluntary cooperation in all areas'. It also urged that, in approaches to 'the disadvantaged,' teamwork be developed across the two sectors. Its overall conclusion, however, was: 'there is no obvious reason for suggesting any variation in the present partnership arrangements'.

On this, however, others were not so sure. In May 1976 *Youth Service* felt able to say 'for certain' that 'despite considerable effort, the traditional youth organisations have not succeeded in retaining many young people over the age of 14/15'. John Ewen – now freed of his NYB constraints – mounted a much more thorough-going critique. This urged the voluntary organisations to recapture ground lost to the statutory sector since Albemarle, particularly by rediscovering and reasserting their genuinely voluntary past. To do this, he argued, they needed to face some unpalatable realities, including the possibility that 'some (had) completed the job they were created to do donkeys years ago'. He saw their claim to be great pioneers as 'a tribal mythology' and accused them of often being as bureau-cratic and as over-professionalised as any statutory agency and of having become over-dependent on statutory funding.

Occasionally, some of these strictures were confirmed from within, as when the Duke of Edinburgh himself acknowledged in May 1976 that his scheme needed to change its middle-class, club-oriented image. At the same time traditional and mainstream organisations continued to stake their claims to continuing relevance. During this period BYC reconstituted itself so that it could more effectively deliver on its commitment to act as the voice of young people. Other organisations again exposed themselves to internal reviews, particularly in an effort to get a handhold

on the Fairbairn-Milson community bandwagon. In 1974 both the Guides and the Scouts announced significant member-ship growth while the latter sought to increase its impact in deprived areas through a Scoutreach programme. NABC started a five-year project designed to get more youth workers involved in the intermediate treatment schemes for young offenders introduced by the 1969 Children and Young Person's Act. BYC, NAYC and NCVYS all undertook developmental work in the field of political education and youth participation while NAYC also pioneered a major new project in response to the mass youth unemployment, followed up its earlier project on work with Black young people and established a Rural Youthwork Education Project.

The voluntary sector mainstream was also being replenished and extended, including by organisations which reflected the changing nature of the wider society and of young people's expressed needs. It was in this period, for example, that the National Association of Indian Youth and the National Association of Young People's Counselling and Advice Services (NAYPCAS) were formed. Endeavour Training emerged to offer residential adventure programmes designed to challenge young people to develop themselves socially and spiritually. In 1977 The Young Volunteer Force Foundation (YVFF), riding the community work tide of the mid 1970s, left behind its rather narrow and (for many of the young people it wished to reach) off-putting identification with voluntary service to become the Community Development Foundation (CDF). Though not getting its

DES headquarters grant until 1979, from 1971 the National Youth Assembly acted as a new networking mechanism for the growing number of local youth councils.

Grass roots activity, and particularly the community activism of the late 1960s and 1970s, also spawned a new breed of local youth working organisations and groups. Many of these, as the Keele research confirmed, were 'less structured and less institutionalised' than traditional youth organisations and were strongly committed to political advocacy on behalf of young people. However, though remaining largely on the periphery of the mainstream service, the emphasis of what later came to be called the 'independent' sector working with young people in need gave a further push to selectivity. Sometimes – as with Street Aid and Centrepoint which provided support and advice services to young people on the streets – they touched a national chord and so got themselves a national reputation. Most, however, worked away in their own localities and on their local issues, coming and perhaps going within the decade as short-term funding from Urban Aid and similar programmes ebbed and flowed.

Adapt and survive thus remained the voluntary sector's guiding principle at a time when, though the rhetoric was often loudly supportive, the material realities were much less encouraging. The warning signs of course appeared early, triggered particularly by tightening economic circumstances and starting with the 1971 cuts in grants for capital projects. By 1975 a Labour Home Office minister, Alex Lyon, was warning the voluntary sector that it

could no longer look to government to raise its levels of assistance: 'the real help for voluntary organisations, if they were to remain voluntary, must be through the public'.

With the arrival of Thatcherite ideas at the heart of government at the end of the decade, the voluntary sector no less than other youth service interests entered unfamiliar territory. Responses shifted from merely rhetorical Commons flourishes to a much more determined and overarching strategy applied as single-mindedly to the youth service as to any other area of educational or welfare provision. Mark Carlisle began to spell this out at the NYB annual general meeting shortly after taking over as Secretary of State for Education in 1979: 'I … believe strongly that there is a potential contribution from private enterprise … which the voluntary youth movement has hardly begun to tap.'

Doorstepping Whitehall

Winning – and losing – national consultative machinery

Well before the real effects of these radical political shifts were felt, however – and especially as the financial climate worsened – the gap left by the demise of the YSDC became a focus of increasing concern and frustration within the service. As soon as Labour were returned to power in February 1974, a campaign began to persuade the new Government and especially its civil servants that some form of national consultative machinery was essential.

By September three of the key national bodies, NCVYS, NAYCEO and CYSA, were raising the issue with Gerry Fowler, who as a full Minister of State at the DES brought greater status to the youth service brief than most of his predecessors. The following February one of his Parliamentary Under Secretaries, Hugh Jenkins, while again cautioning that economic constraints meant that 'practical developments will have to be limited', was telling the Commons of the need for 'all concerned (to) exchange views' on the future of the service. The credibility of this promise was somewhat undermined by being linked to a proposal that NYB organise an under-21s essay competition on 'What Youth Needs Today'. Nonetheless, it was followed quickly by the release of the DES's discussion paper, *Provision for Youth* which recognised 'the widespread pressure for the establishment of some form of national consultative machinery'. It noted too, however, that 'there is no unanimity of view' on how this could be achieved and so, as the way forward, settled for 'much discussion'.

This is precisely what then followed. It was not until May 1976 that even an outline agreement with Fowler began to emerge – and only then after he had rejected proposals for an independent outside chair. Though the new forum was promised for early autumn, Fowler's move to another department and his replacement by a junior minister, Margaret Jackson, further delayed its inauguration.

The 35 members of what was termed the Youth Service Forum who did finally come together in December 1976 represented voluntary and statutory youth service providers from England and Wales and users of the service. (The original terms of reference suggested that at least one-third of the membership should be under 26.) The Minister herself took the chair, DES officials and HMI had non-voting status and the Education Departments of Scotland and Northern Ireland were free to send observers.

The Forum's overall brief was to act as the central arena for considering national youth service policy and for advising national and local government and other agencies concerned with provision for young people. However, some stringent limits were placed on its role. Its overall remit contained at least implicit cautions against its aspirations to develop too expansive a youth affairs agenda. The DES expectation was that 'the advice offered by the Forum will normally be addressed to the Secretary of State for Education and Science'. Only 'on occasion' would the Forum give its views to other government departments, with these non-educational interests being directly represented on the Forum only by invitation. Given the economic conditions of the time, not only were the Forum's own meetings to be limited to three a year, but 'its energies', it was told, 'may be best directed to considering how to make the best use of existing resources'. All this, it was reported, seemed to produce 'considerable anxiety among youth organisations that (the) national consultative machinery will not turn out to be what they had bargained for'.

In the event the Forum struggled from the start: after only its second meeting, in April 1977, members were complaining about lack of progress and poor organisation of its business. However, it did quickly agree to set up a working party with a three-point remit – to consider:

- how young people could effectively influence youth service policy and practice;
- how the youth service should relate to the wider community; and
- what restructuring of 'the system' might need to be considered.

With at least 10 Forum delegates coming as youth representatives, and prompted in part by a BYC discussion paper which even then was talking of 'the alienation of the young and (the need) to enlist their commitment to the political process', it was agreed that the working party should concentrate initially on young people's participation.

Though the initial announcement of the working party suggested that young people would be in a majority, it was chaired once again by Fred Milson, and its report, published in June 1978, was (with a couple of exceptions) produced by the usual kind of adult suspects. What is more, its actual recommendations, far from providing a radical breakthrough in policy and practice, largely disappeared without trace. Notwithstanding the repeated Government rulings on the need to operate within existing resources, its most specific proposals were for more funds to support 'young people's self-determination in their organisations and

groups', local youth forums and the Forum's own research and development work.

The only other concrete outcome of the Forum – a second report, *Resources for the Youth Service* – also produced few ripples. However, it did represent a highly sensitive financial weather vane for plotting the direction in which the, by then dominant, policy winds were driving the service. It, for example, explicitly identified two main types of youth service provision: universal – 'to meet needs common to all young people'; and special – 'for those young people requiring additional degrees of support and help to enable them to achieve the aims of the "universal" provision'. It identified potential target groups for the service, defined not only by age but also according to 'variations in educational achievement' and 'the ability to cope satisfactorily with the demands of adolescence with a minimum of adult support'.

As if to give added credibility to targeting high priority sections of the youth population, the report also gave detailed information on other sources of central government funds 'for support of the youth service'. Clearly, the 'special social needs' seed sown by the Thatcher statement within the youth service in 1971 was growing rapidly into a robust national strategy plant which seemed well on the way to self-generation across the whole of the youth service's funding landscape.

By June 1979, however, for this report and indeed for the Forum as a whole, the

Thatcher connection was much more than just a shadow from the past. In the previous month, in what has been described as 'a watershed election, with the most marked shift of opinion since 1945', Margaret Thatcher had became Prime Minister, having won power on a radical economic and political manifesto. This offered little hope that the two main working party recommendations would even be considered. One was for the DES to make the youth service responsible for initiating and coordinating youth provision for meeting both the universal and special needs it had identified. The other urged the DES to invite LEAs to produce local youth policy statements for their areas.

Once Thatcherism was in the driving seat, such directive policy assumptions – above all for such a peripheral and amorphous area of state provision as this – were entirely out of fashion. Nothing illustrated this better than the reception given, a full year before the election, to a Conservative Party working party report on youth policy, *A Time for Youth*. In calling for a minister for youth and a revitalised Youth Service Forum, it was dismissed by *The Sun*, for example, as reading 'like something dreamed up in Transport House (the Labour Party's headquarters) in the early 60s'.

In this climate, central advisory bodies themselves were hardly popular. As part of a sweeping quango-cull which began immediately after the election, the new Conservative administration did to it what in 1970 its predecessor had done to the YSDC: it unceremoniously abolished it.

(Re)discovering politics

As a body in its own right, the Forum had, according to John Ewen, been 'generally ineffective'. In winding it up the minister responsible, Neil MacFarlane, agreed. He had, he said, seen 'few signs of … collective and constructive thinking … or any strong sense of mutual purpose or direction'. One of his motivations for acting when he did, however, may have been to remove the promise and the opportunity the Forum provided for key youth service interests to develop the very unity whose absence he was deploring. Not only in its making but also during its actual operation and even in its disappearance, the Forum helped to politicise the service's dealings with central government.

The decade had in fact seen a steady movement towards greater professional unity within the service, tinged on occasions with some all-but explicit political motives. In 1970 the YSA's annual conference resolved to start discussion with NAYSO and other relevant bodies, with a view to creating 'one professional association for all those practising in the youth and community service'. After a year of negotiations, in 1971 the YSA and the Community Service Association agreed to amalgamate, while its and NAYSO's local branches started jointly to organise conferences and produce reports. With talk of a possible merger still in the air, in March 1978, CYSA and what had by then become NAYCEO held a joint annual conference in Exeter.

It was thus not altogether surprising that the Forum was partly forced into existence by the combined efforts of NAYSO and CYSA together with NCVYS. By the time abolition came, these organisations were working politically with other national bodies. As a result the angry protest at the Forum's abolition to MacFarlane from Michael Butterfield, chair of the Forum's working party on resources, came not only from his own organisation (NAYC) and the original trio of organisations. It was signed, too, by David Howie, director of NYB and by Peter Mandelson, president of BYC.

Wider developments anyway were demanding that common concerns be identified and agreed positions hammered out and acted on. The new radical right ideology of Thatcherism was, often ruthlessly, reintroducing politics into educational and social policy-making even though the post-war welfare consensus had supposedly removed basic political differences forever. Events as they affected young people specifically were also requiring more concerted action, leading in 1977, for example, to the creation of the new campaigning youth organisation against youth unemployment, Youthaid.

During the 1970s, open and vigorous political debate and organising was by now one of the more striking features of the youth service scene. Indeed, in 1977, CYSA president, David Bellotti – later to become a Liberal Democrat MP – bluntly told the association's annual conference that it was time for it to move to political action. Most striking, however – and notwithstanding its reliance on central government money, in this period NYB repeatedly took up political stances. Its first two directors, John Ewen until 1977

and then David Howie, both saw themselves as needing to operate proactively and indeed politically on the national stage in relation to a wide range of youth issues. NYB's periodicals *Youth Scene* and *Youth Service* on occasions openly condemned, for example, slow government responses to rising youth unemployment; police harassment of Black and Asian young people; the 'harsh deals' meted out by the police and the courts to youth workers carrying out their professional duties; the way the law on cannabis was criminalising young people; and the rapid turn-over of DES ministers with youth service responsibility. *Scene* also gave very forthright support to Ewen's campaign for a more coordinated youth policy.

As Thatcherism increasingly tampered with Britain's pluralistic traditions, the climate became more restrictive and more threatening. However, the relative freedom of expression during most of the 1970s allowed the service's politicisation to take root. Though its effectiveness was uneven, by the end of the decade, it had achieved one concrete and significant outcome: the construction of a youth service partners group committed to exerting collective pressure for action on youth issues at a national level.

One of its first initiatives was to organise a Youth Charter Towards 2000 conference, held in January 1977 at the new Wembley Conference Centre. This was organised by the National Council of Social Service in association with NYB and was actively supported by other key national youth service organisations. Its steering committee was chaired by Conservative

MP Alan Haselhurst who had already demonstrated his youth service commitment by introducing the first of a series of private member's bills aimed at strengthening its legislative basis.

The conference was very heavily hyped from the start: 'potentially the most important youth conference ever staged'; 'a curtainraiser to a major reassessment of youth needs and problems in Britain' whose culmination would be a 'youth charter of positive suggestions for the future'. Most of its substantive impact was intended to be done through follow-up work after the conference itself, in local groups and at other national events. Nonetheless, it attracted a wide range of high-profile keynote speakers including two former prime ministers.

Despite a much-trumpeted commitment to getting extensive participation by young people themselves, initially the 1,500 delegates were given few opportunities to contribute and became 'increasingly critical' of the proceedings. Indeed they produced what the editor of the *Times Educational Supplement*, Stuart MacLure, called in his conference summing up 'a spontaneous youth rebellion of the kind that only good detached youth workers could organise'. The organisers also seemed slow (at best) in responding to the shifting politics of the 1970s, refusing, for example, to take on board young Black participants' protests at their designation as 'young immigrants'.

Though some local activity did result, plans for subsequent national events stumbled while, where attempts to consult young people on these were not simply incompetent, they were judged by some of those taking part to be highly patronising. Within little more than two years, the Charter initiative had all but disappeared off the youth service's agenda.

Other political ploys were attempted from time to time. Though rebuffed, both NAYC and NAYCEO worked hard to get an agreed youth service input into the great education debate then being conducted by the Labour Government in its last two years in office. Unsurprisingly perhaps, NAYCEO's proposal to Margaret Thatcher shortly after she became Prime Minister that she set up a Royal Commission on the youth service was given even shorter shrift!

One political initiative which floated in and out of the service's priorities throughout the decade – and indeed beyond – focused on establishing government machinery, centrally and locally, for coordinating and even perhaps developing youth policy. In 1973 John Ewen, then still head of YSIC, proposed that a small office be attached to the Prime Minister's office for this purpose. This would be directly responsible to a Cabinet minister and would report to a Commons standing committee. Ewen also suggested that parallel arrangements be made within local government, through a youth affairs coordinator based in the Chief Executive's office. These were proposals which were largely endorsed by *Fifty Million Volunteers*.

During 1973 Ewen's ideas were also taken up by a somewhat elite group of individuals involved in children and youth organisations. Their exchange of correspondence with the Prime Minister, Edward Heath, led to a group of youth work practitioners spending an hour-and-a-half at 10 Downing Street. After presenting their views on a range of youth issues, thy also pressed for 'coordinated approaches to youth problems at national and local level'. Neither Heath nor his Education Secretary Margaret Thatcher were converted.

When the 1978 Conservative working party report *A Time for Youth* developed the idea into a proposal for a full-blown Minister of State for Youth, it was no less comprehensively dismissed. However, Liverpool provided an early local example of youth affairs coordination. In due course, too, the commitment to some form of national coordination did gain a more concrete and consistent if weaker and non-governmental expression in what was probably the youth service's most effective collective intervention into the new politics of the late 1970s: an all-party Parliamentary lobby of MPs.

From Youth Service Liaison Group to Parliamentary lobby

The need for some such pressure group was floated as early as the summer of 1977 by Peter Mandelson following a BYC delegation meeting with the then Prime Minister, James Callaghan. At that stage, too, the Education Secretary Shirley Williams expressed some interest in it. With considerable media attention, including, for example, a feature article in *The Guardian*, the lobby was launched in March 1978.

The move was driven by concerns among national youth organisations about, as they expressed it:
- *overlapping (responsibilities), or lack of coordination, between government departments …;*
- *the lack of a coherent youth policy …;*
- *the need to enable young people to be heard …;*
- *the need for parliamentarians to be reliably informed on the thinking of the youth affairs field.*

Its core purposes therefore were to give 'greater prominence in Parliament to issues affecting young people' and 'a much-needed communications link between politicians and young people and those working with them'.

Chaired by Edward Heath, it recruited Gerry Fowler from the Parliamentary Labour Party and Liberal Chief Whip Alan Beith as vice-chairs. No less significant, it brought into existence a liaison group of, as they styled themselves, 'the five main "umbrella" youth bodies' – BYC, CYSA, NAYCEO, NCVYS and NYB. The group also stressed the importance of cooperation with other interested individuals and organisations. It set itself the task of linking parliamentarians (MPs and peers) with those wanting to promote issues through the lobby. Its members thus explicitly committed themselves to collaborative political work on behalf of young people and the youth service – something which, as CYSA pointed out, 'has been needed since the work began'. As Heath made clear at the launch, a high priority was to be given to ensuring that 'young people (had) the opportunity of making clear their own views'. For his part, the Prime Minister James Callaghan wished the lobby 'a long and fruitful life' and promised that his Government would have 'close regard' to the views expressed to it.

By the summer of 1978, the liaison group had issued an *Objectives and Procedures* paper and had organised its first lobby meeting – on 'The Alienation of Young Blacks'. During the autumn briefing papers, other support material and speakers were prepared for three further lobby meetings – on political education, community service and youth homelessness. The group was also actively looking for funds from business or other sources to set up a permanent secretariat and office which was being provided by NYB on a temporary basis. A year later, six of 11 of the group's members were young people (three under 19) who had been directly elected from 24 candidates by nearly 200 delegates brought together at a special meeting in London.

Though criticised by CYSA for its 'further 12 months of inactivity', the group continued to arrange lobby meetings at Westminster during April and May 1980 on youth participation and again on community service. By this time, however, the political energies of the organisations which made up the group had understandably been diverted – first onto the private member's bill on the youth service then going through the Commons; and then the review of the service which was the one concrete outcome of this latest (failed) attempt to strengthen its legislative basis.

Salvation through legislation?

Concern about the adequacy of the service's statutory basis had surfaced periodically ever since it had been given a kind of legislative underpinning by the 1944 Education Act. Though largely disappearing in the optimistic and expansionist post-Albemarle years, uneasiness not only re-emerged during the 1970s but became much more acute. Predicting 'another doldrums ahead for the youth service ... similar to the prelude the Albemarle Report', Gordon Ette pointed in 1972 to the consequences for the service of local education authorities treating it as one of their 'optional responsibilities'. He was writing, too, just as – in response to very serious threats to the state – the youth service in Northern Ireland was being given an unambiguously statutory status.

Ette's conclusion was that:

> Members of the LEAs have produced so many and varied interpretations of the duty phrase that the unevenness of the youth service amounts to inequality and unfairness.

By 1977 Stuart MacLure, summing up the Youth Charter Towards 2000 conference was suggesting that one way to tackle this inconsistency was to give local authorities a legal obligation to spend a fixed proportion of their budgets on the youth service.

As minister with youth service responsibility in Margaret Thatcher's new administration, Neil MacFarlane was unwilling to contemplate any such solution. In 1979, he repeated yet again the obligation placed on local authorities to secure adequate youth service facilities as laid down by the 1944 Education Act, though significantly he seemed to acknowledge that this requirement was only in effect 'technical'. However, he stressed that 'in the absence of any further specification these clauses do not deter-mine the level or nature of the provision to be made'. Even more tellingly, he saw 'the achievement of consensus on common standards' as being 'light years away'. He therefore set his face firmly against being drawn into defining adequacy.

MacFarlane made his statement in response to the first of Peter Mandelson's open letters in which he had referred to the service as 'not among those parts of the education service which LEAs are required to provide as part of their statutory duty'. He therefore called for new legislation to protect it from cuts. A year later, as his parting shot as chair of BYC, Mandelson released a second letter addressed to MacFarlane, this time as a feature article in *The Guardian*. Starting from the proposition that 'Britain lacks any coherent policy ... for all its young working people', he advocated that, to secure the future of the service, 'new obligations should be placed on local authorities'.

Earlier in the decade determined efforts had been made to do just this. As no government, Labour or Conservative, was willing to introduce the necessary legislation, private member's bills sponsored by a sympathetic MP – in all cases Conservative – became the chosen route for achieving this end.

In youth work terms, the motives of the politicians involved in sponsoring and supporting the four youth service bills which resulted were far from pure. Throughout the debates, proposals were repeatedly justified on the grounds that, with teenage violence and vandalism getting worse, the youth service provided a cheaper response than incarcerating offenders; and that, with unemployment rising so dramatically, young people needed to be offered constructive distrac-tions in their unwanted and unsupervised leisure time.

Nonetheless the bills did give the youth service a Parliamentary profile which it had rarely had before. The first was debated in the Commons on 1 February 1974. Sponsored by Alan Haselhurst and with future Labour leader Neil Kinnock as one of its backers, it was described by Conservative Central Office as 'the first legislative action affecting youth work since the 1944 Education Act thirty years ago'. It came, Haselhurst asserted, after he had received evidence 'from almost one hundred voluntary organisations and more than twice as many individuals with youth work experience'. And it was needed, he said, because 'for too long youth work has been the "fag-end" of education departments at both national and local level' and because '(we are) getting our youth service on the cheap'.

The bill itself focused on a range of youth issues then current or emerging, including youth homelessness, community service and provision for young people with special needs very broadly defined. It also sought to set the target age group as 14 to

21-year-olds. At its core, however, were clauses aimed at tightening up LEAs' responsibilities, particularly for the youth service. Thus it laid down that they should be required to:

- establish a joint committee to coordinate their own and voluntary organisations' services for young people in their area;
- establish at least one youth assembly as a forum for discussing youth provision; and
- submit to the Secretary of State 'a scheme for providing or making provision for a comprehensive range of services for young people'.

Unambiguously, the primary focus of such schemes was to be youth service facilities. It concentrated, for example, on social education including for the unattached; recreation and social and physical training; and the appointment of youth and community workers. LEAs were also to be required to plan for the provision of information and advice on welfare services for young people and for international youth exchanges.

Though not meeting full frontal govern-ment opposition, Timothy Raison, the DES Under-Secretary criticised the bill as tech-nically inept – and financially risky. He doubted whether local authorities would be pleased with the bill's proposal that its implementation should not attract rate support grant, and he was adamant that, at a time of cuts in public services, the Government would not accept new legislation requiring increases in public expenditure. At best, he suggested, if passed the bill would need to wait for

implementation 'until the financial situation improved'.

In the event the first general election of 1974 intervened and the bill was lost. Though Haselhurst lost his seat, pressure from the National Youth Assembly among others led to its immediate revival by Ted Brown, only for it again to be cut short by a second general election. Cyril Townsend brought it back to the Commons in February 1975 though, with the new Labour Government reported 'not to be very enthusiastic', its chances of getting through all its Parliamentary stages were always poor.

By April it was dead. Though a junior minister promised to consult with statutory and voluntary Youth Service interests, the Government's own discussion paper, *Provision for Youth* which appeared the following week proceeded as if the bills had never existed.

The fourth and final attempt in this period to go down the legislative route was made in November 1979. Trevor Skeet's bill aimed, as the *Times Educational Supplement* put it, to rectify 'the contradiction of a statutory service without any mandatory provision' – or, still, agreed standards of provision. Pride of place was again given to a requirement that LEAs coordinate youth provision as well as prepare an overall plan for a comprehensive range of youth services. At the very moment that the Government was winding up the Youth Service Forum, it also sought to establish in law 'a central advisory youth and community service committee for England and Wales and for Scotland'.

The good news for the bill's prospects was that Skeet drew eighth place in the MPs' ballot for private member's bills. The bad news was that the new Thatcher Government was under no circumstances willing to contemplate the extra spending which new local authority obligations would entail. (Even Skeet argued that 'we must avoid any kind of requirement on LEAs to spend money'.) Nor would ministers collude with a proposal whose effect would be to increase local authority responsibilities even if they were cost-free since fundamental to the Thatcherite political credo was the commitment to less rather than more government. Finally, as the new Education Secretary Mark Carlisle made clear, the youth affairs perspective which informed the bill had little appeal for the new administration:

> There are limits on the ability of any government to formulate a series of policies corresponding to the many and various areas of our concern with young people. They are not after all a different species ...

Nonetheless, in so far as youth service policy-making ever did this, the bill did manage to stir up something of a political storm. When it reached its committee stage in February 1980, MacFarlane tabled proposals to remove all but one of its 14 clauses. By then, too, the influential Association of Metropolitan Authorities (AMA) was lobbying hard, arguing 'how regrettable this bill is for local authorities'.

Despite such powerful opposition, the bill went much further than any of its predecessors. Wide support within the Conservative Party – including from the Young Conservatives and the Federation of Conservative Students – developed into what *The Guardian* called 'an open revolt' among its MPs on the Commons committee. Outside Parliament, the gains made in political organisation over the previous few years also showed up as the Youth Affairs Lobby Liaison Officer coordinated a joint response from the key youth service interests.

The result was that the bill returned to the Commons for its third reading in July 1980 relatively unscathed. As the debate approached, the possibility that it might pass led to suggestions that Conservative MPs might even be whipped into line. In the event, despite a mass lobby outside Parliament led by Neil Kinnock and Edward Heath, the Government's 79 amendments and a debate of only two hours 20 minutes ensured that it fell, this time never to be revived.

However, to get this 'victory', the Government had to buy itself some respite. In the course of a debate on youth a few days later, again prompted by Skeet, it agreed to introduce its own bill during the lifetime of that Parliament – a promise that was never fulfilled. It also undertook to carry out a new review of the youth service. What in due course the service got out of its Parliamentary efforts of the 1970s therefore was, in 1982, the Thompson Report.

Main references

Mark Carlisle, 'Address by the Secretary of State to the Annual General Meeting',

NYB, 1979

Bernard Davies, 'Priorities in the Youth and Community Service', paper to the CYSA/NAYCEO Exeter Conference, 1978

Department of the Environment, *Fifty Million Volunteers*, HMSO, 1972

John Eggleston, *Adolescence and Community: The Youth Service in Britain*, Edward Arnold, 1975

John Eggleston, 'A Youth and Community Service for the late 1970s', *Youth in Society*, Jan/Feb 1975

John Ewen, *Towards a Youth Policy*, MBS Publications, 1972

John Ewen, 'Up the Voluntary Organisation', *Youth in Society*, October 1979

Catherine Green, *In the Service of Youth: A History of the National Council of Voluntary Youth Services 1936–1986*,

NCVYS, 1986

Gus John, *In the Service of Black Youth*, NAYC, 1981

Peter Mandelson, 'An open letter to the Minister for Youth', *The Guardian*, 2.9.80

Douglas Smith, 'Local Authority Expenditure on the Youth Service, 1975–1980', NYB, 1979

Douglas Smith, ' Local Authority Expenditure on the Youth Service, 1979/80–1980/81', Youth Service' Partners/NYB, 1980

Douglas Smith, 'Expenditure on the Youth Service, 1978–1983', NYB, 1985

Gordon Ette, 'Service of Youth: An Education survey of LEA provision', *Education*, 17.9.76

Michael Thomas and Jane Perry, *National Voluntary Youth Organisations*, PEP, 1975

7 Hitting the Targets

The view from above

Throughout the 1970s, youth culture continued to be treated by many, especially 'official', adults as a foreign territory – viewed from afar, regarded with suspicion and entered only with care. From this somewhat distanced position, policy-makers over the decade subjected its more unreliable and threatening inhabitants to special attention. The result was the development of the increasingly pervasive, top-down targeting of scarce resources on priority groups and those in special social need traced in previous chapters.

In one key respect, however, the analysis underpinning these objectives was deeply flawed: it failed to recognise the boundaries of class and income which continued to block the youth service's access to many of those it wished to recruit. Among key players in this exchange, the result was some deeply contradictory perspectives and starting points.

Thus, for young people, the problems needing to be tackled were most often likely to be *economic and political* – ones, crudely, of too little money and too little power to change their situation. For policy-makers, however, definitions almost invariably centred around the *personal and the social* – even when, for

example, Denis Howell highlighted not just violence, hooliganism and vandalism but truancy, homelessness and unemployment. Yet, most immediately for the youth service, the challenge was *cultural*: how to connect with the values and interests of many more young women and young men from working-class backgrounds and communities and thereby link them into its 'improving' intentions and programmes? Given the service's continuing fierce defence of young people's voluntary participation in its facilities, what it was contending with therefore was not just their exclusion but also their self-exclusion.

A *Youth Service* leader tried tentatively (and somewhat simplistically) to address this credibility gap in 1973. The youth service, it noted, 'is still basically a middle-class service'. As a result 'servicing the needs of deprived and disadvantaged young people is a demanding and often impossible task'. During the 1960s and 1970s this question was broadened out further by the multi-cultural and multi-racial diversity which in many areas infused these traditional culture clashes. As the affluence of the 1960s ebbed away, it also became harder to mask its inherent economic and political dimensions as revealed by young people's growing poverty and joblessness and their loss of control over the transitions to a fully adult future.

Still the unattached ...

Though as the decade progressed targeting became increasingly an imperative of policy, the youth service – in common with other welfare state services and in line with its own historic tradition – rarely took these analytical complexities into its definitions of 'problem' clientele. By therefore – in a phrase used tellingly by the Albemarle Report – often failing to speak authentically to young people's condition, it failed too to address the core realities of the widespread unattachment which still so worried their elders.

Partly as a result, far from disappearing over the decade the problem of the unattached grew – or, no less significant, was seen to grow. In July 1971, for example, Denis Howell – now in opposition – told MPs that the unattached constituted a 'crisis situation' for the youth service. This, he claimed, was affecting between 70 and 80 per cent of young people in the large towns and the main conurbations.

The main study of youth service take-up reported in this period, carried out by the Office of Population Censuses and Surveys (OPCS), seemed to confirm his conclusion. Carried out for the Fairbairn-Milson committees with which Howell was so closely involved, it was reporting evidence collected in the late 1960s. When finally published in 1972 – and with its findings supported by more up-to-date local studies – it touched all the service's long-standing sensitivities. Thus, two of its conclusions were that 'the prevalence of attachment among young people has not

changed markedly since at least the later 1940s'; and that (though with some relevant organisations not covered) the overall attendance figure may have fallen to 26 per cent. It also exposed the service's continuing limitations in reaching and engaging some high priority groups and in holding on to older young people.

The Keele research did something to blur the lines of the debate about the needy or dangerous souls lost to the youth service (see Chapter 6). It, for example, traced a life cycle of membership which confirmed that during their adolescence many young people moved between the categories of attachment and unattachment. It also demonstrated that, even while members, young people's motivation varied considerably. This depended, for example, on how far any young person was prepared to survive the 'stick' of commitment and discipline in order to win the 'carrot' of enjoyable programmes and activities. Significantly in the context of the cultural gap which the service needed to bridge, much depended too on how far her or his expectation for some extension of personal power and meaningful self-image was met by the organisation. Only a minority, it seemed, fully and unconditionally embraced the values of the organisations they joined, and it was they who usually ended up as committee members or junior leaders.

Among policy-makers, however, unattachment was rarely discussed in such sophisticated terms. For them it was the cruder number crunching which made its impact, generating anxieties which clearly, for example, informed those sponsoring the youth service bills. All of these thus sought specifically to charge LEAs simply with setting up 'projects directed to assisting young people who are not members of any recognised youth groups'.

... and the delinquent

As Howell's comments above show, the line between the unattached and the delinquent continued to be highly permeable. In addition, as over the decade the newer incarnations of the old bogeys came to strut the public stage, the range of suitable cases for youth service treatment was extended. Whether these assumed the shape of football hooligan or out-of-control truant or drug-taker, it was only a matter of time before dealing with them, the perceived threat they posed or the ravages they were wreaking on society were added to the service's remit.

This anyway was the period when the forms of intermediate treatment (IT) required by the 1969 Children and Young Person's Act came on stream. Systematic efforts were made to draw youth workers into these – for example, through local conferences and via the work of YSIC/NYB. In 1973 the latter set up its youth social work unit which gave a high priority to bridging the youth work-IT divide. It also published two *Youth Service* IT specials (in 1973 and 1977) and in 1974 compiled a report giving 'a frank assessment of (IT's) progress to date'.

Overall, however, the service resisted this more extreme version of targeting, though less, it seemed, because it objected to the principle of selectivity as such and more

because of a perceived threat to its core commitment to voluntary participation by young people. Its stand was helped indirectly by the courts' own scepticism about the new form of 'treatment' being offered to young offenders, even if this was for some rather different reasons. Even so, the service remained anxious about the threatened growth, topsy-fashion, of an alternative youth service within the new, supposedly community-oriented, social services departments. (In 1979, for example, CYSA referred to IT's development as 'separate – and piecemeal'.)

The NABC report on its five-year intermediate treatment project, published in 1979, in fact revealed that many of its affiliated clubs gave IT a very low priority. It therefore called for more attention to be paid to the needs of young people at risk or in trouble and to training leaders to deal with the specialised needs of those young people. Even then, however, if some deep-seated youth service attitudes were to be shifed, this seemed too little too late. By the time the new Conservative administration began to translate its hard-line law-and-order manifesto commitments into policy and provision in the early 1980s, the possibility of a systematic youth service role within IT seemed barely recognised.

And now – drugs ...

Some specific, often newly fashionable, deviancies did, however, grab the service's attention over the decade. One of these was the growing use of drugs by young people. Though on occasion this included a focus on smoking and alcohol, most of the wider publicity was concerned with illegal drug-taking. Often sensationally, this was treated as self-evidently subversive for the society as well as destructive to the individual. In some areas it therefore became a major concern for youth workers and their agencies, creating in the process a new special target group for the youth service defined by its deviancy. As early as 1970, for example, *Youth Service* carried articles for practitioners on *The Young Drug User*.

The service was not taken over completely by moral panic, however, as it struggled for perspectives which acknowledged the two-way processes at work between young people and the wider society. Thus *Youth Scene*, which was aimed partly at young people, led its April 1973 issue with the banner headline: 'DOPE LEGALISED?'. The piece which followed detected 'recent suggestions made at Parliamentary level' that 'renewed efforts are to be made to remove the stigma presently attached to the smoking of the controversial drug'. In 1978 it again raised similar issues under a headline: 'Pot law creates criminals.'

... homelessness ...

Homelessness, too, concentrated minds from early in the decade, and especially after the public outcry following the television documentary in 1975, *Johnny Go Home*. Some youth service organisations sought to respond early. In 1971, for example, the Youth Development Trust in Manchester won grants from both the Gulbenkian Foundation and the government's Urban Aid programme to extend its city-centre work with 'young drifters'.

These led in 1977 to two reports, published by YDT itself and by NYB. The former described an experimental housing support scheme for young people using youth work approaches; the latter suggested that detached youth work could be very effective in reaching and supporting young homeless people. By the mid-1970s, too, a special advice and support agency, GALS, had appeared in London, targeting young women coming to London on their own and without accommodation.

Homelessness did not feature only as a practice issue for the service, however. In the autumn of 1973, *Youth Service* devoted a whole issue to a 'problem ... (which) has been around for a very long time – a perennial crisis, one might call it'. Its lead article on *The Youth Service and the Housing Problem* damned the service for its 'appalling' complacency, was critical of its failure to grasp the implications of young people's changing lifestyles, and argued that it 'should be concerned, *must* be concerned, to play a vital role in this field'. (Emphasis in the original.)

Perhaps in part as a response to this kind of critique, by the following year 'the development of ways of providing accommodation/support for homeless and rootless single young people' appeared on the list of subject areas to be supported by the new NCVYS/DES experimental projects programme. A clause to guarantee housing to homeless young people appeared in all four of the youth service bills while in 1976 a Department of Health and Social Security Working Group report identified the youth service as potentially an important source of advice and information for homeless young people.

In 1977, NCVYS published its own report which showed that youth homelessness was a national and not just a London problem and that it placed many young people at serious risk. An (unsuccessful) campaign to get young people recognised as a priority group for rehousing in the 1977 Housing Act also drew in some youth service interests. During 1978 the Parliament Youth Affairs Lobby addressed the issue at one of its meetings while at the end of the decade BYC was seeking to keep up the pressure through an examination of the needs and vulnerability of the young single homeless.

... and above all unemployment

The youth 'deviancy' which from the mid-1970s thrust itself most forcibly into the youth service's consciousness was unemployment, producing some startling shifts in thinking and action. At the start of the decade, the service bothered itself very little with young people's involvement in the labour market. When it did, its top-down focus was on their incessant (and unacceptable) job changing; or, bottom-up, on the highly exploitative nature of much of the work young people did. At the decade's end, the question which, it seemed, just could not be ducked was: how could young people be helped into a job – *any* job? Or, if no job could be found, how best could this reality be disguised by inserting them into a special programme with training in its title?

With each of the recessions of the 1960s leaving a bigger residue of young people stranded outside the labour market, anxieties about creeping youth unemployment had begun to appear even in the early 1970s. Indeed, governments of both main parties at the time were sufficiently concerned about the overall state of the UK labour market to support the creation of the MSC as a brand new quango specifically designed to improve labour supply and raise skill levels.

Even so, against a background of three decades of all-party commitment to full employment, the surge in youth unemployment from the mid-1970s left policy makers rushing to catch up with events – and never quite succeeding. In 1974, only 3 per cent of 16-year-olds were without a job. By 1979 the proportion had risen to 11 per cent, including those who had been absorbed onto the government 'holding' measure, the Youth Opportunities Programme (YOP). Another five years on and the equivalent figure was 38 per cent. Equally dramatic increases occurred in the numbers of older and long-term unemployed young people.

NAYC was one of the first youth organisations to take the issue seriously. In July 1971 it made £500 available from its own funds to help coordinate work with the young unemployed. The following October, to provide a national focus on youth unemployment, it brought together a working party, chaired by John Ewen, which included representatives of youth service and prestigious non-youth service organisations such as the Confederation of British Industries (CBI). By 1975 this had been converted into a Standing Conference on Youth Unemployment. The influence of this group was indicated the following year when MSC chair, Sir Richard O'Brien, acknowledged that its proposals had 'proved very useful to us in clarifying our thinking' about a newly announced work experience programme for young people.

Undoubtedly, however, NAYC's greatest coup came in December 1971 when it won a £500,000 government grant to run a one-year pilot for a new scheme, Community Industry. This was to provide education and environmental and community work for unemployed and unqualified 16 to 18-year-olds in England, Wales and Scotland. By May 1972, operating in eight areas of high unemployment, it was two-thirds of the way towards its target of recruiting 600 young people who were facing 'particular difficulties in getting and keeping jobs'. From these small beginnings, and with considerable support from the press, the TUC, the CBI and local authorities as well as other voluntary organisations, the scheme repeatedly had its life and scope extended and its funding increased until it was receiving the largest grant ever given to a voluntary youth organisation. Its political profile also remained high with announcements of its expansion invariably coming through ministerial statements in Parliament including, in 1976, as part of Denis Healey's budget speech.

Once the real youth unemployment crisis struck, other youth service interests also responded. Within the wider political activity described earlier, this included considerable lobbying by NYB, NAYCEO, CYSA and (particularly while Peter

Mandelson was chair) by BYC. This included supporting the establishment of Youthaid in 1977, organising a national rally for the young unemployed in 1981 and exerting pressure through the Youth Affairs Lobby. After at least one earlier failure, in 1978 NYB also finally persuaded the MSC to fund a Youth Opportunities Development Unit whose brief was to provide information and advice on social education and youth work to those working with unemployed young people.

Underpinning this activity at national level was a mushrooming of grass roots initiatives. At the very least clubs and centres opened their doors to unemployed young people during the day to create drop-ins which, though acting as holding operations, often offered few develop-mental opportunities. As the unemploy-ment statistics soared, more strategic responses also built up. The YMCA set up Youth at Work and Training for Life schemes. The Community Development Foundation built on its early YVFF work in areas where youth unemployment had been high for years to set up its own YOP schemes using MSC funding. So too did other voluntary organisations such as NABC, the Methodist Youth Department, NCVYS as well as many statutory youth services, sometimes on a grand scale.

As youth unemployment became another of the decade's moral panics, policy-makers came to see voluntary service by young people as an increasingly attractive way to fill the time of this newly 'leisured' class. Both YVFF and Community Service Volunteers as well as a wide range of more local organisations had continued to encourage it in its more conventional forms, making much, for example, of their close links with schools. However, advocates of the more radical (even compulsory) option of national/voluntary service also began again to raise their voices. Alec Dickson, CSV's inspiration, was 'murmuring' about the need for this early as 1972. In 1975, providing a variation on the theme, Anthony Steen, first director of YVFF and now a Conservative MP, pressed that young people should be allowed to take up community work in return for dole money. By November 1979 the Lords were past mincing their words as they debated a motion calling for 'a universal and compulsory scheme … for all young people after leaving school'.

Ultimately, however, these proved to be sideshows to the main event: the rise and rise of the MSC. Throughout the late 1970s and well into the 1980s the MSC remained the government's supercharged vehicle for tackling youth unemployment. Its growth, certainly until Thatcher's third election victory in 1987, seemed unstoppable. By then its budget was £2,000 million and forecast to climb to £3,000 million – more than double what central government was committing to the country's universities. Its target for the Youth Training Scheme (YTS) which replaced YOP was half-a-million school leavers – plus another half million young unemployed to be recruited on to its Community Programme. Directly and indirectly, it was employing another half-a-million people to run its programmes. One analyst of its impact concluded that:

> On its patronage depended a vast voluntary sector running multifarious programmes without which youth and community work would have collapsed in many areas. In many places north of Watford the MSC was the biggest local employer. In others more and more statutory local authority services were coming to depend on its support.

Strains within the youth service began to show even before 1979. A 1976 leader in *Youth Service* commented for example:

> The Manpower Services Commission to whom (the government) has given new funds is too monolithic to cash in on the immense goodwill towards the young unemployed which exists in the community. Despite being urged to take the voluntary organisation sector seriously, it has taken the MSC nearly a year to recognise the potential of voluntary community groups to provide valid alternative experiences for young people …

After Thatcher came to power, the tensions became more pronounced – though resistance to what the MSC was doing was if anything even less effective.

For the youth service the problems were of both style and values – and were deep-seated. For one thing, when organisations first became entangled, they were likely to presume that they were dealing with a public funding agency like any other – and that therefore ultimately they would be able to 'take the money and run'. In fact, MSC's funding regime was also almost always very short-term – sometimes as little as six months; it was highly prescriptive; and it was underpinned by determined efforts to monitor and keep in line those who were cashing in on its largesse. Often, too, for a small organisation particularly, its operation was dangerously erratic, with goal posts constantly being moved and apparently well-established programmes being aborted at very short notice.

The MSC effect went far beyond the material and the operational, however. It also uncompromisingly set the agendas. Though few economic analysts questioned that mass youth unemployment was the result of a collapse of demand for unskilled or even semi-skilled young workers, implicitly and sometimes explicitly MSC operated on a very different premise: that what had actually collapsed were the motivation and the capacities of the young. This interpretation resulted in a national strategy for reducing or eliminating youth unemployment which was in effect simply training, training, training.

Moreover this was defined in extremely restrictive, not to say mean-minded, ways. It was shaped particularly by the deficiency model of youth on which the MSC worked – its proposition that above all young workers lacked the personal skills and attitudes required by modern employers. This led it, at least initially, to insist that highly prescriptive forms of social and life skills training must be included in its schemes. As Bernard Davies pointed out at the time in an NYB pamphlet which seemed to touch a sensitive chord within the service, though the differences might appear to be merely semantic, such programmes conflicted in fundamental ways with the youth service's declared commitment to person-centred social education.

Notwithstanding such financial, organisational or philosophical pitfalls, youth service organisations became increasingly embroiled with the MSC. In part they were driven on by their anxiety to alleviate the effects of unemployment on so many young people. In part, too, however they saw the MSC as an irresistible source of funds for plugging the gaps left by cuts in their mainstream budgets. Even in the short-term these hopes turned out to be largely illusory. More seriously, in the mid-term some organisations were weakened or even de-stabilised as MSC money was withdrawn and the tactics and strategies required for winning more secure funding remained under-developed.

Initially the MSC was able to act with some degree of independence from government. Increasingly after 1979, however, it became a key instrument for implementing the tough economic and social policies on which Thatcher was insisting. In doing this in more and more hard-line ways, it asserted a definition of youth as a category – and not just for labour market purposes – as defective and in special need. It thus gave a powerful additional push to selectivity within the service's provision and approaches and in some places even undermined its principle of young people's voluntary engagement. Not only did many of the MSC's more restrictive and authoritarian assumptions thus penetrate deep into key areas of youth service thinking and planning until they became part of its commonsense beliefs. In the longer term, its high-pressured colonising style left the service even more confused and divided.

Targeting from below: Towards issue-based youth work

Targeting particular sections of the adolescent population did not emanate only from above, however. Sometimes (albeit unintentionally) reinforcing, sometimes contradicting these strategies were new practice and curricular priorities developed by practitioners – or, more accurately, by constituencies of youth workers who became increasingly articulate and assertive. Usually emanating from the wider liberation movements which emerged (or re-emerged) during the decade, they concentrated their efforts on those who were experiencing the variety of forms of discrimination and oppression still built deeply into British society. They thus injected into the service new perspectives on and approaches to work with young women, with Black and Asian young people and with disabled and (for the first time) gay and lesbian young people. To some extent, too, the needs of rural young people became a focus of such bottom-up pressure.

What follows deals with each of these groups separately. However, on the ground boundary lines could never be clear cut. In 1975, for example, one detached worker, reflecting on the priorities of her work with West Indian young women, emphasised the importance of helping them to gain a stronger sense of their Black history and identity and the need for their distinctive culture to be respected. Similarly, at the 1979 Women

Working with Young People conference, Black women workers defended their right to come together to share their own feelings of alienation by organising their own groups.

Working with girls and young women

As we saw in Chapter 4, at the start of the 1970s even a progressive perspective on work with girls still largely saw them as individuals who, though having many unrealised personal talents, were destined to play a range of 'given' gender roles. At the same time, unease was growing that girls were not just leaving the service early but becoming largely invisible even when they stayed within it. The 1972 OPCS study on who was – and was not – using the service provided some hard evidence on this. So too did the results of another survey done for the Fairbairn-Milson Report on one evening's attendance at 80 youth clubs. Carried out by the YSA's research officer this showed, for example, that:

- less than one-third of the attenders were girls;
- 70 per cent of clubs had 29 or fewer girls present (while only about 25 per cent had 29 or fewer boys); and
- under 3 per cent of clubs had 70 or more girls attending as compared with the 20 per cent of clubs with 70 or more boys.

Six years later, an article in the Inner London Education Authority's youth service newsletter was still drawing attention to the need for more provision for girls and was questioning whether the service's presuppositions about and approaches to them were appropriate.

By the end of the decade, both the terms of the debate on work with girls and young women and some of the priorities for practice had shifted radically. The growing number of women workers in the service, many explicitly identifying themselves as feminists, were increasingly starting from an analysis of women's oppression by men and the institutionalised nature of sexism. Their work thus sought to help young women clarify their collective as well as their individual identities and needs.

As one feminist youth worker noted in 1980, it took time for the impact of the women's movement to be felt: in the early 1970s it was only just re-emerging and still working out its directions. Indeed, at that stage mixed work was if anything becoming more entrenched as the dominant approach. In 1975, for example, the Guides and the Scouts set up a joint working group to consider the integration of their sections for older young people. Though rejecting the proposal, the Guides nonetheless continued to highlight 'help (for) each individual member to develop as a whole person' as well as the 'endless opportunities' the Guides were providing for 'social contact between the sexes'. For their part, the Scouts proceeded to draw up plans to 'mix' the Venture Scouts, their units for older young people.

Nonetheless the Guides' stand may have been motivated by more than organisational defensiveness since by mid-decade, under the influence of a now resurgent women's movement, women workers were bringing overtly political attitudes and aspirations into the service. One expression of this perspective came in a

Youth Service article published early in 1975. It was written by Janet Hunt, then assistant to the director of youth work at NAYC and later, as Janet Paraskeva, director of NYB and the National Youth Agency (NYA). Her starting analysis, shared by many other women workers at the time, was unambiguous:

> Girls will become what we expect them to become. If we do not change our expectations they will remain restricted in opportunity, and so submissive and unfulfilled ... We have programmed girls to believe that they are naturally dependent and helpless, incapable, illogical, highly emotional and unbusinesslike.

She then went on to note Mary Robinson's 1960s definition of girls' roles (quoted in Chapter 4) as a 'budgeter, buyer, cook, dressmaker, interior decorator, nurse, voter, partner and mother' and her suggestion that girls needed separate 'home-making' activity groups. Hunt concluded:

> In the present climate of opinion we must take steps in the opposite direction giving both sexes plenty of opportunity to try out subjects usually restricted to one or the other ... Boys should be included in all domestic and caring subjects.

Within this developing conception of an alternative to mixed work was an even more prominent theme: the need for some separate provision for young women. Freedom from the pressures of male-dominated environments was seen as essential if teenage girls were to become more confident and more autonomous as women, gain greater control over their lives and extend their skills, especially into areas normally seen as exclusively male. Such objectives pointed to the need through their youth work for women youth workers to challenge dominant male assumptions about boys' activities and girls' activities and to ensure that young women were given some male-free space to develop themselves as young women.

The new approaches slowly inserted themselves into existing provision and programmes and generated some special projects. As they took hold, women workers began to create self-help support and development structures. In 1976 the students at Manchester Polytechnic announced that they were forming a Women in Youth Service Group which, they hoped, would 'be instrumental in changing sex role stereotypes which are reinforced in some traditional youth work approaches'. By early 1977 women working within NAYC had come together to arrange all-girl weekend conferences under the title Boys Rule Not OK. These were over-subscribed, had to be repeated – and attracted a double-page spread in *Scene*. They allowed young women to try out activities – motorbiking, canoeing, skateboarding, assault courses, karate, electronics – which 'girls are not supposed to be good at, without fear of being laughed at or labelled "unfeminine"'. Training courses for youth workers on work with girls followed – initially mixed though soon to become women-only.

Though often riven by sharp debates and indeed splits which reflected the wider divisions within the women's movement, by the second half of the decade a national infrastructure for girls' work was emerging

and a national profile being established. In 1977, NAYC created a specialist girls' work post. Articles appeared in the feminist periodical *Spare Rib* and in the *Times Educational Supplement* with the latter suggesting that 'the idea of separate youth work with girls (was) slowly gaining acceptance' and stressing 'the need for positive discrimination'. Local and regional groupings of women workers came into being, clubs and projects organised their own girls-only events, training materials were produced, beginners' guides published and videos made and circulated. In 1981, NAYC started a *Working With Girls Newsletter*.

These developments constantly encountered (at best) indifference and (at worst) outright opposition and obstruction not just from boys using the service, but no less intensely from male workers and officers. Often, the most basic resources were denied the work, including, for example, secure premises and part-time staffing. The women workers involved and the young women taking part were also frequently subject to serious and sometimes violent intimidation reminiscent of the way Scouting was greeted in some working-class areas 60 years before.

At policy-making levels these deeply entrenched interests revealed themselves from time to time in stark and unyielding ways. In 1977, for example, the Cheshire Association of Boys' Clubs was expelled from the NABC because it decided to reform itself as a county federation of youth clubs and register all its affiliated club members – girls as well as boys – with NAYC. A dispute within the London

Union of Youth Clubs (LUYC) which developed into a national *cause celebre* led in 1980 to its field officer, Val Marshall, being sacked because she was encouraging specialist and separate work with young women. LUYC's principal field officer at the time publicly acknowledged that he had taken over the production of the girls' page in the organisation's *Bulletin* because it 'had become too women's libbish and that it ought to be toned down'.

At the time the affair seemed to have all the hallmarks of a local conflict which had got out of hand as the old guard fought a desperate rearguard action to repel this new and threatening girls' work intruder. The opposite may have been true, however. With the 'radical right' in power and gathering itself for an ideological and political counter-attack against feminism, the LUYC confrontation perhaps could be read as marking the high water mark for girls' work as an organised movement.

From immigrant integration to Black consciousness

Feminism was not the only liberation movement during the 1970s to force the youth service into some uncomfortable rethinking, especially on how it focused its resources. A strengthening Black consciousness movement, particularly in the African-Caribbean and Asian populations, had a similar effect, driven by increasingly assertive and articulate Black and Asian responses to the racism within British society.

Throughout the 1970s evidence piled up of the often brutal discrimination being experienced by Black and Asian young people in the education, training and judicial systems and in the housing and labour markets. (One survey in North London as early as 1970 showed that young people of Caribbean origin were four times more likely than the national average to be unemployed.) On the streets, in wholly arbitrary ways, the 19th century 'sus' laws were criminalising more and more Black – and especially Caribbean – young people. This further deepened their resentment and alienation – and demonstrated an oppression not just of individuals but, systematically, of them a group.

Black and Asian young people resisted such treatment in a variety of personal ways. In 1976 it was a senior white officer of the Community Relations Commission (CRC) who noted:

> In the West Indian community there has been a revolt against shit work. Their (young people's) attitude is that the jobs with London Transport were what their parents came to do. It is not the right sort of work for them.

As always happened in groups as alienated as this, the alternative for some Black and Asian young people was indeed illegal activity or participation in the 'unofficial' economy.

Resistance went beyond the personal, however. During the 1970s, Black and Asian groups emerged, including within the youth service, which were increasingly confident of their collective identities and insistent on their own analysis of their problems and their right and ability to define their own solutions. As early as 1971 one study showed that high proportions of Black and Asian young people – in the case of young people of Caribbean origin, over 90 per cent – believed that a Black person 'should be prepared to fight for his rights as a Black man' (sic). In due course, such disaffection began to find more political forms of expression – not least, by the early 1980s, in riots in Bristol, Manchester and Liverpool as well as in a number of areas of London.

Though less violently, signs of this refusal to toe the 'white' line appeared in the youth service – for example, when young Black delegates at the Youth Charter 2000 conference in 1977 rejected the organisers' insistence on labelling them 'young immigrants' and objected to its superficial representation of Black young people and their concerns. It was evident, too, in their demand that they be allowed to present their statement of complaint to the conference themselves rather than having it read for them by the (white) chair.

No less significant was the request of the conference's only Black keynote speaker – the 'statutory Black', as she called herself – that she be allowed to read out the statement so that she could identify herself with it. For, by then, Black workers were coming together and organising politically, with the youth service's relatively flexible structures giving them some additional scope. In 1978 Black youth workers, critical of CYSA for failing to recognise the special needs of Black groups, formed themselves into a Black Youth and Community Workers Association (BYCWA). This prompted CYSA to organise a conference

on youth work in a multi-racial society and in due course to offer the new Association a formal role within its own structure. This was followed up in 1980 through a joint CYSA / Commission for Racial Equality working party and conference and an internal review by CYSA of its own positions and processes.

The core demand of a special discussion paper prepared by BYCWA for the CYSA conference was for more Black youth and community workers to work within Black communities – a position supported quite independently by a Labour Party Race Relations Action Group. To make sure this happened, BYCWA demanded, too, that routes to qualification be opened up. However, the paper also articulated the cultural and indeed class analysis out of which such demands were increasingly being developed:

> The social reality of Black people in British society ... (has) made it imperative that Black communities are served by peers appointed from and by their own socio-economic and ethnic groups. Added to this is the fact that when members of the white community are implanted as leaders, there is a lack of real cultural identity and any meaningful promotion of it.

The paper thus also assumed that Black young people and their communities needed to develop more indigenous provision which as far as possible would be under their own control – and that this should be publicly supported.

Even by the end of the 1970s British policy-makers were rarely ready to concede such a demand. With 'blaming-the-victim' explanations of Black and Asian people's difficulties still being widely adopted, any suggestion that the state and its educational and welfare services might actually be part of the problem continued to be blocked out. Indeed, in taken-for-granted ways, being Black was often still treated as if it were a 'defective' condition. The 1979 Skeet bill on the youth service, for example, followed all its predecessors by linking 'the special needs of young people who belong to ethnic minorities' with those of young people 'who suffer from mental and physical disabilities' and 'the young unemployed'.

Extensive reports on work in progress in *Youth Service* in the early 1970s also illustrated the hold of the dominant message of the YSDC's Hunt Report (published in 1967): that multi-racial provision was self-evidently the best option. Alternative, especially radical, prescriptions – such as those put forward by Gus John in the most comprehensive and critical if extremely dense analysis of Black youth work ever attempted – continued to be ignored, if not actually suppressed. Completed in 1976, it was not published until 1981 – and then only in a highly-filleted version and with a very restricted circulation.

Throughout the decade policy and provision for Black and Asian young people remained a sensitive and contested area for youth service decision-makers. Black and Asian groups and organisations continued to debate both analysis and prescriptions among themselves – often sharply and sometimes divisively. In time they came to exert just about enough

pressure to weaken the credibility and hold of the Hunt Report's purist integrationist strategy. Some establishment bodies, too, if only perhaps for pragmatic reasons, came to accept that Hunt could not be treated as the last word. With more and more Black and Asian young people voting with their feet in areas where Black and Asian populations were concentrated, a self-help (independent) voluntary sector established itself. It thus became increasingly difficult for the youth service, nationally and locally, not to recognise, support and sometimes even positively promote some separate provision.

As early as 1971, a DES report, *The Education of Immigrants*, was recording a widening range of practices in local authority youth services. These included, in one area, the spontaneous establishment of separate clubs and, in another, the deliberate introduction of an 'immigrants only' evening in one centre – though still, it was admitted, with the intention of 'leading members into multi-racial activities on the other nights'. Such trends were confirmed by, for example, a Bedford-shire Education Committee report which recommended, also in 1971, that financial support be given to Black and Asian groups. By the end of the decade the Home Office was ruling that the term 'immigrant' was no longer appropriate in applications for funding for work with ethnic minorities which were being run under yet another of its special programmes – Section 11 of the 1966 Local Government Act.

On what was by then one of the most pressing political as well as social issues of the day, the DES's 1975 discussion paper

Provision for Youth had virtually nothing to say. It confined itself to token comments on the need to 'take account of the special needs of ethnic minorities' and on the service's 'present valuable work with young immigrants'. However, by 1977 NYB, through a leader in *Youth in Society*, was declaring the Hunt doctrine 'somewhat unreal, if not irrelevant'. Even more significantly, in 1980 the CRC published *The Fire Next Time*, an influential report on the condition of (and the potentially violent threat from) Black young people in the inner cities. This explicitly recommended that special provision be made for young people from ethnic minorities. It also urged that full support be given to existing self-help Black groups.

The 1970s did not resolve the struggle over youth service provision for Black and Asian young people: the service was of course too much part of the structures by which so many of them were being oppressed for this ever to have been possible. Nonetheless, some balances were tipped and the ground for that struggle somewhat shifted. This happened above all because within parts of the service, if only for reasons of self-interest among those holding the power, some Black definitions of the problems and their solutions at least partially had to be accepted into youth service discourse and into its planning processes.

From handicap to disability

The 1970s opened with the promise of a major shift in national policy for disabled people: the enactment of the 1970 Chronically Sick and Disabled Persons Act, introduced as a private member's bill by Alf Morris. Writing in 1974 in an issue of *Youth Service* devoted entirely to work with disabled young people, Morris – by then minister for the disabled in the new Labour Government – summed up his objective in one word: integration. (Paradoxically in this context this was the new – though far from uncontested – progressive policy objective which was intended to retrieve disabled people from their highly marginalised position in society.) With the Act requiring local authorities 'to make recreational and educational facilities (available) outside the home', its implications for the youth service were clear.

Within the education field, the Act was reinforced in 1978 by the Warnock Committee Report on provision for what it called 'children with special needs'. This started from the principle that, though approaches and methods might vary, the purposes and goals of education were the same for all children. It too therefore contributed to an overall policy climate in which the service was operating which defined as less and less acceptable barriers to personal development imposed by 'handicap'.

Changes in language became important signifiers of this overall shift. In 1969, for example, even a pioneering organisation like Manchester's Youth Development Trust took it for granted that, in publishing what turned out to be an influential pamphlet on local services for the disabled, its title should be *Young and Physically Handicapped*. By 1974, however, one of the contributors to the *Youth Service* special issue, Paul Hunt, was describing himself as 'physically impaired' and, like most of the others contributing to the issue, adopted the term 'disablement' throughout. This for him seemed to flow logically from his call for a 'shift from an *individual* to a *social* interpretation of disability', on the grounds that '*social* deprivations (are) imposed on top … (of) people's actual individual impairments'. (Emphases in the original.)

In developing his arguments, Hunt also made explicit links with wider 1970s liberation perspectives. His starting point was that 'disabled people are today becoming much more conscious of, and angry about, the grossly restricted lives many of us have to live'. And he went on to suggest that:

> What seems to be happening is the kind of process we are already familiar with in, for example, race relations in this country. The trend is towards the deprived group coming to take more control over its own destiny, deciding its own priorities, and criticising the paternalism of the past … Leaders are emerging who can lay claim both to personal experience of disability and to a closer relationship with other disabled people than the spokesmen and spokeswomen of the past.

On the basis of this kind of analysis he concluded that 'disabled people are today making a plea – or demand – for integration', with many young people, including in clubs and social events, struggling to achieve this 'no matter what the hurts and rebuffs and practical problems'.

Like most other state, or indeed voluntary sector, services, in seeking to apply such ideas the youth service was starting from a long way back. Unintegrated provision remained dominant – indeed, it continued to grow. The Federation of Gateway Clubs, relying mainly on its 4,000 volunteer helpers, was still the largest grouping of clubs for the 'severely retarded'. It had a membership in 1974 of 18,000 young people in over 300 clubs which within two years had risen to 20,000 young people in 350 clubs. The National Elfrida Rathbone Society, working with 'educationally handicapped children', was also expanding and, by 1969–70, had 38 affiliated clubs run by over 200 volunteers and serving 1,000 young people.

However, early in the decade both these organisations were making some early pre-emptive gestures to the new philosophy of integration. In 1971 – the year it affiliated to SCNVYO – the Elfrida Rathbone Society carried out a survey of special schools which revealed that, though only a minority ran clubs, many said they preferred to put their energies into encouraging their pupils to join Scout and Guide troops and local youth clubs. The national development officer of the Gateway Clubs made it clear in 1972 that:

> Ideally it is our plan to … gradually withdraw our special club supportive facilities from those who are ready to become members of ordinary youth clubs and pass them onto other groups.

This move towards integration was demonstrated, too, by the continuing development and raised profile of the PHAB (Physically Handicapped Able

Bodied) movement. In 1973 it received one of the first grants (£6,000) in the DES's programme to encourage experimental work by voluntary organisations. The money was to be used to employ a training and development officer 'to further ... integration in the field of leisure pursuits'. By then, too, with over 100 affiliated clubs, it was beginning to operate on the presumption that the restrictions placed by decision-makers on the education, career training and social opportunities of disabled people made disability 'a social handicap'.

Mainstream youth service organisations also started to anticipate the new progressive ideology. In 1973, for example, the Scouts produced a guide to scouting for disabled young people At its 1974 annual conference the National Youth Assembly, the umbrella organisation for local youth councils, noted 'with great disgust' the inaction of local authorities in providing for the disabled. Two years later the Yorkshire and Humberside region of NAYCEO gave a special working party the remit of considering how obstacles to integrating disabled young people into youth service projects and programmes could be overcome. By then too Merseyside Youth Association had got Urban Aid funding for a full-time field worker to work with the disabled and in Sheffield one club was reported as making an all-out attempt to integrate disabled young people into its mainstream programme.

By the time the United Nation's International Year of the Disabled got under way in 1981 integration was being identified within NYB's monthly

periodical, *Youth in Society*, as 'the key to improved opportunities in education, employment, leisure and social activities' for the disabled. However, despite the specific examples of youth service progress towards this goal, considerable evidence remained of how slow and piecemeal this was overall. In discussions and reports, the term 'handicapped' remained common, if not dominant. A survey of one local authority's provision concluded that many mainstream clubs and organisations were still doubtful about getting disabled young people involved and even the ones that tried often did not cater for them adequately. This was true too of some of the major specialist providers. In its evidence to the Warnock Committee, for example, the Federation of Gateway Clubs rejected integration as inappropriate to its situation on the grounds that previous attempts to introduce mentally handicapped young people into 'normal' youth clubs had rarely been successful.

The few disabled young people who did use the youth service were thus still doing so within separate facilities housed in often inappropriate premises and relying on shoe-string resources and too few staff. The tiny minority who had found their way into mainstream provision would largely have been there by accident, would hardly have been integrated into what it had to offer – yet would be unlikely to have been receiving much attention to their special needs.

Despite some broader shifts towards integration in work with the disabled, the service thus achieved nothing like a strategic change of direction. In all four of the youth service bills there was no more than a token mention of 'young people who suffer from mental or physical disabilities' and the need to include them within the schemes local authorities would have been required to prepare. The 1975 DES discussion paper lumped its one word mention of the handicapped into a section on the 'homeless, ill-housed, isolated, unemployed and otherwise at risk'. It also labelled them all as young people 'who are demonstrably disadvantaged'. The Youth Service Forum, though not surviving long enough to give them detailed consideration, had nothing to say specifically about disabled young people – despite its attempt to clarify what it meant by 'variation of need' among young people. Nor, it seems, did the Parliamentary Youth Affairs Lobby even though, as part of its regular meetings with MPs, it did focus their attention on the unemployed, the homeless, sexism in the service and even gay and lesbian young people.

Even allowing for some impressive breakthroughs locally and by individual projects, within the youth service overall at the end of the 1970s 'disabled liberation' remained as far off as ever.

From the closet to collective action: Responses to gay and lesbian young people

Following the limited decriminalisation of homosexuality in 1967, gays and lesbians in Britain extended the social networks which they had been developing during the 1960s into more political forms of collective action. These were influenced by the American gay and lesbian organisation, Stonewall, as well as by the Black and women's liberation movements. In 1970 the Gay Liberation Front (GLF) drew in both gay men and lesbians. Two years later the Committee for Homosexual Equality (CHE), which by then had 2,000 members and 60 local groups, took the significant step of becoming a campaign.

Despite continuing tensions and frequent splits, collectively and cumulatively the activism of these groups forced gay and lesbian issues out into the open and even onto some public policy agendas. Here, too, in some places youth work provided a relatively 'liberal' space for critical analysis and some progressive action. The youth service was thus one area of provision which was forced, albeit in restricted ways and often kicking and screaming, to start to think 'gay and lesbian' in its policy development and in its practice.

Some tiny chinks in the service's unthinking heterosexist front were just about detectable in the first half of the decade. In 1974 the NCVYS/DES experimental projects were opened up to proposals 'to meet the social needs of homosexual young people'. Later that year a *Youth Scene* article on adolescent suicide – even then a focus of considerable concern within and without the service – noted that one of the questions raised daily by young people contacting the Samaritans was: 'Are homosexual feelings normal at my age?' At about this time, too, *Youth in Society's* Current Awareness Digest began to list publications aimed at gay and lesbian young people, including one published by GLF on *Growing up Homosexual*. One of its 1976 issues also carried an article made up entirely of a conversation among gay and lesbian young people.

In time some youth organisations – very cautiously – began to respond to this changing climate. At the end of 1976 a NCVYS report on young people and homosexuality recorded some of the problems faced by gay and lesbian young people – and the failure of most youth workers to respond to the estimated 50,000 gay and lesbian young people using youth facilities. Though stopping short of proposing changes to NCVYS's own policies, it made broad recommendations for wider improvements. NAYC got into trouble with the popular press in 1977 for responding to a fake letter from a 14-year-old girl to its magazine *Youth Clubs* by suggesting that she might be lesbian. By 1980 a diocesan youth officers' report, published by the General Synod of the Church of England, felt able to concede that 'homosexual relationships should be judged according to the same criteria as heterosexual ones'.

Few if any of these reflections on the position and needs of gay and lesbian young people were simply sparked by spontaneous combustion. By 1976 gay and lesbian youth workers were starting, not just to come out, but to organise. The newly formed Gay Workers Group launched a Sexual Awareness in the Youth Service Campaign (SAYS) and immediately began also to press for CYSA recognition. With five SAYS activists at its April 1977 annual conference, CYSA formally agreed

to do what it claimed it had been doing on a case-by-case basis for some time already – support gay and lesbian workers experiencing discrimination.

Closely linked to these developments was the creation, also in 1976, of the London Gay Teenage Group (LGTG) and of the Gay Youth group in the Merseyside area. These were followed three years later by the National Joint Council for Gay Teenagers (JCGT), set up to help gay and lesbian youth groups develop and establish contacts with each other nationwide. It produced two pamphlets, one of which – a response to a Home Office working paper on the age of consent in relation to sexual offences – acted as the focus for its presentation to the Parliamentary Youth Affairs Lobby in August 1980. Among other proposals it called for a reduction in the age of consent for homosexual sex to 16, a position which had also been adopted by an NAYC young members' conference the previous year.

By 1977 the London Union of Youth Clubs had affiliated the LGTG. However, it was its application for registration as a youth organisation to the Inner London Education Authority (ILEA) which most sharply brought into focus the youth service's deeply entrenched homophobic attitudes – to say nothing of the limitations of some of its more liberal ones. It also illustrated just how bruising the struggle was going to be to get responsive work with gay and lesbian young people firmly established within the youth service mainstream. The application itself prompted an unusually painstaking testing of the water by the ILEA which took a full year to complete. Eventually it did empower area youth committees to judge applications from gay and lesbian groups by the criteria used to vet all applications – a not insignificant advance. However, by delegating responsibility in this way the ILEA's own Youth Committee avoided making its own public stand on what was by then a very hot public issue.

In fact, by then the increasingly organised and vocal activity of gay and lesbian groups was provoking considerable and powerful resistance. During the ILEA's consultations on the LGTG's application, the Metropolitan Police expressed its reservations and one of the high-profile moral crusading bodies of the time, the Festival of Light, made clear its outright opposition.

Most unbending on the issue, however, was the NABC. In 1979 its sought to provide an objective rationale for a position which, certainly as revealed by the public statements of some of its most respected workers and organisers, was underpinned by a virulent homophobia. It suggested, for example, that segregating gay and lesbian young people would 'deepen their sense of isolation from the mainstream of young people'. It also argued that, at a stage when 'youngsters are not completely sexually oriented', they would be exposed 'to the influence of the more adult homosexual who sometimes proves quite militant'. For them to grow into 'well adjusted adults and parents', the NABC believed, they needed to be involved in 'the balanced, lively atmosphere of a boys' or youth club'. Two years later, the NABC's general secretary who

had fronted this campaign made his own underlying attitudes quite explicit when he talked of 'deviant or unnatural sex' which could not be accepted or condoned.

The NABC's views were certainly challenged – by, for example, CYSA through a leader in its monthly magazine *Rapport*, by the Islington and Camden Women Youth Workers' Group and by the chief executive of NAYC. According to a CHE survey on voluntary youth organisations' responses to the 1976 NCVYS report, others including the Salvation Army and the British Council of Churches Youth Unit were at least open to consider a more sympathetic response to specialist work with gay and lesbian young people.

However, as the CHE follow-up survey also revealed, NABC was simply going public with views which many other organisations held just as fiercely and in an equally unreconstructed form. The Scouts, for example, saw the NCVYS report as 'unhelpful and biased … (it) did great harm to the work of NCVYS'. The campaigners talked about 'the real myth of homosexual' being 'the increasing propaganda that such practice is "normal" and acceptable'. Though supportive of the LGTG's campaign for ILEA registration, the Association for Jewish Youth reflected that 'the position in Jewish law of homosexuals is not a happy one'. As the chair of CHE pointed out, though the survey responses showed some progress:

> *… many (organisations) just make respectable noises, denying prejudice but actually doing nothing at all about discussing the issues, let alone actively helping young gays … This survey …*

underlines just how much further we and they have to go.

A lengthy correspondence in CYSA's monthly journal *Rapport* showed just how deeply entrenched in the service (including in sections of the full-time workforce) these views were. A number of its members, including some who were openly gay, argued strongly in favour of work in support of gay and lesbian young people. One, however, hammered home where for many the argument was starting. The unashamed slogan should be, he suggested: 'Minorities – yes; Deviates – NO.'

Rural young people: The missing target

As the economic prospects of the 1970s worsened, political minds became ever more sharply concentrated on the highly visible – and threatening – consequences for the inner cities and the urban council estates. As a result, rural young people largely remained off policy-makers' target lists. As one principal youth officer for a rural county noted in 1975, the Salter Davies report on the problems of rural youth work, produced for YSDC 12 years before, 'could be given reasonable marks for endeavour but not many marks for rousing enthusiasm or creating any sense of urgency'. Even at the end of the decade, in outlining the factors indicating 'consider-able variation of need' among young people, the Youth Service Forum's report on resources had nothing to say on the way in which where young people lived contributed to their disadvantaged status.

Nonetheless, over the decade campaigners working in rural areas gathered and

generated their own evidence on rural young people's deprivation which in due course had some impact on practice and policy. This showed that, like their urban counterparts, young people in rural communities were finding it harder to get jobs – and often in contexts where, with mass youth unemployment unknown or invisible, the unemployed were 'almost seen as lepers'. Even when employment was available, their choices were limited, not least by poor transport. In addition they had to contend with deteriorating medical, educational, recreational and shopping facilities and restricted housing options so that more and more of them (including many of those with the potential to be community leaders) were looking for routes out. All this was happening at a time when the overall perception shaping political attitudes and national policy was, still, of the countryside as the rural idyll – even while young people themselves were labelling it 'a real dump'.

These conditions, and especially the social isolation, inevitably impacted on the availability and use of youth service facilities. On the basis of a small sample, one study early in the decade suggested that over 60 per cent of youth club attenders gave up as soon as they left school. Usually this happened, it seemed, because as one young man put it: 'It's not much cop walking two miles in the wet to play ping-pong with the vicar!'

In the second half of the decade, workers, researchers and planners began in earnest to develop grassroots ways of enabling some of these young people to escape from these doldrums. Less conventional approaches – detached youth work, schemes to encourage youth volunteering, counselling projects – were adapted for rural situations. Broader strategies were defined which, as well as providing for direct work with young people, included political activity and organisational work – for example, to get access to school transport and 'draw in additional volunteers for less conventional activities'. Some workers also constructed support networks to offset their own isolation which 'brings with it the dangers of degeneration and repression of professional standards'.

Perhaps most significantly, however, those committed to developing rural youth work began to campaign nationally for more resources and more provision. At its annual conference in 1978, CYSA passed a motion expressing 'concern about the lack of provision for young people in rural areas'. In supporting the motion, a former Derbyshire youth worker deliberately sought to tap into the sensitivities of his urban colleagues, perhaps indicating in the process how some of the ideas of the new liberationist movements might be quietly driving this new activism:

> The CYSA and its members have always shown considerable concern for minority groups. However, I now wish to make a bid for a significant minority group which to date has received little attention. That group is young people living in rural areas.

This appeal, which came with a proposal that CYSA put pressure on local authorities through its branches, was being made soon after an NAYC national conference on rural youth work, *Not so Rosy*. This produced a Campaign for Rural Youth (CRY), linked to

a research project at Hull University. By late 1979 this was sufficiently developed to enable young people to give a series of three-minute accounts of their experience of rural living to the Parliamentary Youth Affairs Lobby. CRY also presented the lobby MPs with a paper, *Missed the Bus*, written by Michael Akehurst – soon to become director of an NAYC Rural Youthwork Education Project – whose demands were unambiguously political. These included:

- extending existing funding provision for youth work to cover rural projects;
- reviewing European funding arrangements with a view to setting up a rural fund;
- appointing a Parliamentary select committee to examine rural policies;
- recognising rural disadvantage within rate support grant allocations to local authorities; and
- within MSC programmes, making provision for the rural unemployed for travel costs and for setting up small workshop schemes.

By 1980, Akehurst was able to talk of 'the recent snowballing concern for rural youth work' which, he added, 'for youth workers based in the inner city … must seem strange'. As at the start of the 1980s, however, it was less clear whether this emerging concern could be converted into targeted policies which placed rural young people on a more equal footing with inner-city youth and gave them a greater chance of breaking out of their rural traps.

Demand-led versus issue-based work?

Though this applied perhaps least of all to rural youth work developments, much of the impetus for the targeting from below which occurred during the 1970s was influenced by wider self-help campaigning groups and organisations which were aiming to win greater equality and power for themselves. The result was, often overlapping, movements within the service intent on combating the sustained discrimination and oppression experienced by particular groups of young people. If provision for them was to be extended, this was usually seen as inevitably requiring that a challenge be mounted to the attitudes and actions of those who held power and controlled resources within the service and beyond.

Increasingly, these movements had a wider impact. They alerted a broader range of workers not just to the demands of oppressed groups but also to how workers' own prejudicial attitudes and oppressive behaviour as well as those of young people with whom they were working needed to be tackled. Uncomfortable questions then followed about how these had become institutionalised within the organisations for which they were working. These growing – and hardening – insights drew some workers into focusing more of their work on these issues – even to making responses to them their professional and curricular *raison d'etre*. What is more, such tensions sometimes occurred (or at least were seen by others to be occurring) at the expense of commitments – even as an oppositional alternative – to more demand-led social educational curricula directly or indirectly defined by the needs and interests of the young people they were actually working with.

No less than its top-down versions, these bottom-up issue-based conceptions of targeting thus bequeathed another potential source of internal tension – even conflict to a youth service which was anyway struggling to clarify for itself a coherent identity and agreed direction for future development.

Main references

Patrick Ainley and Mark Corney, *Training for the Future: The Rise and Fall of the Manpower Services Commission*, Cassell, 1990

Margaret Bone and Elizabeth Ross, *The Youth Service and Similar Provision for Young People*, HMSO, 1972

Val Carpenter, 'Working with girls', *Spare Rib*, May 1980

HMI, *Responsive Youth Work: The Youth Service and Urgent Social Needs*, DES, 1990

Janet Hunt, 'Introduction: Girls – A fair deal?', *Youth Service*, January / February 1975

Paul Hunt, 'The Changing Face of Disablement' *Youth Service*, July / August 1974

Tony Jeffs and Mark Smith, *Young People, Inequality and Youth Work*, MacMillan, 1990

John Springhall, *Youth, Empire and Society*, Croom Helm, 1977

Lincoln Williams, *Partial Surrender: Race and Resistance in the Youth Service*, The Falmer Press, 1988

Youth Service Forum, *Resources for the Youth Service*, NYB, 1979

8 Losing Direction – and Identity

Beyond emergency training: Two years – or three?

One of the few policy areas on which the Fairbairn-Milson Report's recommendations had a lasting effect was qualifying training for full-time workers. Yet even here it paid the price for taking so long to complete its work. With the life of the National College for the Training of Youth Leaders (set up in 1960 in the wake of the Albemarle Report) guaranteed only until 1971, decisions had to be taken out of synch with the rest of the review. A substantial draft *HMI Memorandum* rehearsing all the arguments for change and the direction this should take was circulating within the DES as early as July 1967. This was followed in April 1968 by a 'confidential' consultative paper whose content quickly became known and was widely discussed and which was eventually reproduced virtually word for word in *Youth and Community Work in the '70s*. By the time this appeared it therefore had little hard news or views on training to deliver to the service.

Nonetheless, the outcomes were of considerable long-term significance. Taking as its starting point the presumption that the Newsom Report would inspire major youth work-oriented shifts in secondary education, the report argued

for easier access for youth workers into teaching as well as for a stronger training link between youth workers and community centre wardens. It also concluded that one-year qualifying courses allowed too little time for improving 'reflective capacities' or the 'basic intellectual skills' demanded by the tasks of the service – that is, the professional skills which Albemarle and 1960s' trainers had so strongly endorsed. It therefore confirmed its 'general agreement' with 'steps already taken by the Department' (the DES) and 'much of the thinking behind them'. Above all, it concurred with the decision to introduce two-year courses from September 1970.

On only one issue did the committee seek, albeit tentatively, to stretch its proposals beyond the DES-imposed boundaries: the majority of its members chose 'to regard the two-year course as an interim step towards the establishment of a three-year course when the resources are available'. Against the background of what was happening elsewhere, especially to teacher training, to have done any less would have risked leaving youth and community work completely out in the cold. From 1969, for example, all graduates were for the first time to be required to undertake training in order to gain qualified teacher status. The whole basis of training teachers was anyway about to come under the very thorough scrutiny of the James Report, published in early 1972. Among other radical recommendations, this sought to point the way to the conversion of teaching into an all-graduate profession – a proposal which by the end of the 1970s was being discussed in terms less of whether than of when it should happen.

Denis Howell – whose commitment to the youth service for well over a decade stands out as exceptional among politicians – was later very open about his regret at not pressing harder for three-year youth and community work training:

> We listened to the silent voices of the Treasury telling us that we couldn't go from one year to three years overnight. Probably wrongly, but realistically, we decided to go to two years.

However, as 'a first step … to a full three-year course', this turned out to be another Fairbairn-Milson aspiration which remained unrealised until during the 1990s, almost by the backdoor, the qualifying courses began to turn out graduates whose professional and academic training was taking three years.

On training, the YSDC report from then on contented itself with discussing desirable course content and how this could be attuned to the shifts in philosophy required by the community approach it was advocating. It also added two rather token paragraphs on further training requirements and on full-timers' pay and career structure.

The new training package was finally promulgated through a DES circular sent out shortly before the general election, in March 1970. Both to meet the service's developing inter-professional requirements and for reasons of economy, the new courses were to be located in polytechnics, where connections with social work could be encouraged, as well as in colleges of education. The National College, with its one-profession focus, was to be closed at the end of its 1969–70 course.

The youth service thus emerged from the Fairbairn-Milson review with six recognised full-time courses – at Goldsmith's College in London, Leicester College of Education (which 'inherited' the National College course), Manchester Polytechnic, Westhill College in Birmingham and courses run by NABC and the YMCA at Liverpool University and North East London Polytechnic respectively. Some colleges of education also continued to offer youth work options though teachers, whether or not they had taken one of these, were still automatically regarded as qualified youth workers.

Obstacles on the route to a professional workforce

Though these arrangements remained the core framework for professional training, a number of inter-connected problems manifested themselves as the decade progressed which impeded the development towards the professional status to which full-time staff in particular were aspiring. Students on the specialist youth and community work courses, for example, were to be given not mandatory but discretionary LEA grants. This resulted in a decade of ineffective protest as LEAs either refused altogether to fund youth work students or, more commonly, paid at minimal levels of grant. The result was that some students could not afford to take up their places while others were forced to survive on poverty-level incomes or had in effect to pursue their courses part-time as they (youth) worked their way through college.

Questions also remained or emerged about whether the products of these courses were the 'right' people. Though the proportion of female entrants reached over 25 per cent by the late 1970s, a very significant gender imbalance in the service overall continued, especially when account is taken of the fact that in 1970 only an estimated 3 per cent of the full-time workforce were women. Then there were serious worries about whether these new recruits were coming into, and then whether they would stay in, the youth service per se. At the start of the decade the evidence suggested that they were. However, DES figures on 133 students finishing courses in 1972 revealed that only about 60 per cent were taking up posts in what was called formal youth work.

Even if all the courses' output had gone into the youth service, however, the supply of 140 newly qualified workers a year would not have met a still growing demand for full-time staff. Large numbers of vacancies were registered throughout much of the 1970s, with employers in 'unfashionable' areas of the country finding it particularly difficult to attract qualified job applicants. Nearly 500 posts

remained unfilled at the end of 1971, prompting CYSA to send a delegation to meet Lord Belstead, the DES Under-Secretary. The response of one of his officials – look more to teacher training as a source of recruitment – led CYSA to press that the issue be taken up through the local authority associations. This clearly had little effect. A NAYSO survey for England, reporting early in 1974, showed that by then 644 posts were either vacant or filled by unqualified workers, representing a shortfall of qualified staff in the service overall of over 30 per cent. The survey also suggested that over the following two years 565 new workers would be needed.

With few trained teachers yet seeing full-time youth work as a viable career option, the personnel gap at that stage was in part being widened by the number of new posts still being created – for 1971 alone the projected figure was over 200. Yet, despite a further rise in the vacancy total in 1974–75 to 674, by 1976 a watershed had, it seemed, been reached. Perhaps as an early sign of the service's reduced financial circumstances and the resultant slow-down in its expansion, for 1975–76 the number of unfilled posts, though still high, had been cut to 419. The growing interest of graduates in full-time youth work may also have been having an effect.

Most significant, however, would seem to have been the number of trained teachers by then wanting to take up youth work. In 1975 an arbitration decision in effect brought full-time youth workers' salaries into line with those of teachers and gave them the same generous salary increases recommended by the 1974 Houghton Report. As the report was eventually applied, too, to youth officers, these negotiations helped enhance career prospects within the youth service.

And so, even though very few teachers did any specifically youth work training within their college courses, by 1975–76 over 1,150 of them had taken up youth work posts. That year they constituted half of the new entrants and, for January – July 1976, 58 per cent. (With recruits from the specialist youth and community work courses being drawn increasingly into the new community oriented social services depart- ments, intermediate treatment schemes and an array of 'alternative' community work projects – the burgeoning independent voluntary sector – the equivalent figure for them was only 19 per cent.) This trend was strongly underpinned by the swing to school-based provision which had occurred post-Albemarle, continued well into the 1970s and had a substantial impact on staffing. One authoritative estimate concluded that in 1972 there were 700 school-based posts – 'and growing'. The NAYSO survey for 1974–75 (on a 95 per cent return) put the figure at 625.

In its one-paragraph reference to training, *Provision for Youth*, the 1975 DES discussion document on the youth service, made no direct reference to any of these more fundamental trends or their possible (unintended as well as intended) con- sequences. The paper's main concern was to enable youth workers to convert to other professions. Perhaps as a way of solving the vacancy crisis – and against some opposition from the established

courses – it did tentatively suggest 'a second tier of professional qualification offering a career in club leadership or management or in activity leadership'. By then anyway the DES had had approved four new two-year courses to start in the September – at Berkshire, Matlock and Alsager (Cheshire) Colleges of Education and at Sunderland Polytechnic.

By then, too, the service was contriving its own solution to its staffing crisis: it was appointing more and more unqualified workers. As early as November 1969 a DES minister was fending off a Parliamentary question from a Liverpool MP supporting the recruitment of 'youth leaders who, although not formally qualified, had demonstrated by their work and experience their suitability for vacant posts in this field'. By 1972 136 such workers were actually in post throughout the service. With 161 new unqualified workers entering the service in 1975 alone, their number had by then risen to 519.

Though in 1978 this figure dropped to 111, the presence of so many 'untrained' and 'non-professional' workers posed a continuing challenge for the service. As many of them were Black, their exclusion from qualified status was interpreted by some increasingly articulate groups as further evidence of the service's in-built racism. More generally, their presence was seriously testing the credibility of youth workers' claims to a 'professional' status tied very tightly to the completion of a qualifying training.

At least one LEA sought to remedy the situation by introducing a local trainee scheme for young unqualified workers. More significantly, in what turned out to be the pioneering move for a much longer-term trend, a part-time course route to qualification for full-time youth and community work was opened up, at Avery Hill College in London (in 1972). (A similar course was also started in Northern Ireland.) Nonetheless, the anomaly of the unqualified worker remained substantially unresolved at the end of the decade and continued to act as a serious irritant within staff relations well into the next one.

Is professional training working?

In responding to this hefty portfolio of concerns about staffing (including professional training), the service began to test out the kinds of collaborative strategies which, as we have seen in earlier chapters, were already being developed for dealing with more explicitly political agendas.

Despite its virtually total reliance on a variety of government grants, NYB came to play a role in these developments which subsequently was seen – not least by government itself – as riskily close to dabbling in pressure group politics. When John Ewen replaced Alan Gibson as director of YSIC in 1969, he found that 'a grand design' already existed for a national body to carry out research and provide information and training services. Even so, against the background of a 'high degree of suspicion in the field about empire building tendencies', it took

four years to create a National Youth Bureau out of YSIC.

Even then, not only was the bureau, as Ewen put it, 'dragged screaming into existence rather than celebrated'. Its longer-term relationship with its field remained ambiguous and sometimes tense. Despite this, special units were added – for supporting work with young offenders in 1973, youth volunteering in 1974, youth work and work with the young unemployed in 1978 – and its staff and facilities became increasingly central to servicing collective professional developments.

One of the first tentative moves towards coalescence among the interest groups involved in professional training – which, paradoxically also exposed some of the divisions among trainers – came towards the end of 1971 with the formation of a Youth and Community Work Training Association (YCWTA). Set up to provide mutual support and an exchange of ideas, by 1975 this had drawn together most of the staff running youth work option courses within teacher training, some of those working on the full-time courses and some local authority training officers. Alongside it, however, a Training Agencies Group (TAG) continued to operate, representing the 'big six' specialist courses, including some which were keeping their distance from YCWTA.

Where all of these interests did come together, however, was in the Joint Consultative Group on Youth and Community Work Training. Formed in 1972, from the start it had in membership CYSA, NAYSO/NAYCEO, NCVYS, the

full-time training agencies and representatives from the community work field and
from the DES. It also provided one of the
clearest examples of the importance of
NYB's servicing role, especially as played
by Alec Oxford, its deputy director and
training services officer.

One of the group's early initiatives, in
1974, was to circulate a consultative
document on full-time training. This
started from the proposition that, given the
NAYSO survey's findings on vacancies, the
service was 'already halfway back, in
terms of full-time staffing, to its 1960
position'. One of its recommendations was
that more and varied training units be
established to provide easy contact with
other professions. A second proposal,
striking in the context of the wider debates
then surfacing, was that 'academic under-
achievers – truly indigenous people – be
recruited and appointed to existing full-
time posts in their own neighbourhoods ...
(and) after x years full-time experience
should be seen to qualify for professional
training'.

The impact of the paper itself was
minimal, not least perhaps because it was
too optimistic in its assumptions about the
community and inter-professional
directions which the service was about to
take. However, inspired by Alec Oxford
and against the background of deepening
uncertainties and confusions about
staffing, the Consultative Group persuaded
the DES to fund a three-year research
project, to be based at NYB. Its explicit
aims were to describe the careers of those
trained on the specialist courses between
1972 and 1978 and to clarify the existing

full-time staffing position within the
service.

However, implicitly at least, the proposal
had other intentions, some highly
pragmatic, others much more principled.
As the project's research worker, John
Holmes, later recorded, it was also driven
by the complaints about the effectiveness
of the full-time courses noted earlier which
were being made most damagingly
throughout the 1970s by youth service
managers. These suggested, for example,
that students leaving the specialist courses:

> ... were too young, too inexperienced,
> unprepared or unable to last a sufficient
> time in any one job, had insufficient
> managerial/administrative skills, and did
> not see their job as relating to other adults
> in the organisation.

Shortly after the research started in 1978,
'the tensions and conflicts between the
training agencies and the field' were
explicitly explored at a day conference
arranged by YCWTA and again serviced by
NYB. This clarified five main sets of
questions:

- *What was "the field" for which students
  were being trained? What priority focuses
  for the training did this require?*
- *Training for what – with four main areas
  identified:*
  - *to administer the service?*
  - *to manage people and resources?*
  - *to create relevant face-to-face work?*
  - *to produce critical and creative people?*
- *What should the priorities for curriculum
  content be?*
- *How should some relevant administrative
  concerns be dealt with, especially in relation
  to placement arrangements?*

- *Where do all the students go – and (implicitly) why?*

The conference resolved little in the time available. However, as well as allowing feelings and attitudes to be ventilated, it did at least offer a framework for a cooler examination of some of the long-standing conflicts which were bedevilling – and continued to bedevil – this key area of youth service activity.

The consultative group's proposal was also formulated just as another and even more searching debate was getting under way: what was this professionalism and how relevant was it within youth work? The notion had by now been embraced enthusiastically and often uncritically by many, perhaps most, full-timers. However, from Albemarle onwards the whole drive to professionalisation had been attacked by some within the service for undermining its long tradition of volunteering and of provision through voluntary organisations. The later critiques of Black and women's groups had taken a different but no less significant or critical tack, pointing to how unbending insistence on professional standards was excluding those who did not fit its dominant (often white and male) definitions of skill and achievement. Overlapping with this critique was one which reinterpreted professionalism's claims to objectivity as unachievable – and as depoliticising youth work practice, turning its practitioners in to 'haves' and distancing them from 'the have-nots' they were supposed to be serving.

Nor was the questioning of the sustainability of a youth work professionalism

coming only from below. Indirectly and probably unintentionally, its possibilities were being reduced, too, by tightening managerial screws. As the economic constraints grew, this was increasingly required by the demand that the same, or even perhaps more, be provided with less – and therefore, that the resources which were available should be used as efficiently and as effectively as possible. During the 1960s, 'we and them' notions of workers and management were largely unknown in the youth service. By at least the mid-1970s, however, youth workers as well as managers were being urged to learn about the virtues of 'management by objectives', about how to 'evaluate practice' – and about how to manage staff.

Indeed, jobs cast explicitly in a managerial mould were more and more widely introduced as adviser posts were converted into officer posts. Line management responsibilities were also firmly put in place via job descriptions and supervision. An increased emphasis, too, was placed on monitoring work in progress while in due course a new JNC-agreed grading structure was to give very formal recognition to the managerial tasks carried by full-time youth workers.

Nor was this tightening of the accountability screw being pressed only for reasons of cost-effectiveness. Impeccable principled arguments were also being developed. In particular it was increasingly being suggested that, in the changing ideological climate, the youth worker's reputation for free-wheeling, not to say maverick, approaches to her or his work could no longer be ignored or benignly tolerated. These were now seen as too often failing to demonstrate that promises were being delivered on the workers' own, to say nothing of young people's, terms. This left the service and its personnel wide open to just the kind of 'woolly liberal' criticisms which were starting to touch genuine chords of recognition among users. Perhaps because professionalised workers did not take ownership of the necessary responses quickly enough, these were also the criticisms which Thatcher and her allies were able to level to such devastating effect after 1979.

In these conditions, the space left open by the 1960s' reforms for the determination of practice objectives through the exercise of professional discretion and professional judgment on the ground was a decade later steadily being closed down. These, even nascent, forms of anti-professionalism inevitably had an impact on the debate about training and qualifications. Indeed, when encountered in this context, it revealed just how far the youth service had moved by mid-decade from the certainties of the Fairbairn-Milson Report:

> What is it (training) intended to do? What is it intended to equip the student for? It implies learning. Learning what? (This is) presumed to go on in courses situated in academic institutions … which lead to relevant qualifications. But is there any evidence that they lead to more effective practice? … To go on into the future mounting more courses and, possibly, of longer duration without evidence that the training provided and the learning done is leading to improved services is both economically and morally questionable.

The report on the Holmes research project, published in 1981, injected some important basic data into the debates on the staffing of the service. For example, it showed that its increasingly heavy reliance on teacher trained workers was not providing the long-term stability which many had hoped for – and expected. Despite their longer training and apparently more credible qualification, they were failing to stay as long in their youth work posts as entrants from the specialist courses.

The research also provided some credible evidence on the uncertain and often contentious state of the service by the end of the decade. Its very title – *Professionalism – A Misleading Myth?* – gave early warning of this, while more detailed findings unpacked some of the underlying tensions. Holmes' identified a split within the full-time workforce which, on one valid reading, could be interpreted as a debilitating identity crisis for the service. Dating back usually to their time on the specialist courses, many workers seem to have placed themselves firmly into one of two opposing camps.

In some respects these mirrored the emergent tensions between demand-led and issue-based work (see Chapter 7). On the one side were those who defined themselves by a commitment to building-based work; on the other those who were community-work oriented in their practice. Apparently each faction was both seeing and seen by the other in very stereotypical ways, with both appearing in effect to operate on the principle: 'If you're not with us, you must be against us.'

Though more speculative, such often divisive debates may at least have been encouraged by a shared, usually implicit but sometimes explicit, belief among the six training agencies that, unlike the National College, they were not obliged to prepare their students for one single profession. Another specific factor may also have been at work. Their contrasting, not to say conflicting, orientations were often shaped by differing interpretations of the Fairbairn-Milson injunction to 'go community'. This too may have fed, even sanctioned, an either-or struggle for the heart and minds of the service throughout much of the 1970s.

Centre-based work in particular was increasingly left out of fashion and under-valued by these debates. It was portrayed by those seeking to distance themselves from it as conservative and conformist – as, for example, trapped in high levels of administrative work and within bureaucratic and hierarchical structures, and as ultimately concerned with controlling rather than liberating young people. By contrast, the community work option was presented by its increasingly vocal advocates as the genuinely enabling and radical arm of youth work which could generate more egalitarian relationships and more person-centre and community controlled forms of practice.

On the ground, however, each of these ideal types often turned out to have much in common. Moreover, as the Keele research revealed, both had their draw-backs. Its findings, for example,

confirmed that 'the statutory agencies tended to display a bureaucratic pattern of administration, in which critical decisions were taken by largely full-time officers clearly aware of their position in an administrative hierarchy'. On the other hand, the researchers wondered whether 'many of the more radical workers … are attempting to move too rapidly and that the slower responses of the "mainstream" bulk of the service may, almost inadvertently … prevent them getting too far ahead of the members'.

This analysis, when placed alongside the Holmes' evidence of a deep ideological and practice split within the ranks of its frontline workers, added up to a discouraging picture of the service as it approached another review of its work. Commitment in plenty remained. However, both these major pieces of research on the service detected high levels of dissatisfaction – not least over the persisting difficulty of convincing other professionals that youth workers were their equal. Staff attitudes were permeated by fears about its long-term future and were increasingly being expressed in the new worker-management language of division, conflict and distrust. National bodies might organise more effectively, indeed politically. MPs might be persuaded to lobby on youth affairs issues. Private member's bills might force themselves into, though not quite through, Parliament. However, at the cutting edge, the mood, it seemed, remained one of low professional self-esteem, self-doubt and drift.

In-service training

Indirectly and perhaps unconsciously, the Consultative Group on Youth and Community Work Training had sought to address some of this culture through an initiative for dealing with another of the service's growing preoccupations: the limited range and variable standards of its in-service training provision. In part this stemmed from a recognition that initial training was too short to prepare workers fully for the demands of the job. It was fuelled, too, by some more specific concerns. These included a need to improve induction for new staff, especially given the requirement that they complete a probationary year; to extend developmental forms of staff supervision (a task also taken up by some YSA/CYSA initiatives); and to provide courses for youth officers and for trainers.

The result in 1976, after two years negotiation with the DES, was an In-Service Training and Education Panel – INSTEP – staffed by a full-time professional adviser, Tom Wylie and based at NYB. Its remit was to:

- *coordinate provision – national, regional and local – and particularly to encourage employers to formulate staff development policies;*
- *validate provision, and particularly to endorse in-service courses and other training run by local authorities, voluntary organisations and educational institutions; and*
- *develop appropriate criteria for fulfilling this validating role.*

Over time the panel proved to be an innovative stimulus to employers to develop in-service training broadly defined. It encouraged even the foot-draggers to taken some action – as well as paving the way for other central validating machinery, particularly in the early 1980s for the full-time qualifying courses.

Training for part-timers and volunteers

While developing this initiative, the Consultative Group was also successfully negotiating for DES funding to review the training of the 300,000 part-time and voluntary workers then estimated to be involved in the service. The numbers of paid part-timers had grown as the service had expanded into the early 1970s while the emergence of 'indigenous' Black workers had produced some new stirrings at the grass roots. Even so, post-Albemarle, the position and status of both these groups remained largely unchanged until in 1976 local groups of part-timers – for example, in Leicestershire, Luton and Walsall – came together in search of mutual support and to demand greater consultation, especially over cuts. CYSA responded the following year by introducing a special category of member-ship which gave them some rights within the union and some access to its services.

The Consultative Group's review of their training was the first since the second Bessey report exactly 10 years before. Designed as a major and systematic enquiry into the policy, structure, content and methods, it was carried out by two experienced sociological researchers, Stephen Butters and Susan Newell. On what was by then a small but significant area of adult vocational training and education, over two years they produced a long, detailed and highly academic report, *Realities of Training*.

Intentionally or not, their report turned out to be much more than was originally envisaged. It provided one of the few systematic attempts to describe and analyse the nature of youth work itself. For those looking for conceptual hooks on which to hang an analysis of youth service practice, it thus subsequently proved to be a constant source of stimulus and ideas. It suggested, for example, that, post-Albemarle, much of this practice had been based within a 'social education repertoire', though with some limited attempts to push beyond this into a 'radical paradigm'. It also sought to explain this practice, not just in the psychological and social psychological terms which had dominated youth work thinking, certainly since Albemarle. Very systematically – and in great detail – it also applied some of the more critical sociological theories and forms of analysis then in fashion.

Its insights into what had happened to the training for part-timers bequeathed to the service by the 1960s were important and at times original. It, for example, gave vivid accounts, warts and all, of local courses still being run in 'the Bessey tradition'. In doing this, it generated considerable original case material from four courses in action based on extended participant observation. More broadly, it demonstrated how, following the 1974 reorganisation of local government, local authorities had sought to make all their training functions accountable to 'senior levels of management best able to judge their effectiveness'. It thus exposed some of the realities on the ground of even notional youth service shifts to community:

> Youth work training was regarded by some educational administrators as potentially an instrument of community education policy, impinging on the running of further education, adult education and community development services ... This created pressures to exert supervisory powers over training officers in the youth and community work service.

The result, Butters and Newell found, was that in a number of formal ways this training had been re-appropriated into the service's statutory service – something which had been happening informally anyway over many years. Effective partnerships with the voluntary sector had in consequence largely withered away, leaving only eight genuine joint training agencies by 1975 out of the 74 which the second Bessey report had listed.

At the time many in the field wrote off *Realities of Training* as too full of jargon – and as too political in its orientation. The fact that it offered no specific recommendations for action also restricted its appeal and made its immediate impact on training practice and management very limited. Though some effective and well regarded provision continued, until well into the 1980s training for part-time and voluntary workers thus remained fragmented and highly variable in quality and lacked any overall developmental strategy.

Contrary pulls and pushes

By the end of the 1970s the jury was still out on whether the youth service had spawned its own distinctive profession of practitioners. The noises coming from the jury room, however, were not encouraging. Serious ideological and methodological splits existed among full-timers. 'Unqualified' workers were still needed in significant numbers – and were undoubtedly making positive contributions across the service to some of its most testing areas of practice. The part-timers and volunteers who were doing most of this face-to-face work continued to be marginalised and devalued and were subject to wide variations in their recruitment, supervision and training. Together these flaws in the youth service's occupational structure seriously undermined the claims of its workforce to professional recognition.

What is more, as wider political events unfolded, it proved to be a particularly bad time to be publicly displaying such a position of weakness and uncertainty. Margaret Thatcher and her New Right colleagues were becoming extremely impatient with these doubtful – perhaps spurious – claims to 'unique professional understandings' even when they came from the big players like teachers, doctors and lawyers. They were seen as adding to the bureaucrats' power over the individual

and so as leading to 'service provision being driven by the professional ... rather than (by) the consumer's views on what they want'. Faced with such ideas, not only did groups such as youth leaders stand little chance of getting the privileges and power of the professional extended to include them. They were going to have to be very credible and convincing even to keep the gains they had already made.

Indeed, as in many other areas of educational and welfare provision, the 1970s was a watershed for youth service policy-making. The relatively liberal and optimistic philosophy and regime of the 1960s which had encouraged notions of professional skill and autonomy slowly gave way to a gloomier set of expectations. In turn these not only seemed to demand that the educational and welfare ship be run in much tighter, more cost effective and more managerial ways. They also required that, sometimes quite radically, it change its philosophical course, too.

At the heart of the service were continuity and consistency, tipping over into rigidity. One of the 'abiding impressions' of the Keele researchers, for example, was of the service's 'amorphousness and lack of boundary'. It quoted one local authority officer as calling it an 'administrator's nightmare' with its 'apparently endless calls ... for new and costly initiatives – detached workers, shop front clubs, community projects'. Moreover this scattergun response to new demands often, it seemed, forced policy makers into 'a policy of "containment" which meant that the organisations received money for established and recognised activities, and only infrequently succeeded in making a case for new ones'. The result, the study concluded, was that 'longstanding practice was seen to be an important determinant of present-day arrangements'.

The consequences of such an approach were highlighted in more practical ways by a survey carried out for *Education* shortly after the Keele research was completed. Of the 86 local authorities responding, for example, 85 were running Duke of Edinburgh Award schemes and 71 voluntary service projects but only 34 were offering forms of sex education; 83 were running activity competitions but only 43 undertaking detached work. As Gordon Ette noted in drawing out the lessons of the survey: 'Tradition, the Establishment and the voluntary organisations can combine to ossify the service by resisting change and hogging the available cash.'

For some in the service, its deepening involvement with formal education since the 1960s had by the 1970s embedded these rigidities even more firmly. The swing to community education had been encouraged, indeed required, by financial as well as educational considerations. Especially once comprehensive education had taken hold and very large secondary schools had proliferated, their expensive 'plant' needed to be exploited to the full. According to researcher Frank Booton, by the middle of the decade much of the youth service's purpose-built provision post-Albemarle had been sucked into these school campuses. In 1977 Booton concluded that, with independent statutory youth units no longer being built and assuming 'a

fundamental difference between schooled and non-schooled provision', the concept of the open youth club was being placed in jeopardy and with it the entire philosophy of social education.

Despite such a bedrock of unchanging practice and provision, from the confusions and then rejection of *Youth and Community Work in the '70s* onwards the service was characterised by uncertainty over what its distinctive role was. Nor were these doubts about its direction and core identity the result only of static or reducing resources. As we have seen, the flirtation with de-institutionalised, if not anti-institutional, community work approaches drew in more and more workers trained on the specialist courses and often led to deep-seated divisions. At best, these provoked tensions over whether too much community meant too little youth work – or vice versa. More damaging still were the meandering discussions on what 'real' youth work was anyway and in particular the contest between traditionalist and building-based and progressive, issue and community-based approaches – and workers.

As local government struggled with the aftermath of its reorganisation in 1974, these debates became overlaid by another contentious issue: would the youth service not sit more comfortably in recreation and leisure, or indeed in social services, rather than education? Though none of the new authorities took the latter option, Avon, Stockport and Nottinghamshire all opted for the former. This further blurring of the service's identity seemed to get some incidental endorsement from the new

Labour government when briefly in 1975–76 it gave responsibility for the youth service to a junior minister at the DES who was carrying the arts portfolio.

Sometimes the anguishing was expressed very articulately and coherently. John Ewen, for example, in a 'valediction' on leaving NYB and the youth service in 1977, saw the (otherwise welcome) arrival of more full-time staff as having brought 'the usual introverted self-protectionism that any newly emerging profession generates'. He also concluded that, by trying to spread itself beyond its youth clientele, the service 'had lost its confidence through being too clever'; and that it had 'lost its excitement and willingness to take risks by becoming middle-aged'.

Two years later the no less influential opinion-former, Fred Milson, in the process of answering his own question 'has the youth service moved to the left?', identified camps of 'conservatives' and camps of 'radicals'. Tarring the latter with the dreaded Marxist brush, he concluded that they had gone too far in their espousal of 'politically aware' innovation and 'activism' and that by 'concentrating on the distant goal' that had been diverted 'from seeking out present opportunities'. The very sharpness of the riposte from Roy Ratcliffe and Tony Taylor, both full-time workers and leading youth work trade unionists, captured as vividly as anything could the shouting across empty voids which by then seemed to characterise much youth service discourse:

> It is this lack of rigour, this absence of integrity, that clearly identifies Milson's cautionary essay as political propaganda.

Influential though they were, Ewen and Milson were still inside players indulging in the game of objective criticism by involved colleagues. Towards the end of the decade, however, an external and much more genuinely detached eye was cast on the service – that of Barney Baker, the DES official with responsibility for its work and development. This offered a very different and much more daring perspective on its current state and future role and prospects which anyway were just about to be reshaped by broader and what turned out to be very radical social policy shifts. Baker also presented his analysis in the succinct and prescient way that sometimes only a thinking civil servant working quietly behind the scenes can achieve.

In June 1978, Baker wrote a 'note' for the Youth Service Forum. In this he expressly denied that he was trying 'to prejudge the work of the Forum or its working parties by establishing restrictive parameters for its discussions'. Rather, he claimed, he was seeking 'to get behind the more tangible questions of resources, kinds of provision, and styles of social education, and pose fundamental questions about the justification of present practice and the needs of the adolescent'.

As a key prompt for these reflections he drew on his experiences of the joint CYSA/NAYCEO conference held in Exeter the previous April, including Bernard Davies's keynote address on *Priorities in the Youth and Community Service*. From the wider participants' discussions at the conference, he identified three main current preoccupations:

- the need to focus on young people's

needs as they saw them and to give them more say in deciding on how to respond to these;

- the need to respond to youth unemployment; and
- youth workers' sense of isolation – and of being obliged to act largely as caretakers for club premises.

What he said he could not detect at the conference was any great concern with 'the antithesis postulated by Davies between young people's needs and aspirations and the (increasingly controlling and disciplining) motives and objectives of sponsoring agencies in providing a youth service'.

For Baker, however, it was precisely this theme which demanded urgent attention. This was partly because of the wider so-called great education debate then going. Initiated in 1976 by the Prime Minister, James Callaghan, this was presented by the Labour government of the time as an attempt to clarify how far the education service was meeting the nation's longer-term economic, and especially its industrial, needs. Baker also thought that Davies's arguments needed testing because, 'with so many competing claims on public expenditure, an increased emphasis on justification in terms of social objectives must be expected'.

For Baker there were also two other reasons for opening up such a debate:
i) *Any assessment of young people's needs involves a social, educational, political and ethical judgment with an application which goes beyond individuals, or even groups or 'sub-cultures';*
ii) *Funding agencies may not be prepared to*

provide the resources for objectives which are not of their choosing and which they may not altogether understand.

He thus 'insisted' that some rebalancing of purposes was essential. On the one hand, he pointed to the client-centred approach advocated over 10 years before by Bernard Davies and Alan Gibson in their book, *The Social Education of the Adolescent* which was still routinely being recommended on professional training courses. On the other, he stressed 'an assessment of needs in relation to society's ... interests'.

Baker wished to describe the kind of outcomes he had in mind in 'less authoritarian though perhaps equally negative' terms. Rather than control and discipline, he therefore suggested 'social prophylaxis' – according to the Oxford Dictionary, 'preventive treatment against (social) disease'. Nonetheless, arguing that 'sometimes there is an advantage in expressing a concept bluntly, even crudely', he concluded that 'society's needs may be defined in terms more or less unpalatable to young people'. And, specifically in relation to the Forum's work, he proposed that, among other things, 'it should attempt to make the case for expenditure on the youth service *principally* by reference to the social objectives which it serves' (emphasis added).

Here, from the subtly functioning heart of government policy-making, was as clear and unambiguous an expression as was likely to be penned of the (just) pre-Thatcherite steer to youth service policy-making which was by then being openly applied to the education service generally. As, once in office, Thatcher gained her confidence and established her power-base, redirection along these lines became increasingly hard line and also explicit.

Indeed, Thatcher's ascent to power represented one of the most clear-cut and radical political break-points of the century which had a profound impact on the youth service as it did on all other public services. Though much less optimistic and much more constrained than the post-Albemarle 1960s, the 1970s had still brought significant growth to the youth service. Even when this was slowed or stalled, the explanations offered were always pragmatic – especially economic. At no point did they start from the proposition that the state should not be involved at all – that it ought not to be investing any money in something like youth work and the institutions sponsoring and supporting it. Prior to May 1979, though weakening under financial pressure, the essential welfare consensus had just about held and so continued to legitimate a substantial statutory contribution to the youth service.

After May 1979, not only could these axioms of educational and welfare policy no longer be taken for granted. Increasingly they ceased to apply as they were explicitly rejected and actively replaced by hard line free market principles.

Main references

M. B. Baker, 'The Future Role of the Youth Service: Note by the Secretary for the Youth Service Forum' (unpublished), 1978

Stephen Butters and Sue Newell, *Realities of Training*, NYB, 1978

Malcolm Dean, 'Ministers rethink Welfare State', *Guardian*, 17.2.83

John Eggleston, *Adolescence and Community: The Youth Service in Britain*, Edward Arnold, 1975

Gordon Ette, 'Service of Youth: An Education survey of LEA provision', *Education*, 17.9.76

Robert Hamilton, 'Don't join the professionals: that would kill youth work', *Youth Review*, Winter 1972

John Holmes, *Professionalisation – A Misleading Myth?*, NYB 1981

John Holmes, 'Is the Grass Greener on the Other Side?', *Youth in Society*, May 1982

Milson-Fairbairn Report, *Youth and Community Work in the '70s*, HMSO, 1969

Youth and Community Work Training Association / Alec Oxford, 'The relationship between the training agencies and the field', NYB, 1978

Key Youth Service Events to 1979

Date	Youth service developments	The wider world
1844	YMCA founded	
1853	YWCA founded	
1883	Boys' Brigade founded	
1907	Boy Scouts Association founded	
1910	Girl Guides Association founded	
1911	National Organisation of Girls' Clubs (NOGC) founded	
1914	Boys' Club 'pioneer' Charles Russell appointed to government post to tackle juvenile delinquency	Start of First World War
1916	Government encourages local authorities to support Juvenile Organisation Committees (JOCs)	
1918	Education Act empowers local authorities to make grants to clubs and youth groups	First World War ends
1921	Board of Education circular empowers local authorities to set up their own JOCs	
1925	NABC founded	
1926	NOGC becomes National Council of Girls' Clubs (NCGC)	
1936	SCNVYO set up	
1937	Physical Training and Recreation Act	
1938	Club Leaders' Association formed	

1939	KG Jubilee Trust report *The Needs of Youth* published	Start of Second World War
	Circular 1486 – 'Service of Youth' released	
	National Youth Committee set up	
1940	Circular 1516 – 'Challenge of Youth' released	
	National Conference of Youth Service Officers established	
1942	NCGC becomes National Association of Girls' Clubs (NAGC)	Compulsory registration of all 16 to 18-year-olds
	Board of Education Youth Advisory Council set up	Beveridge report *Social Security and Allied Services* published
1943	Youth Advisory Council first report *Youth Service after the War* published	Board of Education White Paper *Educational Reconstruction* published
	Publication of *Training and Service for Girls of 14-16*	
	HMI inspection of youth organisations introduced	
1944	1944 Education Act: Sections 41 and 53	Board of Education becomes Ministry of Education
	NAGC becomes National Association of Girls' Clubs and Mixed Clubs (NAGC&MC)	
	McNair report *Teachers and Youth Leaders* published	
1945	Second report of Youth Advisory Council *Purpose and Content of Youth Service*	Second World War ends
		General election - Labour Government
	MAYC founded	
1947		School leaving age raised to 15
		Central Advisory Council on Education report *School for Life*
1948	BYC established	

1948	PEP report on *Service of Youth Today*	
1949	Jackson report *Recruitment, Training and Conditions of Youth Leaders and Community Centre Wardens* published	
1950		General election – Labour Government
1951	Fletcher report *Recruitment, Training and Conditions of Service of Youth Leaders and Community Centre Wardens* published KG Jubilee Trust Ashridge Conference: Sir John Maud defines youth service aims	General election – Conservative Government
1955	*Citizens of Tomorrow* published by King George's Jubilee Trust	General election – Conservative Government
1956	Duke of Edinburgh's Award scheme launched	Bill Haley film *Rock Around the Clock*
1957	House of Commons Select Committee on Estimates report on the youth service MacAlister Brew's *Youth and Youth Groups* published PHAB clubs started	
1958	Albemarle Committee appointed	Nottingham and Notting Hill 'race riots'
1959	House of Lords debate on youth service	Crowther report on secondary education General election – Conservative Government Colin McInnes novel *Absolute Beginners* published Mark Abrams: *Teenager Consumer Spending* published
1960	Albemarle Report published YSDC set up	End of National Service

1960	First issue of Ministry of Education Bulletin *Youth Service*	
1961	NCTYL opened	
	NAGC&MC becomes NAYC	
	Ray Gosling's *Lady Albemarle's Boys* published	
	Joint Negotiating Committee for Youth Leaders and Community Centre Wardens set up	
	Building Bulletin 20: *Youth Service Building - General Mixed Clubs* published	
1962	First Bessey report *Training of Part-time Youth Leaders and Assistants* published	Immigration Act
	Community Service Volunteers established	
	NABC: *Boys' Clubs in the '60s* published	
	London Federation of Boys' Clubs: *Boys' Clubs and Girls* published	
1963	Youth Service Association formed out of National Association of Youth Leaders and Organisers and National Association of LEA Youth Leaders	Newsom Report: *Half our Future* published Robbins Report: *Higher Education* published
	Building Bulletin 22: *Youth Club – Withywood Bristol* published	Children and Young Persons Act
	Elfrida Rathbone Society established	
	Mary Robinson's *Girls in the '60s* published	
1964	Youth Service Information Centre set up	General election – Labour Government
	Jalna Hamner's *Girls at Leisure* published	Smethwick by-election
	Life of NCTYL extended to 1970	

1964	Haynes Committee report on Boys' Brigade published	
1965	Mary Morse's *The Unattached* published	
	YSDC report: *Service by Youth* published	
	Salter Davies report on rural youth work published	
	Medical Research Council Study of delinquency and the youth service	
1966	Second Bessey report *Training of Part-time Youth Leaders and Assistants* published	General election – Labour Government
	Advance Party report on Scouts published	£500 million public spending deflation package
	BYC reconstituted	Introduction of Section 11 Funding
	Commission report on MAYC published	Home Secretary Roy Jenkins' speech on integration of 'immigrants'
1967	Hunt Report: *Immigrants and the Youth Service* published	Ministry of Education becomes Department of Education and Science (DES)
	YSDC reconstituted	Plowden Report: *Children and their Primary Schools* published
	Fairbairn and Milson YSDC subcommittees set up	
	Goetschius and Tash's *Working with Unattached Youth* published	Ministry of Housing: *Needs of New Communities* published
1968	Young Volunteer Force Foundation launched	Enoch Powell's 'Rivers of Blood' speech
	Community of Interests on youth work and community education in Scotland published	Race Relations Act
		Seebohm report on social work published
	University of Keele research project into the youth service commissioned	White Paper *Children in Trouble* published
1969	Milson-Fairbairn Report published	Children and Young Persons Act – intermediate treatment introduced

1969		Community development projects started
		Skeffington Report *People and Planning* published
		First 'Black Paper' on education published
1970	NCTYL closed: two-year qualifying courses set up nationally	General election – Conservative Government
	House of Commons debates on the youth service	Chronically Sick and Disabled Act
		First national conference of Women's Liberation Movement in Britain
		Gay Liberation Movement founded in Britain
1971	Ministerial Commons statement: DES rejects Fairbairn-Milson Report; YSDC disbanded	
	DES ends 50 per cent grants to voluntary capital projects	
	NAYC sets up Community Industry	
	YSA and Community Service Association merge to form CYSA	
	Youth and Community Work Training Association formed	
1972	SCNVYO becomes National Council for Voluntary Youth Services (NCVYS)	DES White Paper: *Framework for Expansion* published
	Bone and Ross's *Youth Service and Similar Provision for Young People* published	Campaign for Homosexual Equality founded
	Avery Hill College introduces part-time route to professional qualification	
	Joint Consultative Group on Youth and Community Work Training established	

1973	NYB set up: absorbs YSIC; sets up Youth Social Work Unit	Manpower Services Commission established
	Haselhurst Youth and Community Service Bill	
	Youth service lobby for 'minister for youth'	
1974	Townsend and Brown Youth and Community Service Bills	Miners' strike
	University of Keele Research Report: *Adolescence and Community* published	Two general elections – Labour Governments
		Local government reform: at least three authorities transfer youth service to leisure/recreation departments
	NYB Young Volunteers Resources Unit set up	
		Houghton Report on teachers' pay (applied to youth workers)
1975	DES discussion paper *Provision for Youth* published	
	NAYSO becomes NAYCEO	
	PEP Report: *National Voluntary Youth Organisations* published	
	NAYPCAS formed	
	Four new two-year qualifying courses approved	
1976	Youth Service Forum established	Sterling crisis: IMF loan; spending cuts
	Prince's Trust established	
	Gay youth groups started in London and Merseyside	Prime Minister James Callaghan launches 'Great Education Debate'
	NCVYS report on 'young people and homosexuality' published	
	In-service training panel (INSTEP) set up	
	BYC restructured	
1977	Youthaid established	Holland Report: *Young People and Work* published
	Youth Charter 2000 conference	

1977	Boys Rule Not OK conference NAYC appoints girls' work worker	
	Part-time workers admitted to CYSA membership	
1978	Youth Affairs Lobby set up	Youth Opportunities Programme launched
	Butters and Newell: *Realities of Training* published	Warnock Report *Special Educational Needs* published
	NYB Youth Opportunities Development and Youth Work Units established	
	Black Youth and Community Workers Association set up	
	Campaign for Rural Youth launched	
1979	Youth Service Forum abolished	General election – Conservative Government
	Skeet Youth and Community Service Bill	
	Joint Council for Gay Teenagers set up	

Main reference

Doug Nicholls, *CYWU: An Outline History of Youth and Community Work in the Union, 1834–1997*, Pepar Publications, 1997

Index